GROUPS,
LEADERSHIP
AND MEN

_____

Research in Human Relations

GROUPS,

LEADERSHIP

AND MEN

Research in Human Relations

Reports on Research Sponsored by the
Human Relations and Morale Branch of
the Office of Naval Research 1945–1950

EDITED BY HAROLD GUETZKOW

NEW YORK / RUSSELL & RUSSELL

*These papers were derived from the
United States Navy's Conference of
Its Human Relations Advisory Panel
and Research Contractors at Dearborn, Michigan, September, 1950*

301.155
G938g

TABLE OF CONTENTS

v

Research on Leadership

Research on Individual Behaviors

Appendix

PREFACE

BEGINNING IN 1945 the Office of Naval Research of the United States Navy has engaged investigators in basic research under government contract. The Human Relations and Morale Branch of the ONR convened a conference of its Advisory Panel and these research contractors during September, 1950 at Dearborn, Michigan, to report progress made to date. Representatives of some of the large foundations and of human relations research units in the other armed forces also participated in the meetings. In initiating this conference, the members of the Navy's Human Relations Advisory Panel felt that the contractors needed opportunity to become more familiar with each other's work. This report from the conference endeavors to make details of the Navy's research in human relations known to all those who may be interested. It is the first over-all report to be issued since the program's beginning in 1945.

It may be surprising to many to find the Navy supporting basic rather than applied research in human relations. The Chief of Naval Research, Admiral T. A. Solberg recently stated: "Almost 90 per cent of the ONR contracts are in basic research with no 'applied' strings attached, for the Navy is fully aware that a sound basic research policy is the foundation of later developments on the applied side. Most of our projects come in as research proposals originating with the individual scientist. These projects are selected and supported within the limitations of the budget and the policies of ONR. The scientific investigator is then given full freedom to follow his own bent in completing his work. ONR feels that such projects pay off in basic scientific data and new techniques which can then be analyzed and applied to Navy needs." The guide used by contractors for making research proposals is presented in the appendix.

The papers included in this volume were prepared for this pub-

lication by the contractors at the conclusion of the conference. They
differ from the oral reports in some cases by covering their projects
more thoroughly. In a number of instances they have been revised
in light of the rough-and-tumble discussions which took place at
Dearborn. They present projects in all stages of completion, as must
necessarily be the case when an on-going program is being surveyed
in its entirety. In order that the results might be made usefully accessible to a wide audience, the material was consolidated and many
of the more technical details were omitted. Severe limitations were
thus placed upon the contributors. The professional social scientist
may follow up the overviews through the more specialized references
included at the end of each report. Although the contractors cooper-
ated well in minimizing the use of specialized terms, they are scientists and necessarily use the vocabulary of their trade. A short note
on the general meaning and significance of some of the technical
terms employed by the various investigators is included in the appendix as an aid to the general reader.

The papers are published in approximately the order in which they
were presented at the conference. The proceedings were arbitrarily
divided into three large sections: Group Behavior, Leadership, and
Individual Behaviors. At the conclusion of each grouping, one of
the non-contractor participants presented an oral summary and comments. Dr. E. Lowell Kelly of the University of Michigan handled
the projects on Group Behavior; Dr. Leland C. DeVinney of the
Rockefeller Foundation summarized the research on Leadership,
and Dr. John C. Eberhardt of the National Institute of Mental
Health treated the reports on Individual Behaviors. The chairman
of the ONR panel, Dr. John G. Darley, consolidated aspects of these
on-route summaries into a final paper, which highlights some of the
controversies of the conference. In no way does his paper represent
conclusions agreed upon by all the contractors, nor does it concern
matters upon which Panel or official ONR endorsement would be
relevant. Darley's final paper has caught something of the free give-
and-take spirit of the conference, even though, as he clearly states,
his overview of controversies at times reveals his special point of
view. It was adapted by him directly from his notes and the steno-
typed report.

Throughout the conference, partly stimulated by ONR officials
and by representatives of the other armed forces, there was considerable discussion of the problems involved in translating research
results into practical military applications. Drs. John W. Macmillan

and Howard E. Page, who are responsible for the immediate direction of the Navy's human relations research, consented to report on this matter. Their analysis is included as the final paper of this volume.

The conference exhibited the same remarkable freedom from governmental interference which has characterized the Navy's administration of its basic research program during the past five years. The contractors felt that the working policy of Macmillan and Page, giving all possible technical assistance yet free from bureaucratic intrusion, provides a relationship conducive to successful research. The fact that this report is being published under academic auspices is again testimony to the ONR's concept of collaboration with already existing agencies for pursuance of common goals. It is indeed unusual to find a military organization at the research frontier, helping to build in an atmosphere of complete academic freedom the foundations of our social sciences.

PITTSBURGH   H.G.

GROUPS,
LEADERSHIP
AND MEN

────────

Research in Human Relations

FIVE YEARS OF SOCIAL SCIENCE
RESEARCH: RETROSPECT AND PROSPECT

JOHN G. DARLEY

Assistant Dean of the Graduate School and Professor of Psychology,
University of Minnesota. Chairman of the Advisory Panel
on Human Relations, Office of Naval Research.

My TASK IS TO PROVIDE a general setting for the conference to be held this week. It would be presumptuous for me to review in any detail the several research projects that will be reported here by the principal investigators. I believe I may speak, however, with some first-hand knowledge of the events leading up to our presence together on this occasion.

The Advisory Panel on Human Relations for the Office of Naval Research is charged with responsibility for reviewing research proposals in the broad category of the behavioral sciences, and recommending research programs and amounts of financial support that will most effectively serve the fundamental interests of the Navy.

In March, 1950, the Panel met to consider contract renewals and new projects. We had at hand narrative progress reports for renewal contracts. These documents so impressed the Panel members that the idea of a working conference of contractors emerged as a unanimously accepted and desirable method of integrating and accelerating the Navy's program in the areas under consideration. We were impressed not only by the very evident progress revealed in the solution of major problems facing the research teams, but also by the possibility of generalizing to a more systematic conceptual framework the variety of abstractions latent or emergent in the reports. At the same time we were tantalized by the technical and methodological problems which could be only lightly touched on in the narratives. It seemed to us therefore that a conference of principal investigators might be expected to have at least three desirable outcomes:

1. The cross-education of a highly able and highly motivated group of research workers with respect to emergent theory and to basic methodology.
2. The identification of gaps in the research which might be filled by projects designed in the light of a review of the total program to date.
3. The strengthening of the Navy program which might be expected to emerge from a five-year synthesis and review of progress, since ultimately the basic research must be translated to a form of social technology with reasonable utility.

Because of the plans for early and widespread publication of the transactions of this conference, we may view it also as a device to minimize the publication lag with which we are all too familiar in our respective fields. It is our hope also that early and widespread publication will have some impact in shaping research in the social sciences elsewhere by setting forth our strengths and weaknesses in these various projects.

The Advisory Panel is grateful to the University of Michigan and to Dr. Marquis for their willingness to accept responsibility for the management of this conference. Although the Michigan staff is heavily involved in research commitments of many kinds, they felt as we of the Panel felt—the conference idea afforded an excellent opportunity to expedite developments in the behavioral science field.

This, then, is the immediate reason for our presence here. It is the first time, I believe, that a major program of research, operating in many separated centers, has been administered to permit an interim review and stock-taking of the entire enterprise. From the vantage point of five years of hard work we shall have the chance to review our efforts and to lay down the broad lines of development which may be followed for some time to come.

So much for the immediate past. But before completing this footnote to history, I should like to touch briefly on the development of the Panel itself, since it has some archetypical features in the realm of behavioral research programming. The Advisory Panel was organized late in 1946, under the Medical Sciences Division of what was then the Office of Research and Inventions. This location was no more than a historical accident related to the fact that the only two persons remotely resembling social scientists in ORI happened to be on duty in the Medical Sciences Division. These auspices were fortunate, however, in that we had the whole-hearted and continuous support of both Captain Conrad and Captain Vorwald, then major figures in ORI, in setting up the program. As demobilization progressed and as personnel changed within the Navy, the fully-staffed civilian advisory panel emerged as a natural evolution, since the Navy in embarking on this new research venture deemed it wise to rely heavily on civilian consultants, as it was doing in many other major research fields.

Imagine for a moment the early meetings of this advisory panel: representatives of anthropology, economics, political science, sociology, psychiatry, and various schools of psychology are thrown into a situation demanding administrative and policy-making decisions of considerable magnitude, with insufficient prior opportunity to learn each others' language, to establish compatibility relations, or to maintain one's ego-supports. By some further happy accident, each panel member is an eminently skillful verbalist.

The early meetings had an Alice-in-Wonderland aspect that I can still recall. On some occasions we resembled nothing so much as a group of belligerent tom-cats arriving in an already crowded neighborhood. The various psychologists sometimes seemed more divergent in their views than the representatives of other disciplines.

Yet out of this situation, which today few of us would dare undertake with our new knowledge of group dynamics, we were able to arrive at a *modus vivendi* in which I believe real progress was made. A substantial amount of our success was due to the yeoman efforts of Lowell Kelly as panel chairman and John Macmillan as ONR representative, general wet nurse, and guardian for the Panel.

The Panel is equally indebted to the continuous and generous administrative support of a substantial number of Naval officers, including Captain Schilling, who have patiently borne with these strange social scientists and who have protected the program as a free and unrestricted research enterprise. Successive Chiefs of ONR have publicly, officially, and with conviction, maintained the Navy's sponsorship of and interest in behavioral research. To my knowledge, no contractor has experienced any invasion of his basic research program or any modification that would weaken or pervert the enterprise.

Over the years there have been some changes in the membership of the Panel. Those of us who have been connected with the program since its inception know well the personal and professional loss we suffered in the deaths of John G. Jenkins, Kurt Lewin, and Ruth Benedict, each of whom was an original and vital member of the group. Even with the changes in membership and the changing interests of the group, it is safe to say that after five years the members of this Panel represent a fairly high order of interdisciplinary integration, at least at the level of administrative and programming considerations. For myself, certainly, and I think for other members of the Panel, participation has been a challenge and a definite growth experience.

A measure of our development should take its departure from the research outline that was prepared by the Panel in October, 1946. I paraphrase it here from the article published by Dr. Macmillan in the Monthly Research Report of the Office of Naval Research. The Panel proposed the following research areas as a framework within which the program should develop:

1. *Comparative study of different cultures:* To provide a basis for understanding the behavior and goals of groups, research in the economic, political, cultural, psychological, and sociological structure of nationality grouping is . . . essential. These factors condition and set limits upon the extent to which cooperation is possible between national groups. This series of research studies should also include the description of the motives, habits of mind, and strong social values that various cultures pass on to their individual members. . . .

2. *Structure and function of groups:* It is apparent that our society calls upon the individual to operate efficiently as a member of a wide range of groups varying in size, purpose, structure, and interest. . . . It must be the aim of the research to study the productivity, structure, and development of these various groups in relation to their assigned tasks so that we can arrive at more effective selection, training, and management procedures for group relations. . . .

3. *Problems of communication of ideas, policies, and values:* Between nations, between groups within a nation, and between individuals within a group, the effectiveness of communication is of paramount importance. Not only do we deal with problems of different languages, but even where the language is common to all participants, the meaning of words, the values being sought, and the receptivity of individuals often combine to create misunderstanding, mistrust, and conflict. . . .

4. *Leadership:* Just as all individuals at some time must operate within a group, so these groups operate under various forms of leadership. Whether the leader is selected by higher authority, elected from within the group, or emerges spontaneously under pressure of combat or immediate crisis, his contribution is often a determining factor in the group's effectiveness. . . .

5. *Growth and development of the individual:* While it is generally true that the individual is molded by the culture and

society in which he holds membership, he still brings to that relation considerable individual variability as a functioning member of his society. . . . Thus no over-all pattern of research in human relations can provide workable answers unless it includes studies that are focussed on the development of individuals' capacity to participate in group life. . . .

This was the framework hammered out by the Panel on a Saturday morning at one of its earliest meetings. It was an interim document to serve not only administrative needs in reviewing contracts, but also to state for our Naval sponsors and in understandable terms the scope of the new social science research program.

Today this 1946 outline is only a fair guide, for obvious reasons. We ourselves were not able enough to foresee the dimensions of things to come or skillful enough to know all the resources upon which we could draw; our prospective contractors, it turned out, did not always share our emphases or enthusiasms for particular areas; and finally, even with substantial financial backing, we could not hope to cover the entire range of research bounded by the outline.

If now we try to classify the present research contracts within our original five interest areas, certain disproportions are immediately evident, in part for the reasons cited above. Five of the reports fall in the area of leadership studies; five more deal with group structure and function; two are concerned with communications problems; one represents a comparative study of cultures; and the remaining five deal in some way with individual behavior as it may relate to successful functioning. Before the principal investigators rise en masse to question my categorizing of their work, let me hasten to state that many other rubrics could be imposed on the data. I use the present set of categories for historical and administrative comparison only.

It might appear that we have underemphasized problems of communication and comparative cultural analysis, at the expense of some overemphasis in the remaining three areas of our interest. Alternatively it may be that our original five categories were by no means of the same order of generality and to that extent were deficient. Communication processes and problems will, for example, crop up frequently as we review the projects in the areas of group function and leadership, and in a few instances as we discuss the effects of group pressure on individual judgments.

Another set of factors that may account for the divergence of our 1946 program outline and the 1950 program actuality with respect to research resources in the country can be adduced from a brief consideration of the projects *not approved* by the Panel over the years. For obvious reasons, these must remain in the category of the unnamed though not unnumbered dead. I might add that a few of these arose from the dead several times, before they were laid permanently to rest so far as this Panel is concerned.

I have found in my files thirty-nine of the total number of research proposals that have been rejected over the past four to five years. So far as my classifications of them are accurate, you may be interested in their primary orientation:

7 were oriented as anthropological investigations;
8 were oriented as sociological investigations, including problems of race relations;
2 were oriented around traditional physiological psychology;
2 were oriented as straightforward psychiatric studies;
11 were organized in the area of individual psychology, including psychometric studies, clinical studies, and polling studies;
9 were organized in the area of group psychological studies.

By another system of classification that does not attempt to account for all thirty-nine proposals, eleven of them dealt with race and class conflict, including ethnic groups; seven more corresponded to group dynamics research projects; and an additional four dealt with leadership phenomena in some form.

With respect to traditional departmental or disciplinary lines, it would appear that the Panel has dealt most severely in rejecting and most generously in approving projects from psychologists. Adjacent or related disciplines have not fared so well in getting Panel support, nor have so many projects come to us for consideration from these disciplines. The favored situation for psychology stems from several causes: the probable greater publicity of the Panel's work within the field of psychology; the membership and connections of the Panel itself; and the more rapid and sophisticated orientation within psychology to the areas of the Panel's interest.

Beyond the obvious administrative criteria of overlapping or duplicating proposals, and spheres of interest relevant to the Navy, three major factors appear to have led to Panel rejection, singly or in combination: the rejected projects tended to originate in institutions that appeared to be weaker, less well-organized, or less concerned with respect to integrated behavioral research; the rejected projects tended to be less well-designed and presented; the rejected projects dealt to a lesser degree with fundamental research problems, often concerning themselves with solutions to practical problems or aiming at a kind of social reform or amelioration.

If we now consider both the approved and rejected projects, with full recognition of the multiplicity of the criteria used in their evaluation over the years, it is possible to characterize, at least partially, the strengths and weaknesses of the program supported by the Navy and by this Panel. The following points emerge from my own review and consideration of the work of the Panel; other observers might stress other parts of the total picture.

1. The approved projects originate in institutions that tend to have well-integrated and active programs of behavioral research, with adequate administrative support locally.

2. The approved projects tend to be somewhat superior in their basic experimental designs and somewhat more oriented toward fundamental research than toward social reform or pragmatic outcomes.

3. The projects generally involve problems that are reduced to testable hypotheses.

4. The projects are characterized by a minimum of classic psychometric theory. This area of research, heavily supported during the war at the developmental level, is still being supported elsewhere as an end in itself; but psychometric theory in the present program is more largely a means to other ends.

5. The projects, whether conceived in the field or laboratory setting, tend to deal with crucial socio-psychological situations; they have both a "real life" flavor and a dynamic orientation.

6. The generalizations are for the most part tentative and limited with some rigor to the data actually involved, with a notable absence of intuitive and sweeping conclusions, historically or observationally buttressed.

7. The need for some synthesis and slightly higher order of concept formation and generalization is continuously apparent. Too often variables are named and then reified by use of a particular assessment device.

8. The experimenters tend to accept, implicitly or explicitly, the same general standards of evidence and proof via the methods of statistical test, replicated experiment, and predictive outcome. Even when the raw data do not lend themselves immediately to such treatments, the need for such treatment after the crude observational phases of research are completed is frequently made explicit.

9. While relatively few new methods or technics appear in the projects, old methods and technics are applied with considerable insight and sophistication.

10. The projects are in need of integrative theory, as Bruner has already pointed out in his general review of the field of socio-psychological research.

11. The projects are still a long way from quick and easy translation to a social technology.

In more general terms, what we appear to have in this program is not a transcendent or pretentious "social science" to which all disciplines must be expected to subscribe and assign their sovereignty. Rather we see the slow, arduous, painstaking processes of science generally, involving observation and delimitation, preliminary investigation, formulation and testing of tentative hypotheses, correction and reformulation, and still later, the attempts at prediction and control. The exciting part of all this is that these processes are occurring at widely separated centers, on vital socio-psychological phenomena, and with an increasingly large number of able people involved to the extent that the contractors consciously make use of young graduate students or young research workers in the actual conduct of the investigations. While we may be impatient for the necessary synthesis and slightly higher order of generalizations that wait to be drawn from the data, such progress can only be made when there exists a sufficiently large and dependable pool of observations with which to deal in theoretical or conceptual terms.

It is significant, too, to consider the disciplines absent from this program and to consider the implications of this absence for social science and social theory. Traditional economics, political science, and history are not found. There are many pragmatic and special reasons for this, but we may reasonably question whether their continued absence will represent a healthy state of affairs in the broad domain of socio-psychological research, although we cannot here deal with this problem in detail.

One cannot view the range of projects we shall discuss without some awareness of the tremendous burden of responsibility that has devolved upon our segment of the social science enterprise. Certainly the research that we are to review is only a part of the Navy's own program of research, and only a small part of the total of similar research supported today from a wide variety of sources. Later scientific history will set the Navy's program and contribution in proper perspective. But equally certainly the Navy program is both symbolic and representative of a major scientific movement throughout the country. For an indefinite moment, psychologists, anthropologists, and sociologists are enjoying a *succes d'estime* that is heady and gratifying. In a simpler figure we are eating remarkably high off the hog. We have been given the chance to produce our equivalent of the atom bomb; if we fail, or as is more likely, if the gap between our product and the expectation of it is too great, we face the possibility of rather aggressive rejection, at many levels.

It may be well therefore to consider some general problems of such research before we turn to detailed consideration of the research projects. I might add that the Advisory Panel has at various meetings uncomfortably faced these issues and I believe that some awareness of them is essential on the part of all of us who share to any major extent in the building and strengthening of the various social sciences.

While the applications of physical science were most dramatic and telling, World War II can also be said to have been a social scientist's war. Since the war, increasing demands have been made upon social scientists to produce workable solutions to problems of human relations and intergroup behavior. We may grant that the social sciences, as separate disciplines, have contributed significant research and knowledge over the years; but we are still not too well prepared to cope with the group phenomena toward which our attention has been forcibly directed by world affairs and national pressures. We are being asked to help society bring its human relations in line with the technological advances provided by the physical sciences. Many outstanding physical scientists have indicated a real willingness to give us the opportunity to produce; the speeches and cooperative actions of a Conant or a Bush or an Oppenheimer represent reasonable and moderate expectations of our probable contribution.

Several institutions have embarked upon programs of organized social science research; many effective and productive teams of investigators are available in the country. From the standpoint of resources and acceptance today's social scientist is well favored.

In his vitriolic review of the first two volumes of *The American Soldier,* the younger Schlesinger describes this situation somewhat more briskly: ". . . Bursting on to University campuses after the war, overflowing with portentous if vague hints of mighty war-time achievements (not, alas, to be disclosed because of security), fanatical in their zeal and shameless in their claims, they persuaded or panicked many university administrations into giving their studies top priorities. Needless to say, they scored an even more brilliant success with the foundations. . . ."

As further evidences of "the mark of the beast" he mentions the "remorseless jargon . . . the idea of research by committee . . . the fetish of 'inter-disciplinary' projects . . . (and) . . . the whole hap-pily subsidized by the foundations, carrying to triumphant comple-tion their ancient hope of achieving the bureaucratization of Amer-ican intellectual life. . . ." One detects a possible suspicion of jangled nerves and fiscal envy in the otherwise placid atmosphere of Harvard, but nonetheless this eminent historian has provided us with some documentation, however grudging, of post-war developments in social science.

There is another interpretation of the present-day prominence of the social scientist. It is characteristic of our American culture to set lofty goals and to subscribe to generalized ideals as guides to conduct, at the same time as our day-to-day behavior falls well short of these goals and ideals. Myrdal has pointed out this dilemma of the Ameri-can creed versus the American reality in relation to the specific prob-lems of the Negro minority; Curti, in another context, has traced the threads of culture and belief that intertwine to give a pattern to American thought. This gap between ideal and reality is not neces-sarily a manifestation of national hypocrisy. When conditions be-come too strained, we tend to revert to the national ideals and we defend them and implement them with a vigilance that attests to their power as a force in the conduct of human affairs.

Two components of this American creed involve: a fair amount of faith in the ultimate attainment of rationalism in human affairs; and a kind of pragmatic idealism generally subsumed in the belief that Americans can make a technology out of anything, as they have done so well in the engineering and other applied science fields. On these two currents of American thought the social sciences are presently being carried.

The sweep of events in which the social scientist suddenly finds himself occupying a position of considerable social visibility has had its counterpart in the separate social science disciplines. Bruner, in the first issue of the *Annual Review of Psychology*, discusses this problem in relation to psychology as such; he mentions the imbal-ance between theory construction and production of investigation results; the improvement in methodology and the absence of a con-ceptual framework. Among other major trends, he cites the consoli-dation of social psychology and the psychology of personality; the focus on groups as units of analysis; and the search for or place of values in the research structure. He concludes: "the critical shortage in social psychology is not in its lack of zeal for data but in its paucity of integrative theory." I imagine that a review of the literature in the other social sciences would show similar concern with rapid change.

It seems to me that one real danger exists in the overexpansion we have experienced: if we fail to deliver at least some of the goods on the major order placed with us, the consumer will become sufficiently frustrated to reject us and seek delivery elsewhere on a shoddier product. Yet it is equally clear that we cannot revert to an earlier day when ten dollars' worth of Hollerith cards or several hundred test scores would keep us happy for months on end. As social scientists we can only move forward with the tide of events, maintaining some awareness of our weaknesses.

Consider first the problem of achieving verifiable and usable knowledge in the behavioral sciences. We talk about interdisciplinary research as a more effective means to that end. But such an idea is by no means new. We have lived through the Yale Institute and its descendants; we have seen the evolution of child development experiment stations with their related and teamed specialists; in fact, the very atmosphere allegedly characteristic of a university is that of a community of scholars presumably interacting in a productive manner. How then does the 1950 interdisciplinary model differ from the earlier models? Do we consult with each other; do we work out experimental designs together; do we merely penetrate our colleagues' fields; do we merely borrow their concepts as glib generalizations; can we actually work together in the data-collecting stages of research?

At the level of descriptive or quasi-explanatory concepts, frustration-aggression, acculturation, learning theory, stratification, psychoanalytic theory, and psychometric methodology may all be found in varying degrees of utility in the journals of anthropology, sociology, and psychology. But withal, many questions remain unanswered. Does increased productivity actually result from research participation by disparate social scientists? Are some disciplines sufficiently sophisticated and advanced either in methods or concepts so that harnessing them to less precise or less sophisticated disciplines may actually retard progress in the short run? How shall we bound and delimit the problems rather vaguely referred to as "group dynamics" and "human relations?" For what general order of problems is an interdisciplinary attack most productive? What must we do to train research social scientists with due regard for the contributions of the several disciplines? How shall we discharge our responsibility at the local institutional level for pacing and aiding our colleagues in the disciplines not presently as favored as we are?

Charles Dollard, addressing the 1949 meeting of the American Sociological Society, says we have tended to bypass "the hard grinding work of developing a nucleus of men, each of whom was master of more than one discipline," even though the need for collaboration among the social sciences is still paramount. Furthermore, when we talk so easily about interdisciplinary research, we forget that the ordinary academic emphasis has been that of increasing and more intensive specialization. The road to academic respectability, if not to glory, is crowded with individual scholars working over increasingly minute segments of their respective fields. Thus, there is some likelihood that the product of the interdisciplinary research group will approach the average potential of the group rather than the potential of the more gifted members of the group, unless we find Dollard's nucleus of men who are masters of more than one field and unless we can find a way to break with our academic tradition.

It is therefore necessary for us to demonstrate the presumed advantages of an interdisciplinary emphasis in creating new knowledge. Social scientists are not genetically or by tradition excellent or productive cooperators. A brilliant exception to this pessimistic generalization is the recent article by S. P. Hayes, Jr., in the *Psychological Bulletin*, entitled, "Some Psychological Problems of Economics."

In reviewing the projects sponsored by this Panel, it may be of significance to note that while many are of necessity carried out by teams of research workers, few teams involve any range of disciplines. At the risk of some heresy, it might be suggested that for the present at least the interdisciplinary effort contributes most to a general formulation of a behavioral problem, but when the real work of hypothesis formulation, data-collecting, and testing begins, the disciplines contribute in the order of their familiarity with classic and time-tested experimental methods, including methods of quantification and statistical design.

As a second problem for the social scientist, consider our dependence on our constituency. The consent of society was not asked for the invention of the electric light, the telephone, the automobile, the atom bomb, or, so help us, television. Applications of physical and biological science in engineering and medicine are awaited and accepted by the public generally. But without the consent, support, and active participation of human beings, the social scientist's ideas and findings cannot result in significant social change. How then are we to cross this barrier, even assuming that we can produce a body of verifiable knowledge permitting prediction and control? We need translators, synthesizers, integrators, teachers, and public relations specialists concentrating upon the task of putting our findings to use. Our task here will be made no easier because of the prevailing belief of the non-specialist that he is his own social science expert, simply by virtue of being a human being and living in a society.

A third problem is found in the fact that the raw material of social science research not infrequently involves highly controversial issues —issues around which the individuals in our society have built up strong feelings, or pat solutions, or deep hostilities. We cannot escape what Bruner speaks of as the search for a place of values in our research, first because they are ever-present and intrusive variables in the raw data, and second because we would be quickly accused of a managerial emphasis in our work, for hire under any philosophy and for any ends. We should not lightly, for example, present our findings by characterizing them as "the democratic method," enhancing their acceptability by the tie-in with a loaded value term and giving them a currency beyond their true worth. We should, by the same token, be extremely cautious regarding the research findings we believe are ready for public consumption, lest we bring about undesirable social side-effects in moving from experimental settings to social change settings. We should be equally cautious about stating our finding in any way that may permit overgeneralization or false deductions in the realm of public policy or premature administrative use.

I have taken the time to spell out these issues because, while I believe them important, I am sure they will not and possibly should not emerge in the discussions of research findings, research methods, and theory-making that represent our real task as a working conference.

I know I speak for all members of the Advisory Panel in welcoming to this meeting the principal investigators and their staffs, as well as the representatives of interested agencies who are here as observers of the results of almost five years of research in the behavioral sciences. The urgency of our work is stressed by the daily headlines we read. I am sure you will share the faith of the Panel that we are beginning to emerge with a body of testable and verifiable hypotheses upon which scientific progress can truly be made.

DETERMINING SYNTALITY DIMENSIONS AS A BASIS FOR MORALE AND LEADERSHIP MEASUREMENT

RAYMOND B. CATTELL

Social Psychology Research Institute
University of Illinois

ANY ATTEMPTS AT SCIENTIFIC PREDICTION of group behavior must employ some scheme of measurement of group characteristics and performances, *i.e.*, of traits of the group as a whole. An infinite number of possible variables exists. Consequently, for the sake of economy as well as to insure interaction among various researches, it is necessary to settle upon a limited number of important parameters. To get effectiveness as well as economy, it is necessary not only to agree on a limited set of standard parameters but also to discover those which correspond to functional unities in group response behavior and structure.

By these scientific canons some of the early group research has got off to a false start by arbitrarily assuming such popular dimensions as degree of sociability, of democratic organization, of democracy, strength of morale, general group ability, degree of aggressiveness, *etc.* It may *seem* enough if such variables are sufficiently operationally defined to be reproducible in other experiments, but (1) they are generally lacking in such precision: the criteria of democracy, for example, have been different in different experiments on this supposed parameter; (2) even when precisely reproducible it is questionable whether a certain dimension or factor loads the same individual variables in the same way in different groups—just as we measure intelligence by different tests in nursery school children and adults, so morale may weight certain observations differently, for example, in large and small groups; and (3) a variable may avoid both of the

16

above objections and still be of no particular relevance or predictive value on group behavior. To say the variable is relevant to a theory is not particularly impressive, since at this stage of perception, theories are far more likely to be wrong than right. The field of variables needs to have some of its structure revealed before we can profitably make tentative hypotheses or theories.

At the time this research was begun, no proof had been offered that the operational measurements used to measure any of these descriptive categories constituted a unitary pattern other than in the experimenter's imagination. The basic research now to be described sets out to measure groups on a wide variety of performances and characteristics, to intercorrelate these group variables, and to determine by factor analysis what *functionally unitary "traits" exist for groups* of the given size and organization.

The pursuit of any comprehensive research upon this problem of determining what may be called group *syntality* dimensions (syntality meaning for a group what personality does for an individual) is best planned in two stages, as has been done in the corresponding inquiries on factors in individual *personality*. The first and more flexible stage is a survey of the verbal categories and symbols that have come into popular use in describing groups of all sizes and sorts. The second calls for greater precision by passing to objective measurement of the variables finally chosen as most important and representative of the pragmatic verbal field and by introducing factor analysis to order these variables. Thus the first "rating" stage reconnoiters the whole situation and gives a perspective within which the exact behavioral measurement can proceed.

As a matter of research strategy, we may note parenthetically that the *behavioral* measurement research will at first hold constant some of the multifarious directions of variation found in the *verbal* survey, e.g., size, membership motivation, degree of overlap with other groups. In this vaster task of determining objective measurement parameters, studies must proceed in planned rotation or sequence, holding some sets of variables constant in each, as, for example, age has been held constant in most of the initial factorizations of ability in the individual personality. Thus each experiment must confine itself to a population of groups of fixed size and type.

At the time the present objective measurement research began (1948), some verbal surveys were already started elsewhere, notably at Ohio State, which fortunately issued in a very comprehensive and well organized set of dimensions [11]. However, our variables were already set up partly on the basis of a pioneer study in our own Social Psychology Research Institute [5], and it remains for our further experiments to take advantage of some of the realms of variation uncovered by these verbal studies. Incidentally we shall distinguish in the rest of this article between variables and dimensions. Dimensions are special variables which have been selected by factor analytic or other methods to represent more variables than themselves, to be substantially independent of one another and to correspond to the chief significant directions of variation which characterize the entities measured.

At present the hundred or more variables recorded in the objective study subtend all three "panels" of group characteristics, namely, (1) performances of the group acting as a whole, (2) particulars of internal structure and interaction, and (3) characteristics of the population (mean and sigma on various personality factors and attitude-interest measures). The first we shall call "syntality" variables; the second, "structure" variables; and the third, "population" variables. Later we shall attempt to get crisper definition of factors by factorizing these three realms in isolation, but in this initial exploration it seems desirable to intercorrelate all in a single pool to determine the over-all functional relations.

These three panels require little further definition. Population variables are simply means of the personality factor or other measures of the component members. By contrast, syntality variables deal with emergents from the population variables. Thus a group of low general intelligence with a highly intelligent leader may have a lower population measure but a higher syntality measure, on intelligence. Structure variables are harder to distinguish from syntality variables because they also characterize the group as a whole, but syntality can be measured without any observations on the *internal* interaction of the group.

Examples of the three classes of variables from the present study are as follows:

1. *Syntality variables:* Accuracy of conclusion in committee-like debate on given data; reduction of strength of pull when tug-of-war rope is electrified (a "morale" variable); time to construct a large wooden structure to given specifications; extent of cheating in competition with other groups; extent of deviation from prior group decision as a result of emotional appeals.

2. *Structure variables:* Degree of formalization of leadership; assessment of leadership along a directive-non-directive continuum; orderliness of behavior; amount of expressed criticism

of the group; amount and kind of interaction, as determined by an interaction-process analysis; permissiveness of atmosphere; degree of change of individual opinions after expression of group opinion; degree of emergence of "lieutenants" between formal "captain" and rest of group; frequency of change of formal leader at periodic voting; and a variety of sociometric scores.

3. *Population variables:* Here we attempted to determine the more important dimensions of personality by the fewest possible measurements. Consequently, we assessed such ability, dynamic and temperament factors as general intelligence, emotional stability (vs. neuroticism), surgency, schizothymia, as well as interests and attitudes on some important issues, *e.g.,* radicalism-conservatism, and some background data. The present research was aided by recent advances in the degree of definition of these factors through a research for the United States Public Health Service simultaneously being carried out by this Research Unit. Most dependence has been placed on the 16 Personality Factor Questionnaire [14]. For each group the mean and the dispersion (sigma) for some twenty personality aspects of the population were thus obtained directly and some twenty more were obtained from individual behavior observed in the group.

About one hundred and fifty variables, comprising some sixty syntality variables, fifty structural variables, and forty population variables, were thus measured for eighty groups of ten men each. An attempt was made to get a wide range of subjects and finally the eight hundred persons were taken about equally from Air Force officer candidates (courtesy of Air Force Human Resource and Development Branch), university students, and men enlisting in the Navy.

It seems important, in spite of difficulties, to insure that in experiments on groups, the groups formed are real in some sense other than that of being arbitarily brought together for the experiment. This does not mean that they must have traditions or long duration, but they must have real dynamics. Our definition of a group is *a set of people who satisfy their needs consciously and unconsciously through the existence and instrumentality of this set of people.* That is to say, the group must operate as the best means by which each individual can satisfy certain individual desires. In this experiment, each individual hoped to gain ten dollars which he could do only by joining up in one of these groups. In addition to three to four hours of individual testing, each individual shared nine to twelve hours of group activity and testing which was divided into three sessions on three different days spread over a week or more. The present study is thus confined to *traditionless groups* which for the first session were *with-*

out, and in the last two sessions *with formally elected and defined leadership.*

The observations on the group performances were made by an experimenter, Dr. Stice, and an observer in suitable detachment from the group, using recording apparatus and various prepared scoring schemes, including an interaction process analysis chart developed at Illinois, with some debt to Bales [2]. These observations, now scored and tabulated but not correlated, permit of analysis both from the standpoint of emergent processes in group formation, *i.e., longitudinal study* of structural growth, and also *cross-sectionally* to determine group dimensions as stated above. It is our aim to make the cross sectional analysis first, in order to discover the important syntal dimensions in terms of which to deal with developmental or other problems.

As we are now only at the threshold of the year in which the statistical analyses are to be made, no results are available. A glimpse of what may emerge in regard to group dimensions is, however, foreshadowed by the pilot studies of Wispe [5] and Gibb [10] on about twenty groups. There we find about nine factors, three of which operate in the realm of what is popularly called morale; one is a general group ability factor; one is a kind of "group self-possession" correlating with freedom of group self-criticism, and so on. As illustration of the pattern of a single factor among the variables it influences, we may take what has been called "Morale III." This is something which produces among the syntality variables high performance in the following:

1. The electric shock situation.
2. The solution of arithmetical problems.
3. Orderliness of behavior.
4. Mutual permissiveness of atmosphere. } Structure variables
5. Low dominance of the leader.
6. Low neuroticism.   } Population variables
7. Good intelligence.

The almost innumerable further problems to which a positive solution is opened up by a sound factorization of group dimensions may be illustrated by issues going popularly under the rubric of leadership problems. Our thesis is, first, that the effectiveness of a leader is only to be measured in terms of *the performance of groups under him.* As part of the preliminary exploration, Dr. Saunders in this Unit is making an analysis of variance in group performances to see what fractions are associated respectively with leader variance and with population variance. When this is done we propose to correlate syntality measurements, *e.g.*, on the morale factors, the general ability factor, *etc.*, with the measured personality factors in leaders, the structural (sociometric) characters of the group, and the mean value of these characteristics for the population.

The kinds of questions which the comprehensiveness of the data in this study will enable us to answer in quantitative terms may be illustrated by the following outstanding ones:

1. To what extent do the syntal characters of the group depend upon population characters? We already have evidence that the mean individual level in general neuroticism is strongly correlated with the level of group morale obtained.

2. How are the syntal characters related to leader behavior dimensions, *e.g.*, domination, imitation, integration, as worked out by the Ohio researchers [12]?

3. What is the correlation between syntal dimensions and measures of interpersonal communications as worked out, for example, by Festinger, Schachter, Back and their co-workers [9]?

4. What are the correlations between syntality measures and various sociometric measures of internal interaction (other than strictly communication variables as in (3)? This may link up with the study of administrative conference process by Marquis since two of the situations in which our groups were tested were designed to involve administrative kinds of activity.

5. What are the personality characteristics which distinguish leaders from non-leaders statistically broken down with respect to various types of group syntality, particularly with regard to successful and unsuccessful groups as measured on various dimensions? This aspect of the analysis can be brought into close relation with the work of Carter [3] on leadership personality in relation to other variables.

6. How is the degree of shift of individual toward group opinion related to (a) division of opinion in the group as in the work of Asch [1], (b) the personality characteristics of the individual, and (c) the syntality dimensions of the group?

7. What is the relative rate of learning on various performances and internal integrative activities (comparing our third with our first session) of groups of different syntality, leadership structure, and mean population characteristics? This integrates with the morale and productivity studies of French and Katz.

It will be seen that in general the analysis seeks to interrelate, without prejudice as to the direction of causation, three measured aspects of the group: syntality, internal structure (deduced from function), and population characters.

Our argument is that really effective hypotheses can best be formed when factorization has structured the variables in these areas into a dozen or so putative functional unities, any one of which is likely to extend across all three areas. These factors will themselves be interrelated and can profitably form the basic concepts for more precise and interpretative hypotheses dealing with the manner of their interrelation. Prior to this revelation of the main factor structure, it would seem as unprofitable to attempt ambitious hypotheses as to speculate about cellular structure before the use of the microscope.

The above argument may perhaps best be illustrated by taking the subject of leadership measurement as a rider on the use of syntality dimensions in research. According to the definition given in the initial introduction to this report, leadership is to be measured by the syntality changes which the leader is able to produce. That is to say, the principal dimensions of a particular group would need to be measured under a wide array of leaders giving a normal distribution of leadership powers, so that each leader could be assessed in standard scores on the deviation which his leadership produces on each of the syntal dimensions from the mean for that dimension. At first sight, this may seem somewhat perplexing since our common sense analysis of the operations of a leader are that he (1) finds means whereby the group can obtain some agreed goal, and (2) attempts to find and make explicit some agreed goal in order to give the maximum satisfaction possible to the group in the circumstances. It might seem, if one thinks of syntality or personality in terms only of ability dimensions, that changes of syntality would represent only operations of the former kind. However, we must remember that syntality includes dynamic dimensions too, and that consequently a change produced in the goal of a group will show up as a change in certain dynamic dimensions.

To clarify this further it is necessary at this point to connect the theory of group behavior with the methodology of handling dynamic traits or attitudes in terms of ergic vectors [7]. Psychological forces have direction as well as strength and must accordingly be represented as vectors. It has been suggested that the coordinates which are most important for defining the direction of dynamic traits are those of the primary drives or ergs [7]. Thus, according to the ergic theory of attitude measurement, any given attitude, interest or dynamic trait is representable as a vector, in relation to about nine co-

ordinates corresponding to the ergs or drives. This is illustrated in
Figure 1.

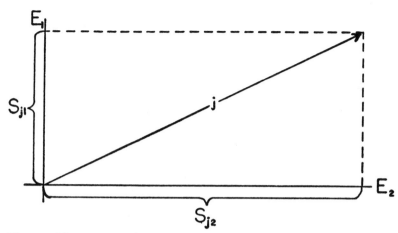

Figure 1. Measurement of an attitude vector in situational index projections
upon ergic coordinates.

From the standpoint of group psychology this ergic theory of attitude measurements leads to the generalization that group synergy is
itself a vector and that it may be obtained by summing the vectors of
the attitudes of the individual members of the group to the group,
i.e., their particular interests in the group.

It is, of course, possible to speak of the amount of energy, *i.e.*,
a force operating over time, in abstraction from the direction of
the force. But such a use of disembodied force—or an energy
orphaned from its biological parentage—is probably of very limited
use in group psychology. In any case it cannot be arrived at without
first experimenting upon forces with direction and then abstracting
it from calculations of that kind.

For in general it is important to know *what* drive is involved in the
group activity, whether it be learning, sublimation or conflict. Different drives may behave differently in regard to their plasticity, their
goal gradients, the tempo of their energy release and their responses
to frustration. Attention to ergic qualities is particularly important
because group activities may be selective with regard to quality. The
activities of a group are likely in the first place to be such that the
synergy is a special selection from among the possible satisfactions of
the individual. For example, with the exception of the family group,

most groups are selective against sexual drive in the sense that they are organized so that it achieves little direct satisfaction through the larger group as such.

To clarify the next point, it is necessary to introduce the concepts of synergy, maintenance synergy and effective synergy. By synergy we mean the total interest which goes into the activities of a group, and this will be the vector sum of the individual attitudes to the group. Thus the synergy of a group will depend on the number of people in it, the intensity of their interests in the group and the particular qualitative nature of those interests. Now a group uses up part of the energy which the individuals put into it merely in maintenance activities. For example, a missionary society has the effective purpose of sending out missionaries into the field, but only a fraction of the subscriptions it gathers actually go into that activity, some being used up in maintaining the organization of the group, its office expenses, *etc.* That part of the synergy which goes into mere maintenance we will call maintenance synergy, and we shall define the effective synergy as the total synergy minus the maintenance synergy. Pursuing the argument above about the importance of knowing the ergic quality of the synergy which goes into a group, it is easy to see that a certain amount of segregation goes on as between the maintenance and effective synergy, in that the maintenance synergy is likely to use up more sociability and good will, leaving over more hostile and aggressive impulses for external expression in the effective synergy. The selective dependence of certain cultural activities upon particular drives has also been emphasized by Freud. Advance in this area will obviously be possible only with advance in techniques for objectively measuring motivation and dynamic traits generally. The experiments of McClelland [13], Cofer [8] and others [7] seem to promise that we are on the brink of obtaining such objective means of measuring dynamic traits, and if so, the foundation will be laid for obtaining regularities and laws in regard to the disposition of synergy and the leadership operations which affect it. For example, it seems likely that one criterion of good leadership will turn out to be the ratio of effective to maintenance synergy under his organizational activities.

The definition of a leader as "A person who has a demonstrable influence upon group syntality" has certain corollaries which may not be immediately evident. In the first place it is no longer possible to speak simply of good leaders and poor leaders, but instead we are required to view the problem in terms of whether a leader is good or bad with respect to a specific syntality dimension. For example, a certain leader may in general increase the dimension of group general ability, reduce its dimension of morale and increase its dimension of dictatorialness of atmosphere. Secondly, it indicates that every man in a group is to some extent a leader in so far as every man has some effect upon the syntality of a group. Thus leadership can no longer be considered an all or nothing phenomenon, but even when it is formally organized in terms of a leader and followers, there is for each person an index showing the extent to which he is leading.

Conclusions

The theoretical points and practical research activities described in this report may be summarized as follows:

1. A group is better defined dynamically, in terms of an instrument of individual satisfactions, than in terms of interaction, communication, boundaries or organization.

2. The description of any group requires attention to three panels: (a) population, (b) structure and (c) syntality. The latter requires the definition of any given group in terms of quantities with respect to a limited number of dimensions. These dimensions may be obtained by factorization of a great variety of variables.

3. An experiment is described in which eighty groups of ten men each are factorized with respect to their performances and characteristics on some 150 observed variables. A preliminary analysis suggests that there will be about a dozen dimensions, some of which have meanings in the realm of morale, others in the realm of ability and so on. Syntality can be defined by analogy with personality as that which permits a prediction of what the group will do when the situation is defined. Thus it takes the general form:

$$R = f(O, S)$$

where R is the reaction of the group, O is the definition of the group as an organism, *i.e.*, its syntality, and S is the stimulus situation. This may be expressed more completely in the following expanded formula, which corresponds to the general factorial specification equation:

$$R_j = S_1F_1 + S_2F_2 + \ldots S_nF_n + S_jF_j$$

where R_j is the reaction in the particular situation j, the F's are the various factors which define the syntality, and the S's are the situational indices or factor loadings which define the meaning of the situation with respect to each of the factors.

4. A leader is to be measured by the extent to which he changes the syntality of the group from its mean syntality. Thus his leadership capacity would be defined by a series of measurements as follows:

$$L = F_{1x} + F_{2x} + F_{3x} \; etc.$$

where the F values are the positions which the individual X produces on the various dimensions. Thus the prediction of how a group will behave under the leader X is possible by inserting these F values into the specification equation with the situational indices already worked out for leaders in general and for populations in general.

5. The synergy of a group is defined as the vectorial sum of the individual vectors corresponding to the attitudes of the component individuals toward the group to which they belong. That is to say, it is the sum of the interests of the individuals in the group in the group's activities. This synergy may be divided into maintenance synergy and effective synergy. Some evidence of the existence of a factor corresponding to the amount of synergy in a group has been produced recently by Hemphill. From inspection, it also seems likely that the concept of cohesion used by Cartwright, Festinger and others is operationally defined in terms of phenomena which are consequences of the magnitude of synergy in a group.

6. Since a leader has the dual functions of finding the best way to reach a goal which the group has agreed upon and of getting the group to agree upon a goal which will give it greater satisfaction, it is necessary to measure group syntality with due regard to the inclusion of dynamic variables so that the second of these activities can be adequately registered in terms of the change in ergic dimensions of syntality under the leader.

7. The reference of various applied problems to these syntality dimensions when they are adequately defined, stabilized and standardized for measurement will have the result of generalizing the concept of leadership, in so far as we shall find it necessary to regard every individual in some degree as a leader. Also it will require the rather composite concept of goodness of leadership to be re-examined from the point of view of "goodness for what?" which will require attention to the expression of leadership in quite a number of independent dimensions, not all of which will obviously have value judgments attached to them. As far as the empirical findings yet available indicate, it also requires us to think of morale not as a single dimension,

but as expressed in at least three independent kinds of morale, some of which are good for some operations and others for different purposes.

8. The crystallization of these functional unities among variables which we have called dimensions above, by making it possible to describe a group in quantitative terms at a given moment, will open up possibilities of making more precise statements about developmental, longitudinal changes in groups under various influences.

BIBLIOGRAPHY

1. Asch, S. Effects of group pressure upon the modification and distortion of judgments. This volume.
2. Bales, R. F. *Interaction Process Analysis.* Cambridge, Massachusetts, Addison-Wesley, 1950.
3. Carter L., Haythorn, W. and Howell, M. A further investigation of the criteria of leadership. *J. abnorm. soc. Psychol.,* 1950, *45,* 350–358. 358.
4. Cattell, R. B. Concepts and methods in the measurement of group syntality. *Psychol. Rev.,* 1948, *55,* 48–63.
5. —— and Wispe, L. G. The dimensions of syntality in small groups. *J. soc. Psychol.,* 1948, *28,* 57–78.
6. —— The dimensions of culture patterns by factorization of national characters. *J. abnorm. soc. Psychol.,* 1949, *44,* 443–469.
7. ——, Heist, A. B., Heist, P. A. and Stewart, R. G. The objective measurement of dynamic traits. *Educ. psychol. Measmt.,* 1950, *10,* 224–248.
8. Cofer, C. N. Verbal behavior in relation to reasoning and values. This volume.
9. Festinger, L., Back, K., Schachter, S., Kelley, H. H. and Thibaut, J. *Theory and Experiment in Social Communication.* Res. Cent. for Group Dynam., Michigan University, 1950.
10. Gibb, C. A. The emergence of leadership in small temporary groups of men. Champaign, Illinois, University of Illinois Library, 1949.
11. Hemphill, J. K. The measurement of group dimensions. *J. Psychol.,* 1950, 29, 325–342.
12. —— Situational factors in leadership. Bureau of Educ., Res., Columbus, Ohio, Monograph No. 31, Ohio State University, 1949.
13. McClelland, D. C. and Liberman, A. M. The effect of need for achievement on the recognition of need-related words. *J. Personality,* 1950, *18,* 236–251.
14. The 16 Personality Factor Questionnaire. Champaign, Illinois, Institute for Personality and Ability Testing, 313 West Avondale Street, 1949.

INFORMAL COMMUNICATION IN SMALL GROUPS

LEON FESTINGER

Research Center for Group Dynamics
University of Michigan

SPONTANEOUS, INFORMAL SOCIAL COMMUNICATION is a vital part of the functioning of groups. It appears, when we consider group action from a theoretical point of view, that the sharing of information, the exertion of influence and other such processes whereby one part of a group communicates with another part are very basic. A better understanding of the dynamics of such communication points, in turn, to a better understanding of how groups function and the ways in which they affect their members.

The program of research in social communication which we shall describe has thus attempted to focus on various types of communication and various aspects of the communication process. It is not possible to give here a detailed account of the experiments and findings related to the several problems of communication which we have pursued. We shall, however, list briefly the various problems on which we have worked and examine more fully the work on one of these problems, namely, communication as the exertion of influence.

1. *The transmission of rumor and information in groups:* A number of studies have been conducted which were concerned with discovering the factors which determine when rumors or information will spread, and the direction of the transmission of such rumors. One such study was done by following up the transmission of a rumor which started spontaneously in a community [4]. Two other studies were conducted by following up the transmission of rumors which were deliberately planted within a group in a prearranged manner [5,2].

2. *Restraints against communication in hierarchies:* Studies have been performed on the determinants of the direction of communication and the kind of information which does or does not get communicated in hierarchical structures. One such experiment was done in a functioning organization [2]. Two experiments were performed in artificially created hierarchies in which we studied the communication process which existed between and within the hierarchical layers thus created [7,9].

3. *Communication and influence:* The first study related to this problem investigated the determinants of group formation and the development and maintenance of group standards in a housing project [5]. As a result of it, numerous new insights and hypotheses were gained concerning the part that communication plays in small groups. In order to clarify and add to our knowledge, a number of laboratory experiments were performed to test and elaborate some of the specific hypotheses which had emerged [1,6,8]. We shall in the ensuing pages describe in detail the development of the research on this problem.

SOCIAL PRESSURES IN INFORMAL GROUPS

There are many beliefs and attitudes that people hold which cannot be checked with objective data. Yet people are in need of support for these beliefs and one method employed to gain it is by agreement with others. The attempt to get such support, that is, the attempt to have others in a group, of which one is a member, agree on a given opinion or belief or behavior pattern, leads to a process of influence among members of the group and consequent mutual adjustment of opinion. An individual may try to influence others to accept his beliefs or he may be willing to be influenced by others. Under appropriate circumstances the result of such a process of influence by communication is that a number of people find support for their opinions by achieving a state of relative uniformity within a group.

It is, of course, not necessary that everybody accept a certain opinion in order that it seem correct and valid for a particular individual. We tend to refer our opinions to certain groups and not to others. In general people tend to hold opinions which are accepted by the people with whom they associate. Such considerations, then, seem to be important for the formation of groups and for the influence processes which act in these groups. An attempt was made to investigate these phenomena in groups that had developed in a housing project [5].

The housing project consisted of one hundred houses arranged in courts. These houses were all occupied by the families of married veteran students at the Massachusetts Institute of Technology. About half of the families had children, in almost all cases, one child per family.

After achieving a working knowledge of the kind of people who lived in the project, the type of social life they led, and their interests and backgrounds, it seemed appropriate to study the conditions for friendship and group formation within this neighborhood community. When our data were assembled, the most striking item was the dependence of friendship formation on the mere physical arrangement of the houses. People who lived close to one another became friendly while people who lived farther apart did not. Mere accidents of geography such as where a path led or whose doorway a staircase passed were major determinants of friendships within this community. The small face-to-face social groups which formed were, to a large extent, limited to the number of people who lived in the same court.

Certainly other factors operated. If two people did not like each other they did not become friends even if they lived right next door to one another. It was impressive, however, to see how large a part mere physical arrangement did play. Since the courts did play such an important role in determining friendship formation and, consequently, the formation of social groups within the community, we were able to study other aspects of the functioning of these groups, considering each court as a potential social group. We could then examine to what extent these potential groups had become actual psychological groups and how membership affected people's attitudes and behavior.

We were fortunate in being able to study these processes in connection with a new issue which arose in the community. A few months after our investigation had begun the tenants spontaneously formed a tenant organization. We were able to study the growth of this organization and to observe, from the beginning, the development of attitudes toward it and the participation in its activities by the residents of the project. The fact that the organization would affect equally all sub-groups in the project made relevant an investigation of the ways in which different group standards had developed in the different courts and the factors which affected their strength and nature.

Both the qualitative and quantitative data which we gathered in this community pointed clearly to a high degree of uniformity within each of the courts in the project concerning attitudes toward and activity in this tenant organization. They also pointed to great differences between courts in this respect. Each group, it seems, had developed more or less strong group standards concerning this issue and exerted strong influences on its members to conform. How effectively this influence was exerted on its members depended to a great extent on how cohesive the small social group was. Those groups to which the members were strongly attracted were able to exert strong forces on their members to conform and those toward which the members were little attracted were not able to maintain uniform group standards. Furthermore, the people who did not conform to the group standards of the court in which they lived were not as integral a part of the group as those who did conform. These nonconformers tended to have fewer friends in their own court and fewer friends in the project as a whole.

In attempting to explain the data which we obtained in this study we were led to the following interpretations. The informal pressures which a group exerts on its members are frequently subtle ones which are difficult to localize. The weight of other's opinions, the gradual change in one's ideas of what is the "normal" thing to do simply because every one else does it, and the mutual influences of people on one another are the kinds of things that serve effectively as pressures toward conformity with the behavior pattern of the group.

Under such circumstances the consequences of nonconformity are also subtle. These consequences may merely be the tendency to prefer those people who are not "different." There was no indication in this project that there was any overt or formalized pressure on court members to conform to their court standards. Many of the residents realized that the people in their court were different from the people in some other court, but the influences which created and maintained these differences among courts were indirect and the residents were not aware of them. Members of the courts were influenced in their opinions and behavior merely by virtue of their association with others without any formalized "group intent" to influence.

The strength of the influence which the group could effectively exert in this manner depended partly upon the attractiveness of the group for the member and partly on the degree to which the member was in communication with others in the group. No matter how attractive a group is to a particular person, it will be impossible for the group to exert any influence on him if he is never in communication with the group. In general there seem to be three conditions under which individuals would be able to resist group influences of this nature.

1. The member may not be strongly attracted to belong to the group. Under these circumstances the relatively weak influence which the group exerts cannot overcome personal considerations which may happen to be contrary to the group standards. This person may, if the influence attempts become overt, simply leave the group.

2. There may not be sufficient communication between the member and others in the group. Under these conditions the pressures from the group are simply not brought to bear on the member, although, if they had been exerted, they might have been effective. In such instances the non-conformer may not even be aware of the fact that he is different from most of the others in his group.

3. The influence of some other group to which the person belongs may be stronger than the influence which the court is able to exert on him. Under these circumstances the person who appears as a non-conformer is one only because we have chosen to call him a member of the court group. He does deviate from his own court but he conforms to some other group to which he actually belongs.

In order to understand more fully these group processes involving communication, the following three questions must be asked and answered: (1) When do pressures toward uniformity arise in groups and what are the conditions for the effective exertion of influence in response to such pressures? (2) How does perceived group membership, attraction to the group, and strength of pressure toward uniformity affect the direction of communication? That is, upon whom are influences exerted and upon whom are they not exerted? (3) What determines when a non-conformer is or is not rejected by the group?

These three questions were investigated in three separate laboratory experiments specifically designed to answer them.

The Exertion of Influence Through Social Communication

On the basis of the results of the previous study, the hypothesis may be advanced that pressure towards uniformity in a group, the amount of influence exerted and how effective the exertion of influence will be is a function of how attractive the group is for its members. In order to test this hypothesis specifically, Back [1] conducted an ex periment with the following focus:

1. Determination of the exact relationship between attraction to the group and the accomplishment of influence.
2. Determination of whether these same relationships will exist irrespective of the particular source of the attraction to the group.

In the experiment in question three sources of attraction to the group were experimentally varied. In some groups the source of attraction was the personal liking among the members, in some it was the possibility of a reward which could be attained by membership in the group, and in still others the source of attraction was the prestige which the group had in the eyes of the experimenter. For each of these sources of attraction to the group some high cohesive and some low cohesive groups were created. There were then, in all, six different types of groups employed in the experiment.

The procedure which was followed attempted to control other variables which could affect the influence process. In essence the pro cedure was as follows: Pairs of subjects of the same sex, who did not know each other prior to the experiment, were scheduled to appear in the laboratory at the same time. After the subjects were introduced to each other they were each taken to a different room and were each given a set of three photographs. They were told that the pictures had been taken from a film strip and formed a sequence which they were to reconstruct and then write a story connecting the pictures. They were also informed that after having written the story they would have an opportunity to discuss their ideas and their stories with the other person in the group and afterwards they would be able to write a final story. It was emphasized that their story should be closely tied to the pictures and should make use of the available clues that were present in the set of three pictures.

At this time each subject was also given additional instructions which, depending upon which of the six experimental conditions he was to be in, was calculated to increase or decrease the attraction he felt toward being in this group. While it would not be feasible to go into the details of this manipulation of the attraction to the group, suffice it to say that there is evidence that the strength of the attrac tion to the group was successfully manipulated for each of these three types of attraction.

When they had completed their stories, the two partners were brought together to discuss what they had written. Before this discussion they were reminded that the object of it was to help them improve their own story. It was emphasized that they were not going to write a common story and that they could stop the discussion at any time when they saw its usefulness at an end. The length and manner of the discussion were therefore left entirely to the subjects.

After they had concluded the discussion the subjects returned to their separate rooms to write their final story. They were instructed to "write what you now think to be the best story." They could not see the pictures again and, therefore, could not check information which they had received from their partners.

The data obtained from this experiment fall into three categories:

> 1. Data obtained from observing the discussion process which went on between the two members of each group.
> 2. Data showing how much each member had been influenced by the discussion. This was obtained from coding the initial and final stories and counting the number of changes which could be traced to the partner's influence.
> 3. Data from an interview with each subject conducted at the end of the session.

Summarized, the major results are the following:

1. *Patterns of discussion.* On the basis of the observations of the discussion in each group, ratings were made in terms of whether or not the discussion seemed to be an active attempt at influence. Of the 30 high cohesive pairs, 16 were rated as actively attempting to influence each other, while only 7 of the 30 low cohesive pairs were thus rated. Consistent with this is the finding from answers to questions in a post-experimental interview. The subjects were asked whether or not they felt pressure from their partners to change their story. Out of the 60 subjects in the 30 high cohesive groups, 36 reported that they did feel such pressure, while only 21 members of the 60 low cohesive subjects reported that they felt such pressure to change their opinion. We may thus conclude that stronger attraction to the group did make for greater pressure towards uniformity as seen by the amount of influence which was attempted.

2. *Reaction to partner's influence attempts.* After the experiment was finished each subject was asked the question, "If your partner had tried all he could, do you think you would have accepted his story?" For each of the different sources of attraction to the group the members of the high cohesive groups reported feeling less resistance to

influence from the partner than did the members of the low cohesive groups. In other words, the members of the high cohesive groups, irrespective of the source of the attraction to that group, tended to report more readiness to change their opinion in response to pressure from their partner.

3. *The effect of cohesiveness on the amount of influence actually accomplished.* We have seen that in the high cohesive groups the subjects tried harder to influence their partners and were also more willing to accept their partners' opinions. We may therefore expect to find more influence accomplished in the high than in the low cohesive groups. This is indeed the case. Irrespective of the source of the attraction to the group, the high cohesive pairs showed more change which could be attributed to the influence of their partners than did the low cohesive groups.

This experiment, performed under controlled laboratory conditions, with experimental manipulation of the variables with which we were concerned, substantiates the hypothesis arrived at in our field study of a neighborhood community. We may now state somewhat more precisely the hypotheses emerging from these studies. The greater the attraction of members to a group, given some discrepancy in opinion concerning a relevant issue, the more pressure towards uniformity will develop within the group and, consequently, there will be greater attempts to influence others in the group and greater readiness on the part of the members to change their opinions in line with the opinions of others. The result of this, of course, is more rapid progress toward a state of uniformity.

INTERPERSONAL COMMUNICATION IN SMALL GROUPS

With the establishment of the theory that groups tend to exert pressures on members to change their opinions when difference of opinion exists, we must look further and examine the determinants of the direction of communication, that is, upon whom in a group will such pressures be exerted. It would seem that if a group has the property of moving toward uniformity, then any discrepancy among the different parts of the group will give rise to pressures which will be exerted differentially on the parts of the group to effect a change in order to re-establish uniformity. The strength of these pressures is a function of the magnitude of the tendencies toward uniformity which the group possesses. In a group where the tendencies toward uni-

formity concern an opinion about a particular issue, the exertion of
pressures on persons to change their opinion must make itself felt
through a process of communication among them.

What can we infer about this process of communication?

> 1. If we assume that the magnitude of pressure applied to any
> member of a group is a direct function of the discrepancy be-
> tween that person's opinion and the opinion of the rest of the
> group, it would follow that within a psychological group we
> would expect communication to be directed mainly toward those
> members whose opinions are extreme as compared to the opin-
> ions of the others.
>
> 2. The less the pressure toward uniformity in a group, the less
> should be this tendency to communicate mainly to the extremes
> of the opinion range within the group. We would also expect
> to find here, in line with the results reported in the preceding
> pages, that the less the pressure toward uniformity in a group,
> the less will be the actual exertion of influence and the less will
> be the actual accomplishment of influence within that group.

The experiment by Festinger and Thibaut [6] which we shall
summarize here was specifically designed to test these hypotheses under controlled laboratory conditions. Groups of volunteers ranging
in size from six to fourteen members, all of whom were strangers to
one another, assembled in the experimental room. Each member was
asked to sit down at one of a number of small tables arranged in a
circle. Each member was identified to the others by a letter printed
on a card placed on a stand in front of him so that all others could see
it.

After all the members were present the group was given a problem
to consider. The problem was such that opinions concerning it could
be placed on a suggested seven point scale. The members were
instructed to consider the problem and then each to place on a stand
in front of him a card which would indicate to the others in the group
what his opinion was on the problem. Thus, at the start of the experiment all members had formed opinions and were aware of what
the opinions of everyone else in the group were. The problems which
we used in this experiment were chosen so as to produce adequate
dispersion of opinion within each group.

When these preliminaries were over the experimenter described to
the group the manner in which the problem was to be discussed.
Paper pads were distributed to the subjects and they were informed
that discussion about the problem was to be restricted to writing
notes to one another. They were free to include anything they liked

in the notes. They could address a note to only one person at a time, but they could write as many notes as they pleased. As soon as a note was written the experimenter would take it and deliver it to the person to whom it was addressed. It was emphasized that, in order to have the discussion proceed sensibly, if any member of the group at any time changed his opinion he should change the card in front of him so that everyone in the group would be aware at all times of what the opinions of the other members were.

In addition to this general procedure, instructions were given which attempted to manipulate the magnitude of the pressure toward uniformity operating in the group. Some were given instructions calculated to produce rather high pressure toward uniformity, other groups were given instructions calculated to produce moderate pressure toward uniformity, while still others were given no additional instructions. In the last groups any pressures toward uniformity which existed would be spontaneously generated.

The results obtained were as follows:

1. *The direction of communication.* It is possible to examine the direction of communication by examining the number of communications addressed to those individuals whose opinions were at the extreme of the range in the group, to those whose opinions were one step removed from the extreme of the range, two steps removed from the extreme of the range and so on. It is found that uniformly 70 per cent to 90 per cent of the communications are addressed to persons whose opinions are at the extremes of the existing range of opinion in the group. The number of communications received falls off very rapidly for those people whose opinions are closer to the middle of the range. This result is uniform. It is true for all groups irrespective of the particular problem they were discussing. We may conclude unequivocally that the volume of communication directed toward a group member is a function of his proximity to the extreme of the existing range of opinions.

2. *The effect of increasing the pressure toward uniformity.* It was possible to calculate an index for each group which would reflect to what extent the communications were being directed toward the extremes of the opinion range. We can consequently compare these indices for groups in which high pressure toward uniformity had been induced with those in which medium pressure toward uniformity or low pressure toward uniformity had been created. The results show that there is least tendency to communicate to the extreme

opinions in the "low pressure" groups and there is the greatest tendency to communicate to the extremes of the opinion range in the "high pressure" groups. The "medium pressure" groups tend to fall between the other two in their tendency to communicate to the extremes. We may conclude therefore, that the higher the pressure toward uniformity the greater will be the proportion of the communications addressed to the extremes of the psychological group.

3. *The relation between pressure toward uniformity and amount of influence accomplished.* It was possible in this experiment to check once more on the hypothesis with which the Back experiment [1] was concerned. In this experiment cohesiveness was varied and consequently the pressure toward uniformity was indirectly manipulated. In the present experiment pressure toward uniformity was manipulated directly. To be consistent it is clear that one should find the same difference between the high pressure and the low pressure toward uniformity groups as was found between the high cohesive and the low cohesive groups in the Back experiment. We would expect then, to find greater actual change toward uniformity, the greater the experimentally induced pressure toward uniformity.

In order to test this hypothesis a measure of the amount of change toward uniformity was calculated for each experimental group. In all of the comparisons the "high pressure" groups showed most change toward uniformity, the "medium pressure" groups showed the next largest amount of change toward uniformity and "low pressure" groups showed the least amount of such change.

We may conclude that pressure toward uniformity in a group has the following effects:

    1. The greater the pressure, the more is influence exerted on extreme opinions.
    2. The greater the pressure, the more influence is actually accomplished.

DEVIATION, REJECTION AND COMMUNICATION

In the light of the effects of pressures toward uniformity which we have already examined, we may now try to formulate, more adequately, the various types of reactions to such pressures which a group may show. We have already seen that one response is to attempt to exert influence on other members of the group and another is to be more amenable to influence and more ready to change. Both of these act to move the members of the group closer towards uniformity. There is still a third reaction to pressures toward uniformity which also, in a sense, acts to hasten the achievement of uniformity. This type of behavior is the rejection from the psychological group of those individuals who do not conform or do not agree with the others. In the extreme instance, of course, if one excludes from the group all of the divergent opinions, one then has already achieved uniformity within the psychological group. The existence of three simultaneous tendencies whenever pressures toward uniformity exist may then be postulated:

1. A tendency to attempt to change the opinions of others.
2. A tendency to be ready to change one's own opinion.
3. A tendency to reduce one's dependence on those who disagree.

It is the last tendency which gives rise to the overt symptom of rejection from the group.

An experiment by Schachter [8] was designed to measure the extent to which the existence of pressures towards uniformity makes for the rejection from the group of nonconformers or deviates. It is, of course, of importance in this connection not only to know that once pressures toward uniformity exist those who deviate are rejected, but also to know the conditions under which the rejection of deviates is stronger or weaker. The experiment by Schachter was designed to test the hypothesis that the strength of rejection of deviates responded to the same factors which increased tendencies to influence others and greater readiness to change one's self. Specifically, that the higher the cohesiveness of the group and the greater the degree of relevance of the issue to the group, the greater would be the magnitude of the rejection of members who do not conform on that issue.

The experiment was conducted as follows: students on the campus of the University of Michigan were offered an opportunity to join various clubs that were being organized. Each of the clubs eventually consisted of ten members who were to meet for discussion purposes. Interest in joining these clubs was stimulated by making the discussion topics and the purposes of the discussion attractive to potential members. When each club group actually met, among the ten members were three trained participants who were instructed to behave in certain patterns.

Each group was given a topic to discuss which was in line with the members' reasons for joining. This topic was selected so that almost everyone would have opinions about it which would cluster closely together. One of our confederates was instructed to take an extremely deviant position with respect to the opinion on this issue and to maintain it throughout the course of the discussion. Another of the confederates was instructed to adopt a very deviant opinion but gradually, as others tried to get him to change his opinion, to yield so that by the end of the discussion he would agree with most of the others. The third trained participant was instructed to adopt that opinion which most of the other members of the group supported and to remain at that opinion.

Again a full description of the way these experiments were performed would be inappropriate. We proceeded, however, to create some groups which were highly cohesive (that is, there was a strong attraction for the members to be in the group) while other groups were made into low cohesive groups. Similarly, the variable of relevance of the issue to the functioning of the group was manipulated. For some groups, both in high and low cohesive conditions, the issue was very relevant to the performance and purpose of the group. For other groups the issue which they discussed was made largely irrelevant to the functioning and purpose for which the club had come together. The course of the discussion was observed and records were kept of those who spoke, of whom they spoke to, and what kinds of remarks were addressed to various people. After the discussion, in the guise of electing officers and committees to insure the continued successful existence of the club, measurements were obtained from which could be inferred the degree to which members of the group rejected others. From these data it was then possible to analyze the extent to which the variables of cohesiveness and relevance operated to affect rejection by the group of members who deviated.

1. *Factors determining degree of rejection from the group.* We may first look at the extent to which the confederates who played different roles in the group were rejected by the group. It should be pointed out that, of course, the trained participants were rotated from role to role so that the effect of personality would be cancelled out in the analysis.

It is of course not surprising that the confederate who started out agreeing with the other members of the group, and continued to agree with them, was not at all rejected. He was accepted by the group as were the other members. It is also interesting to note that the paid participant who at the start of the discussion held an extremely divergent opinion, but who gradually was influenced by the others so that he ended up agreeing with the group, was never rejected by the group. He too was accepted as well as the other members and as well as the trained participant who had always conformed.

On the other hand, the consistent deviate, that is the accomplice who had started out voicing extremely divergent opinions and remained divergent throughout the course of the discussion, was consistently rejected by almost all of the groups. The variables of cohesiveness of the group and relevance of the issue to the group did affect the degree to which the deviate was rejected. The highly cohesive groups rejected the deviate considerably more than the less cohesive groups. Those groups where the issue was relevant rejected the deviate more than did those groups where the issue was largely irrelevant to the functioning of the group. These two factors acted together so that in the low cohesive groups where the issue was irrelevant there was virtually no rejection of the deviate.

2. *The pattern of communication.* In order to be sure that the same factors are indeed operating here which acted in the other experiments we have examined, we may look to see if we can corroborate some of the results which we had found previously. It will be recalled that in the Back experiment [1] there was evidence from the observation of the discussion that the high cohesive groups attempted more actively to influence the members than did the low cohesive groups. This was true in the present experiment. There is observational evidence of the same kind that the high cohesive groups tended to exert more influence in the discussion than the low cohesive groups and that the groups where the issues were relevant tended to exert more influence in the discussion than the groups where the issues were irrelevant.

It will also be recalled that in the Festinger and Thibaut experiment [6] it was found that the great majority of the communications tended to be addressed to those whose opinions were extreme with respect to the range of opinion present in the group at the time. We would then expect to find in the present experiment that the great majority of the communications were addressed to the consistent deviate. This is indeed true. In all groups many more communications were addressed to the consistent deviate during the course of the meeting than were addressed to any of the other members of the group.

An additional result was obtained with regard to the communications addressed to the deviate. If we examine changes in the communication pattern as the discussion proceeded in the high cohesive groups where the issue was relevant (the group in which rejection was strongest) we find differences to exist between those members who do and those members who do not reject the deviate at the end of the meeting. Those who do not reject the deviate steadily increase in the frequency of communications addressed to him as the discussion proceeds. This same set of data for those members who do reject the consistent deviate at the end of the meeting shows quite a different pattern. As the discussion progresses the number of communications addressed to the deviate increases to a maximum and then drops steadily off. The maximum was reached when the discussion had gone on for about twenty-five minutes. The number of communications addressed to the deviate by those who reject him at the end of the meeting decreases steadily from then on.

This would seem to indicate that as long as a nonconformer is still included in the group and accepted as a member of the group, the great majority of communications will be addressed to him in an attempt to get him to change and conform to the group opinion. Once he is rejected from the group, however, or when the tendency to reject him becomes strong, there will be a corresponding decrease in the number of communications addressed to him. This reinforces the interpretation that the bulk of communications intended to influence the opinion of others are addressed to the opinions that are extreme within the psychological group. They are not addressed to extreme opinions held by persons who are not considered part of the group.

It seems clear then that the same factors which affect the amount of influence exerted and the readiness of members to change their own opinion, also affect the tendency to lessen one's dependence on those who disagree and to reject the disagreers from the group.

SUMMARY

We have discussed in detail a number of research studies on processes of influence by communication in small groups and the effects of these processes. In brief we have explored the following problems:

1. What are the determinants of the magnitude of pressures to attempt to influence others?
2. What determines just what persons one attempts to influence within a group?
3. What are the determinants of how much change is accomplished by an influence process?
4. What are the determinants of rejection of members because of non-conformity?

It is interesting to note the relationship between this program of theoretically based research and another program which has oriented itself more at the level of finding applications in actual life settings. Many of the findings from the program in informal social communication and much of the theory which has been developed in connection with these researches has had great practical value in studies of industrial productivity, and in leadership training. Many of these studies are reported by Dr. French in the following paper. It is to be hoped that continued development of basic areas of knowledge concerning the communication process in groups and the continued application of such findings will lead to a firm and fruitful body of data which will offer many more possibilities of application to problems of group functioning and group life.

BIBLIOGRAPHY

1. Back, K. The exertion of influence through social communication. *J. abnorm. soc. Psychol.*, 1950 (in press).
2. Back, K., Festinger, L., Hymovitch, B., Kelley, H. H., Schachter, S., and Thibaut, J. The methodology of studying rumor transmission. *Human Relations*, 1950, *3*, 307–312.
3. Festinger, L., Informal social communication. *Psychol. Rev.*, 1950, *57*, 271–282.
4. Festinger, L., Cartwright, D., et al. A study of a rumor: its origin and spread. *Human Relations*, 1948, *1*, 464–486.
5. Festinger, L., Schachter, S., and Back, K. *Social Pressures in Informal Groups: a Study of a Housing Project.* New York: Harper & Bros., 1950.
6. Festinger, L., and Thibaut, J. Interpersonal communication in small groups. *J. abnorm. soc. Psychol.*, 1951 (in press).
7. Kelley, H. H. Communication in experimentally created hierarchies. *Human Relations*, 1950, *4* (in press).
8. Schachter, S. Deviation, rejection, and communication. *J. abnorm. soc. Psychol.*, 1951 (in press).
9. Thibaut, J. An experimental study of the cohesiveness of underprivileged groups. *Human Relations*, 1950, *3*, 251–278.

GROUP PRODUCTIVITY

JOHN R. P. FRENCH, JR.

Research Center for Group Dynamics
University of Michigan

THE PRACTICAL PROBLEMS OF GROUP productivity are both well-known and widespread. Many important activities in business, government, education, and in the armed services are conducted by small groups; there is, however, general dissatisfaction with the inefficiency of committees, the low productivity of work groups, and the common ineffectiveness of groups in "getting things done." Even in those groups that function more successfully, one observes difficulties in reaching decisions, personality clashes, ineffective leadership, wrangling, dispute, and wasted motion in moving from discussion into action.

For a long time it has been recognized that such bottlenecks in the operation of groups can be reduced by good leadership, but it is only in the last decade that experience has demonstrated the significant improvement which can be achieved through the specific training of leaders in the skills of human relations. Such leadership training is especially important in the armed services where large numbers of civilians must be trained for the military leadership role without previous experience of this kind. To discover, therefore, how the productivity of groups may be improved, particularly by means of more effective leadership training, has become the practical purpose of this project.

As a scientific problem, group productivity is not well understood. Very little research has been done; no solid body of theory has been developed; and even the methods of measurement and investigation are in the pioneering stage. Therefore, the scientific purposes of this project are: (1) to devote in the initial stages a relatively large proportion of energy to defining the problem in terms amenable to empirical testing, to isolating the major variables involved, and to devising methods of measurement and experimentation; (2) to discover the determinants of group productivity (including the nature of leadership), and (3) to discover the principles and techniques for improving group productivity (including leadership training).

The general methodological approach for accomplishing these research objectives was based on the fact that we had very little precise, quantitative knowledge about group productivity and no very adequate techniques for studying it. Thus, it was planned to start with field studies, including actual field experiments where possible, in order to diagnose the major variables determining group productivity and explore possible techniques for changing it. At this point it was planned to devote considerable attention to the problem of measuring both group productivity itself and the variables affecting it. Once we had secured an initial diagnosis of the pattern of major variables, we were to proceed to more focused laboratory experiments to discover the exact relations among these variables.

This broad strategy has led to a sequence of six interrelated studies: (1) a broadly conceived field experiment at the National Training Laboratory in Group Development, (2) a laboratory experiment on the effects of cooperation and competition on group productivity, (3) a laboratory experiment on the effects of acceptance of expert knowledge, (4) a field experiment on changing group productivity through participation, (5) a laboratory experiment on self-directed training, and (6) an experiment on the effects of role-playing as a training method.

After the completion of our initial experiments, we began to redefine the problem of group productivity in terms more amenable to research. We found that a project which focuses on the *face-to-face* group must, of course, be conscious of the interpersonal relations and interactions within the group; but it must also concern itself with the kind of members composing the group and the nature of the larger organization of which it is a part. However, organizations and the groups within them have differing major purposes of work out-put, problem solving, planning, training and education; yet along with the unique factors there are some common factors which determine the progress that a group will make. It is these common factors which make possible the development of systematic theory concerning the determinants of group productivity.

The productivity of a group then, may be defined for scientific purposes as the speed of locomotion of the group toward its goals. This general definition implies both the quantitative aspects of goal achievement (for example, the number of products produced per unit of time) and the qualitative aspects of goal achievement (for example, how good these products are).

Our first two studies indicated further that when groups have multiple goals, the investigation becomes highly complicated. The subsequent studies, therefore, focused upon groups with primarily one goal, in order to allow more consistent analysis of the factors which influence success or failure in reaching the goal.

Our first experiments have led to further refinements. The problem of *changing* group productivity is not only separable from the overlapping problem of the determinants of group productivity, but it is also in some respects a different type of scientific problem. Essentially, the solution to this problem of changing group productivity involves two types of scientific laws: laws stating the determinants of group productivity and laws stating how these determinants can be varied to produce a change. Because of its logical priority, the study of these determinants is now the major focus of the project. However, the manipulation of these variables in order to effect and control a change is of great interest from a methodological point of view as we try to devise laboratory experiments to study group productivity in a more controlled way.

The procedure for measuring group productivity will vary with the type of group, the nature of its goal, and the nature of the task or activity. We have made use of a combination of the following types of measures: the quantity and quality of the final product produced by a group; the nature of the group process while working on a task, including the amount and the kind of contribution by members to the work process.

In terms of our definition, these latter measures are more properly viewed as intervening variables, for our research has shown that the sum of individual contributions does not always correlate highly with the out-put of the group composed of these individuals. The measures have involved the use of such techniques as standardized performance tests, the coding and evaluation of group and individual products, observer ratings and questionnaires filled out by the subjects.

THE DETERMINANTS OF GROUP PRODUCTIVITY

THE TRAINING LABORATORY

In the summer of 1947 there was held at Bethel, Maine, the First National Training Laboratory in Group Development under the joint sponsorship of the Research Center for Group Dynamics and the National Education Association, and with the financial support of six universities. Each summer since, one hundred delegates (from various social agencies, educational, industrial, and health organizations) have joined with approximately fifty members of the training and research staff for a three-week period of training and research in the processes of group functioning.

The initial study of this leadership training workshop was designed to explore the factors outlined above and to get preliminary data on the training process as well as the changes produced by it. Many of the data collected during the summer of 1947 concerned five matched groups which received the same general pattern of training in the problems of human relations. The major findings revealed the over-all effects of training, the internal processes of the groups, the structure of the groups, the effects of individual personality on the contribution of each and the influence of the Laboratory as an institution [1].

The effects of the total pattern of training on the delegates were marked. As measured by interviews and questionnaires given at the beginning and again at the end of the Laboratory and by a follow-up questionnaire nine months later, the changes were startling. There was a more democratic ideology about human relations, an increased understanding of group dynamics, greater skill in group leadership and membership, a willingness to utilize such specific techniques as role-playing, group productivity observers, and action research methods, and a better understanding of the relation of one participant to another.

The productivity of the groups was measured through the Group Productivity Test (a performance test yielding a group product). Three out of four groups showed improvement in such dimensions as flexibility of planning, time perspective in planning, and skill in motivating others and encouraging their activity. There was, however, no consistent change in total productivity scores.

The internal processes in each group were measured by recording the content of discussion, the types of activities and the interactions among members. These interactions were recorded in twenty precoded categories describing the quality as well as the quantity of behavior for each member. The quality of the behavior in all groups was predominantly geared towards "getting things accomplished." Within each group there were very large individual differences in the quantity of participation, with a tendency for this hierarchy of participation to become stable over a period of time. Above all, there was evident a general eagerness to attend to the task at hand and an orientation toward productivity.

Study of the quality and quantity of member interaction revealed, as indicated by correlations, that the amount of member participation is an inverse function of the quantity of the leader's behavior. It was also found that the total amount of activity initiated by a member correlates very highly (.91 to .99 in the five groups) with the amount of behavior received from others; and further that the behavior of an individual is determined considerably by his perception of the reactions of the others in the group to him.

The kind of activity is another determinant. A significantly greater amount of participation becomes evident for educational rather than procedural action. Again, activities such as role-playing result in more aggression among members than do other activities. The official role of the person, such as leader, observer, or trainee, affects both the behavior initiated by the person and the kind of behavior he receives from others. However, this influence of the role on behavior varies from one activity to another.

The internal structure of the groups was measured by weekly sociometric tests requiring choices of most productive group members and choices of friends. From these data two types of group structure were determined: the informal prestige structure and the friendship structure.

Some important characteristics of the way in which a group is formed became clear. Both the prestige and the friendship structures tended to become stabilized during the three weeks of the Laboratory. Cliques based on friendship developed at all levels of popularity. Although considerable similarity exists between the two types of structures, the group is decidedly more aware of the prestige structure than of the structure based on friendship alone. This is probably related to the fact that the former has more hierarchical stratification with a few members receiving most of the choices while others receive no choices at all.

The more important determinants of group structure were examined and it was found that the position of a member in the prestige structure of the groups is determined by the amount of his contribution to the locomotion of the group towards its goal, as well as by his official role in the group (the leaders had the highest and the research observers the lowest prestige in the group). In the friendship structure, the position of a person depends primarily upon his ability to satisfy the individual needs of other members. Friendship choices are made mostly on the basis of similarity of occupation, personality characteristics, and the extent of actual and expected reciprocation of the choice.

Research techniques for investigating the internal processes and the structure of groups have been mainly restricted to categorizations of behavior and to sociometric methods. As an attempt to get at less overt aspects of these group attributes, a procedure similar to the Thematic Apperception Test was developed for use with groups. In this projective test a picture of a group (ambiguous in terms of its structure and emotional tone) is presented to a group with instructions that the group must arrive at a description of what is going on in the picture. A method for analyzing the group responses to this picture has been developed. Each of the groups in the Laboratory took the test early and late in their history, and the resulting quantified products have been related to other measured attributes of these groups. More work will be required before this test is standardized but results to date suggest that it will be a useful measurement technique.

In general, the personality determinants of the productivity of the group members were not as influential as those already mentioned. Individuals rated as highly productive by other members of the group (as contrasted with those who were rated low) showed certain distinctive personality characteristics as measured by the Rorschach and by the Runner-Seaver personality tests. The former indicated that the more productive members had greater intelligence, more originality, and were less stereotyped in their attitudes and ways of thinking. They were emotionally responsive yet with better emotional control. On the Runner-Seaver test, there was evident in this group a greater sociability and initiative with less obstinacy and anxiety.

In addition to the conventional ways of analyzing sociometric data, a method of intergroup sociometry was developed to study the relations among such independently defined subgroups as: the training faculty vs. the research team vs. the delegates vs. the marginal members of the community; also each training subgroup vs. other subgroups.

The intergroup sociograms showed that the relations among the training faculty, the delegates, the research team, *etc.*, were complex and changing with time. In general, those subgroups high in the official table of organization were high in the prestige structure and in the friendship structure of the institution. The training faculty was definitely the subgroup with most prestige.

In general, the prestige structure and the friendship structure of the institution are determined by the same factors, though there are some differences. Some of the determinants both types of institutional structure may have in common are: the ideology of the person, his occupation, his sex, his official role in the institution (for example, belonging to the community council), the training subgroups to which he belongs, and even the location of his living quarters at the Laboratory.

During the three weeks at the Laboratory both types of structures showed distinct growth and development. The prestige of the training faculty increased. Significantly those determinants of the institutional structure which referred to the pre-Laboratory environment of the person either dropped out entirely or became less important as determinants. For example, occupation at the end of the Laboratory no longer determined prestige, and the sex of the individual became less important.

Institutional standards, that is, those pressures toward uniformity of attitudes, beliefs, and behavior among members of the institution, developed at the Laboratory. As measured by the ideology test, the delegates not only changed their values in the direction of the central norm of democratic collaboration, but there was also a significant decrease in individual differences in respect to this central value. And what is more, those members of the institution who did not conform to this value tended to be rejected as friends.

The Influence of Cooperation and Competition on Group Productivity

On the basis of previous field studies it appeared that productivity and group processes were particularly affected by the nature of interpersonal relations as connected with the rewards for performance in the group. In order to study these effects [3, 4], groups were placed in two contrasting environmental situations: first, a cooperative situation where the reward was equal for all members of the group and depended on the productivity of the group as a whole in intellectual tasks and in solving human relations problems; and second, a competitive situation where each member received a different reward depending on his own relative contribution.

The groups in the cooperative situation showed more coordination of effort, diversity in the amount of contribution per member, division of labor, attentiveness to their fellow members, mutual understanding of their communication, willingness to accept and agree, orientation to the goal and orderliness of procedure, productivity per unit of time with a better quality of product, quality in discussion with friendliness during it, favorable evaluation of the group and of its products, and obligation to others in an effort to win their respect, than those in the other group. Group harmony appears to be disrupted when members see themselves competing for mutually exclusive goals. Greater group productivity will result when the members or sub-units are cooperative rather than competitive in their interrelationships.

THE EFFECTS OF ACCEPTANCE OF EXPERT KNOWLEDGE

The specific focus of this laboratory experiment was the relationship between the way in which the group utilizes its intellectual resources and its ability to solve problems. The hypothesis being tested was that, where individuals differ in expertness, successful group problem-solving is contingent upon attitudes of acceptance toward the ideas of other group members.

The group problem was a jig-saw-type puzzle involving several parts of graded difficulty which could be scored for the number of solutions and for the number of errors. Information which would, if accepted, facilitate the solution of the problem was systematically introduced into the group by a trained confederate playing the role of the "expert." A condition was created where acceptance of cognitive content introduced by others was favored and imposition of the member's own cognitive content was inhibited, while the opposite effect was sought in a second variation. It was found that in groups where restraining forces to take the initiative and driving forces to accept ideas of other group members had been induced, there were produced significantly less incorrect solutions than in the contrasting groups. However, there was no significant difference between the two treatments in the total number of solutions produced.

CHANGING GROUP PRODUCTIVITY

THE EFFECTS OF PARTICIPATION

A major technique for improving group productivity taught at the Training Laboratory has been collaborative participation in making decisions which affect the members of the group. The effect of this variable on industrial production was studied in a field experiment which was financed primarily by the Harwood Manufacturing Corporation [2].

Technological changes in production methods were introduced through group meetings using three different degrees of participation: total participation by all members in the collaborative planning of the changes; participation through the election of representatives to plan the changes; and no participation but careful explanation of the changes and the reasons for them.

The major finding revealed that the level of production after the change is a function of the degree of participation. The differences were very large. The level of production resulting from total participation was about 50 per cent higher than the level for no participation. These effects are produced primarily by creating different group standards. Further, the amount of resistance to the change and the aggression against management is an inverse function of the degree of participation. The rate of turnover of employees also decreases with increasing participation.

Changing Productivity Through Training Methods

The field experiment on the Training Laboratory had indicated the effectiveness of a pattern of training in which the trainer gradually delegated to the group more responsibility for leading the discussion. In this laboratory study, a similar pattern of self-directed and self-motivated training was contrasted with a directive method of training. The purpose of the study was to compare the influence of these two training methods on the productivity of the groups in solving complex problems of human relations. Although both types of groups showed increases in productivity, there was no significant difference in gains between the two types of training. The effect of training was found to depend, however, on the extent to which the group accepts or rejects the training method. Comparing the two methods by including only those groups which accepted the training, the self-motivated training method resulted in greater interest in the problems, greater clarity of the goal, more cooperation and more efficient use of manpower.

The Effects of Role-Playing

Both the research data and observations by the trainers in the first study indicated that role-playing was one of the most effective techniques of leadership training. Its effectiveness, moreover, seemed to depend on the degree of involvement in the role. A preliminary study was therefore designed to test this general hypothesis by measuring certain predicted effects of three different degrees of involvement in a role: actually participating in acting out the key role in a socio-drama; watching the scene with instruction to identify with the key role; watching the scene with the instruction to observe "what is going on" in the group.

As measured by a subsequent questionnaire, our hypothesis was confirmed. The greater the degree of involvement the greater was the salience, clarity, and degree of differentiation of the person's perception of the role, and his liking for and his identification with it. Measures of the discussion following role-playing revealed that greater involvement leads to more frequent and more intense participation in subsequent group discussion. All of these variables, in turn, might be expected to result in "deeper" and more extensive training effects.

A replication of the experiment confirmed these findings concerning the effects on discussion. Together, the two experiments show a clear pattern of the effects of the degree of involvement in a role on the perceptions, feelings, and behavior of the trainee. In addition, they demonstrate the value of new uses of role-playing; for example, assigning members of the group to identify with the role of the leader in a scene is an effective technique for securing criticisms and alternative suggestions concerning the behavior of the leader.

SUMMARY AND EVALUATION OF PROGRESS

Important methodological progress has been made in the measurement of group productivity, the development of the group Thematic Apperception Test, the ideology test, intergroup sociometry, and particularly in developing experimental methodology for studying productivity and methods of changing productivity.

A very large number of determinants of group productivity have been discovered: *process variables* such as the amount of contribution and participation by members, the coordination of activities, the effectiveness of communication, and group standards; *group structure variables,* as the cohesiveness of the group, the prestige structure, and the functional role structure; *personality variables* as indicated in the Runner-Seaver dimensions and the Rorschach patterns; *environmental variables* such as the structure of the task, and the pattern of rewards producing cooperation or competition; *cognitive structure variables* such as goal orientation and the perception of abilities of other members.

Much progress has been made in discovering the interrelations among these five types of determinants of group productivity. We have found, for example, that the amount of participation by different members is very closely related to their position in the sociometric structure of the group. There are too many similar interrelations to summarize here, but it is clear that they are the important facts upon which a theory of group functioning may be constructed. Emphasis upon this aspect of the project is necessary since our understanding of group productivity and of the nature of leadership is now limited primarily by inadequate theory concerning the functioning of the group.

Finally, the project has already had great practical value to many important leaders and groups. The studies of existing groups, such as the Training Laboratory, have improved the productivity level and have trained several hundred leaders including officers of the United States Navy and Air Force. The training methods and techniques for the improvement of productivity have been communicated to a much larger audience through our publications and programs of teaching.

BIBLIOGRAPHY

1. Bradford, Leland P. & French, John R. P., Jr. (Eds.) The dynamics of the discussion group. *J. soc. Issues,* 1948, *4,* 2. (Six articles on the Training Laboratory study).
2. Coch, Lester & French, John R. P., Jr. Overcoming resistance to change. *Human Relations,* 1948, *1,* 512–532.
3. Deutsch, Morton. A theory of cooperation and competition. *Human Relations,* 1949, 2, 129–152.
4. —— An experimental study of the effects of cooperation and competition upon group process, *Human Relations,* 1949, 2, 199–231.
5. French, John R. P., Jr. Field experiments: changing group productivity, in *Experiments in Social Process.* New York: McGraw-Hill, 1950.
6. Lippitt, Ronald. A program of experimentation on group functioning and group productivity, in *Current Trends in Social Psychology.* Pittsburgh: U. of Pitt. Press, 1949, 14–49.
7. —— The strategy of socio-psychological research in group life, in *Experiments in Social Process.* New York: McGraw-Hill, 1950.
8. Group growth and educational dynamics. Bulletin No. 2 of the National Training Laboratory in Group Development, 1948.

A SOCIAL PSYCHOLOGICAL STUDY OF
THE DECISION-MAKING CONFERENCE

D. G. MARQUIS, HAROLD GUETZKOW, AND R. W. HEYNS

Conference Research
University of Michigan

WHEN THE RESEARCH STAFF UNDERTOOK THE ONR-sponsored large scale study of conferences, it immediately became obvious that the project could be given focus only if the area to be investigated were carefully delimited. First there was the necessity of restricting the investigation to one type of conference. Such widely diverse groups as academic seminars, social discussion groups, labor-management conferences, and executive committee meetings were unlikely to have enough in common so that a set of research findings could be applied to all. Consequently we decided to limit our investigation to decision-making conferences in which the participants are affected by the decisions and are involved in carrying them out.

Having selected our population, the question remained: What did we wish to find out about these groups? The practical goal of the project was to discover ways of improving conference procedure. Such a goal in a research project, however, required the formulation of criteria of a "good" conference which could be measured and whose relationship to various group characteristics could be ascertained. Since the groups studied were not comparable in terms of the problems they dealt with, it did not seem feasible to design an external, objective criterion measure of the quality of the group decision applicable to all the groups. Our observation and the responses of executives to questions concerning the ways in which they used conferences [4, 6] indicated that there seemed to be no single over-all criterion of conference effectiveness which would be both easily obtained and generally acceptable. As a result, the project has deliberately concerned itself with more than one criterion. The results summarized in this report make use of three criteria: (1) The satisfaction of conference members with the meeting, (2) the productivity of the meeting, and (3) the amount of disagreement with the decisions at the end of the meeting.

METHODOLOGY

In a new area of research such as this, it is of immediate interest to know the kinds of data the investigators were able to collect. In this section we shall describe briefly some of the dimensions we attempted to measure, the instruments used, and the success we had in using them.

The project has completed several experimental investigations of conferences in which factors such as leadership style, success and failure, and size of meeting were systematically manipulated. Also, during the past two years, we have made an intensive field study of seventy-two actual conferences held in business and government. Since most of the techniques found useful in previous studies were utilized in this field study, this section will be concerned with a description and evaluation of the methods employed for collecting data from conferences under field conditions. The field observations were directed by J. N. Peterman and executed by L. Berkowitz, N. T. Fouriezos, J. W. O'Brien, R. W. Heyns, H. Guetzkow, and others.

The conference groups studied met five requirements: (1) Meetings to be observed had to be those that took place in conjunction with the administrative and operational processes in industry, business, or government. (2) The meetings to be observed had to be decision-making in character; that is, at least 50 per cent of the meeting time had to be devoted to the consideration and resolution of problems, and had to have as their main purpose the reaching of decisions. (3) The group had to be composed of not less than five participants, including the leader, nor more than seventeen. (4) The participants who made up the group had to have worked in previous meetings with each of the other members. (5) No more than two groups were observed in any one organization, nor were any such groups taken where two or more of the participants in one group were also members of the second group.

Data obtained during the actual conference were recorded by four observers. Since we had included in our sample of conferences only those which had decision-making as a primary function, we were particularly interested in describing the problem-solving process during the conference. To do this, eleven categories were devised into which the verbal participations of a conference discussion could be classified as to their function in the problem-solving process. These included such functions as "problem proposing," "goal setting," "solution proposing," "opposing," and "supporting." One observer was responsible for classifying each participation in the conference in the appropriate problem-solving category and also noting which conference member made each remark and to whom it was addressed. The reliability of this coding was determined by correlating the scores derived from the recordings of two independent observers for the same conference. A correlation of .72 so obtained on the basis of the participations of twenty-four conference members, indicates that these scores have sufficiently high reliability for the purposes of this study. Previous research had indicated that problem-solving coding could be done as reliably in direct observation as from a typewritten record of the meeting.

A second major area of interest in this research was that of the self-oriented needs of conference members. It was felt that the degree to which conference members exhibited behavior which was prompted more by their own needs than by the requirements of the group task, would have a profound influence on the conference outcome. There was considerable doubt, however, as to whether such observations could be made in a group situation with any reliability. Clinically oriented colleagues felt that such ratings could not be made without prior knowledge of the personalities of the participants. We were encouraged in preliminary research to find that an observer who secured such prior knowledge of a participant through interviews and projective test results made ratings on self-oriented needs exhibited in a group situation which were in substantial agreement with those of another observer who had no prior knowledge of the participant. Consequently the recording and rating of such needs was made a part of the field study. In the field, the self-oriented need ratings by two observers correlated .73 [1].

In order to have a record of the substantive aspects of the conferences, a third observer traced each agenda item from its initiation to its disposal, recording a description of the item, time spent on it, and conflicts precipitated by it. A comparison of the summarized data of two observers recording the same conference show substantial agreement.

A fourth observer made a seating diagram of the conference, noting the identity of each participant. He also kept a tally of the number of times each participant said "I" or "We" (the latter only when it referred to the immediate group). Correlation of scores derived from two independent observers' I-We tallies was .67 in our reliability sample of conferences.

After the conference, three kinds of data were collected. The observers, who during the conference had been recording the data just described, each made independent ratings of the conference as a whole on a number of variables covering motivational, procedural, emotional, and other aspects of the meeting. The average of the observer ratings was used as a final score after it was found that this method yielded results which were almost identical with ratings which had been arrived at in a pooling conference. The correlation between ratings by different observers, averaged over all variables, was .72.

The remaining data were gathered from the participants in two ways. A questionnaire was given them right after the conference. On this questionnaire each participant indicated on an eleven-point graphic rating scale his degree of satisfaction with aspects of the meeting such as procedure, decision, leadership, and the meeting as a whole. Within a day or two of the meeting, the participants were each personally interviewed. Answers to most of the interview questions were also given in terms of eleven-point ratings, with open ended probes which gave the respondent's reasons for his opinion. Some weeks after the conference, but no more than two months later, a delayed measure of member satisfaction was obtained by mail from almost all the participants.

These participant ratings were averaged to give a group measure on each variable rated. Since the bulk of our analysis was to be in terms of group measures, we were interested to discover how stable these mean participant ratings were. This was done by means of a split-half reliability technique. For each conference the ratings of the participants were split randomly into two groups. The participant ratings were then averaged for each sub-group and the two scores thus derived for each conference were correlated for a sample of conferences. Most of the correlations were sufficiently high to indicate that group measures thus derived were reliable. However, there was some indication that ratings which required the participant to give his own reactions to aspects of the meeting had a somewhat lower split-half reliability than those which sought the participant's estimates of characteristics of the group as a whole. For example, the split-half reliabilities of participant ratings of feeling of being accepted, feeling of being free to talk, and estimate of own influence on others in the conference, were lower than ratings of such things as the importance of the problem and the power of the group.

In general, these methods of data collection have been used both in the laboratory and in the field studies. Our data indicate that trained observers can reliably perform such functions as the classification of participations into problem-solving categories, observation of the extent of self-oriented needs in the behavior of conference participants, I-We recording, observation of conferences from the standpoint of content, and rating of conferences on a number of variables such as communication adequacy, amount of overt conflict, and procedural resourcefulness. There is also evidence that participants are, for many aspects of the conference process, sources of reliable data.

RESEARCH FINDINGS

It is impossible to present in any detail the results of the nine experimental and five field studies made by the project. The findings to be presented will be based primarily on the field observation of seventy-two conference groups in business, industry, and government. Whenever it is appropriate, evidence from experimental studies will be mentioned. Within the field study itself, there has been selection with respect to the variables which will be discussed. We will deal with three outcomes or criteria: the satisfaction of members with the meeting, the productivity of the group, and the amount of remaining disagreement among the participants with respect to the decisions. The variables discussed in some detail are those which are significantly related to one or more of these criteria. There will be a brief discussion of some variables which on theoretical, common sense, or other grounds might be expected to relate to the criteria but which do not show a significant relationship to them. This selection of criteria is, of course, arbitrary, since any investigator or practitioner may be interested in treating as dependent variables those which we have classified as independent variables. The results presented, the manner in which they are organized, and the conceptualization concerning them are tentative, since analysis of the data is still incomplete.

THE PREDICTION OF MEMBER SATISFACTION

This section deals with the question: What factors are related to member satisfaction? The group satisfaction score was the average of member responses to the question: In general, how satisfied are you with this meeting? Responses to probe questions attempting to deter-mine the factors which were taken into account by the participants in rating their satisfaction indicate that the way in which the group proceeded and the quality of the group decisions were heavily weighted. The probe analysis results are confirmed by high correlations between items related to satisfaction with group process and decision, and meeting satisfaction.

1. *Cohesiveness:* Cohesiveness has been defined by Festinger as the resultant of all the forces keeping the members in the group. The principal factors making the group attractive to the members are the need-satisfying properties of the group. In the groups which we observed there were undoubtedly a wide range of needs being satisfied, or left unsatisfied. It seemed worthwhile, however, to attempt to measure the cohesiveness of the groups by characterizing each group on a series of dimensions along which the attractiveness of the group for its members would theoretically vary. That is, if there were theoretical or empirical reasons for thinking that groups whose members like each other are, other things equal, more attractive to their members than groups not so characterized, the group's score on personal liking would be an index of its cohesiveness.

The observers made ratings of the groups on five variables, all of which, so it seems to us, meet this criterion. These variables include such characteristics of the group and its functioning as (1) the extent to which the group was supporting and accepting of its members; (2) the pleasantness of the affective atmosphere; (3) the extent to which the members of the group seemed to like each other personally; (4) the cohesiveness of the group; and (5) the extent to which the members of the group seemed frustrated. The actual instruction to the observer on the last item was to make an estimate of the extent to which the needs of the members of the group in the areas of communication, problem-solving, as well as personality needs were being satisfied. All five of these items show high correlations with each other; the lowest coefficient is .61. All of these variables can be conceptualized as dimensions along which the attractiveness of the group for the members could vary. Accordingly, a simple arithmetic average of the ratings on each of the five items was computed and is called a cohesiveness index.

This interpretation of the cohesiveness index of the group as a measure of the attractiveness of the group is supported by the fact that it correlates significantly with a composite score which represents the extent to which the participants were satisfied with aspects of the group process. The participant score was derived from participant responses to four items: (1) the extent to which they perceive the participants as forming a unified group; and their satisfaction with (2) the way the group went about its business, (3) the quality of the decision, and (4) their own performance. The cohesiveness index also correlates significantly with the participants' rating concerning the freedom they felt to say what they wanted to say.

The cohesiveness index correlates significantly with member satisfaction with the meeting, both immediately after the meeting and after a period of time. The more cohesive the group, as rated by observers, the more satisfied the group is with its meeting.

2. *Self-oriented needs:* Another variable which is closely related conceptually to those which make up the cohesiveness index is the extent to which the conference was characterized by expression of personal needs and tensions. This was a rating made by observers. The observers made judgments as to whether the behavior of the members was induced primarily by the requirements of the group situation or whether the behavior was generated primarily by the personal need systems of the individuals. To put it another way, were the members task-oriented or self-oriented? High scores on this variable indicated the presence of considerable self-oriented behavior. The ratings on this dimension are significantly related to satisfaction of members, both immediate and delayed. The relationship is negative; the more the group's process was characterized by self-oriented behavior, the less the satisfaction of members.

3. *Degree of procedural control:* Three observer scores describe the extent to which the group's process is systematized and regulated—the degree of procedural control. The first is the extent to which the leader behaved differently, performed different functions, than did the other members of the group; the second is the extent to which the leader exercised control over the group process; the third was a rating of the orderliness of the group in its treatment of topics—the extent to which it was characterized by orderly, systematic procedure and interaction. All of these variables correlate significantly with member satisfaction and in a positive direction. Groups with a good deal of procedural structuring or control, defined in these terms, are more satisfied with their meetings than groups which are less orderly in their procedure, whose leaders exercise less control and differ less in their behavior from the other persons in the group.

This probably means, more than anything else, that leaders who are formal and exercise a good deal of control are meeting the expectations of most of the members in the sample. The meeting is being conducted by the designated chairman as meetings are supposed to be conducted. This interpretation is corroborated by the experience of persons who have attemped to introduce changes in the process of existing groups in industry; there are strong expectations concerning leader control and formality. These findings indicate that in the kinds of groups we were dealing with, a more or less formalized procedure with strong, leading behavior by the designated chairman makes for satisfied members.

4. *Participation:* Manuals of conference procedure make a great deal of the variable of participation. The leader is warned to insure a spread of participation among the members. The rationale for this emphasis, not always explicitly stated, is that spread of participation makes it more likely that the group product will indeed be a group product, members will have the feeling of having contributed and be more likely to come back, and so on.

An index of spread of participation, which indicated the extent to which the participation pattern deviated from equal participation, showed no relationship to member satisfaction. This finding is consistent with the results in several of our laboratory studies, where we find no relationship between the amount that a member participates and his satisfaction with meeting and decision.

It may be that actual verbal participation is not necessary for satisfaction so long as the members feel that there is adequate opportunity for them to make whatever contributions they desire. Indirect evidence on this possibility was obtained by asking each participant the following question: "Sometimes in a meeting, a person wants to talk, but can't. He just does not get an opportunity to talk. To what extent did you have an opportunity to say what you wanted to during this meeting?" The correlation between responses to this question and the individual's actual amount of participation is .02. However, the average of member responses to the opportunity question correlates significantly with satisfaction with meeting.

THE PREDICTION OF GROUP PRODUCTIVITY

The problem of measurement of group productivity is a difficult one and the project has made a number of different approaches to the problem. As has been indicated, one of the observers recorded each agenda item and noted the disposition made of it; *i.e.,* whether it was completed, not completed, or postponed to a later meeting. The measure to be discussed here is the proportion of agenda items which were completed of those which were attempted. The measure is objective and has some comparability from group to group. It admittedly does not adequately control the variable of problem difficulty. In common sense terms, we are calling a productive group one which finishes what it starts. This measure correlates only .28, significant at the 5 per cent level, with member satisfaction with meeting.

One of the measures which was mentioned earlier as significantly correlated with member satisfaction also is significantly related to productivity: the extent to which the group process is characterized by self-oriented need behavior. The relationship is negative. The more the group process evidenced self-oriented need behavior, the less productive the group.

Two variables which are significantly related to productivity combine a characterization of the problem and the group. The first is one which characterizes the problem motivation of the group: the urgency of the problem. Both participants and observers responded to the question: "How necessary was it that the group arrive at a decision at this time?" Both indices of problem urgency correlate significantly with productivity. The more urgent the problems, the more productive the group.

The second variable in this area is a measure of the extent to which the problem lies within the power domain of the group. Each participant was asked to indicate whether he felt the group had sufficient power to handle the problems it considered. Scores on this item correlate significantly with productivity. The more adequate the power of the group, the more productive it is.

In the light of current emphasis on the importance of the cohesiveness dimension, it is of interest to note that the cohesive groups were no more productive, as measured here, than were less cohesive groups. Thus, while member satisfaction increases with cohesiveness, group productivity is unaffected by variance in cohesiveness.

Mention has been made of the fact that groups characterized by a good deal of procedural structuring, leader differentiation, and control were the most satisfied with the meeting. The suggestion was made that this relationship may be due to the fact that expectations of members concerning "good" group process were being met. It is interesting to note that these groups, while more satisfied, were not any more productive than groups whose mode of interaction was more informal and in which the leadership function was shared. The results indicate that shared leader functions and informal group procedures, patterns of functioning which are often resisted by groups because they are regarded by members as inefficient, did not reduce group productivity.

The process descriptions of the groups by the observers indicate that the most productive groups showed more adequate communication (in terms of audibility, understandability and freedom to participate), were more orderly in their treatment of topics (*i.e.*, showed a minimum of backtracking and simultaneous discussion of more than one topic), and made a more penetrating attack on the problems than did the less productive groups.

The Prediction of Member Disagreement with Group Decision

As has been mentioned, it is frequently very important to secure a high degree of agreement among group members with respect to the decision, or to put it in terms of the actual measures used, to reduce the amount of residual disagreement. To obtain a measure of amount of agreement, each participant was asked: "How much difference was there between your final opinion(s) on the question(s) discussed and the decision(s) which the group reached?" The average of all the participant responses represents the amount of disagreement which remained after the meeting.

The relationships between this variable and the other criteria which have been discussed are as follows: groups whose members report agreement between their own final opinion and the decisions arrived at by the group are neither more nor less productive than other groups, neither are they more satisfied immediately after the meeting. They are, however, more satisfied with the decisions reached and with the meeting after a period of time.

The relationship between residual discrepancy and decision satisfaction corroborates the results of three studies made by members of the Conference Research staff. Sperling asked groups of college students to decide which of five negative characteristics was most appropriately applied to the faculty of the college. He found, when other factors were experimentally eliminated, a high relationship between participant satisfaction and what he called the "loser's score," the difference between the participant's final opinion and the group decision. Heyns and Levin report the same result in two separate studies of conferences in which clinical psychologists arrived at group decisions concerning the ratings to be given clinical trainees.

There is evidence in the field study data obtained from observers that residual disagreement is presaged by evidence of disagreement throughout the meeting itself. Observer scores indicate that high residual disagreement groups show significantly more conflicting behavior, do more opposing of each other's contributions, and spend more time in conflict situations.

Several of the observer scores shed some light on the factors which are responsible for residual disagreement. High residual disagreement groups are characterized by the observers as disagreeing as to goals and means to goals. They also show significantly more self-oriented need behavior on the part of participants.

Groups with relatively high agreement are characterized by observers as being relatively more orderly and efficient in their problem-solving. These relationships may be, of course, a reflection of the absence of conflict in the group in the first place. There are, however, certain relationships which seem more likely to be important in the reduction of conflict. The communication process was more adequate in the high agreement groups; the members understood each other better. There was more attention to group process in these groups; that is, the number of contributions which related to the way the group was functioning was relatively greater. This suggests that these groups were more sensitive to what was happening than were high residual disagreement groups.

From the standpoint of the participants, those groups showed the most agreement with the group decision after the meeting whose members felt accepted and supported and whose members felt the group had sufficient power to deal with the problems before the group.

These results may be interpreted tentatively as indicating that differences among participants as to goals and means to goals, self-oriented need behavior, and a feeling of participants that they are not accepted and that the group lacks power to deal with the problems increase the likelihood that residual disagreement will be large. The continued presence of goal conflict and conflict in other areas indicates that there will be more final disagreement. The data suggest that greater agreement can be attained, in addition to reducing the amount of goal disagreement and self-oriented need behavior, by more adequate communication among members and more attention, by way of explicit reference and greater sensitivity, to the process of the group itself.

RESUME OF RESEARCH FINDINGS

Incomplete analysis of data from a study of seventy-two business, government, and industrial conference groups permits the following conclusions:

> 1. The three criteria which have been discussed—the satisfaction of members with the meeting, the productivity of the group, and the amount of residual disagreement after the meeting—are relatively uncorrelated.
> 2. Member satisfaction with the meeting increases with the cohesiveness of the group, the amount of procedural structuring, and decreases with the incidence of self-oriented need behavior on the part of participants. Member satisfaction has no relationship to spread of participation among group members.
> 3. Group productivity increases with the urgency of the problem, with the power of the group to deal with the problem, and decreases with the incidence of self-oriented need behavior. The productive groups are more orderly in their problem-solving process and have a more adequate communication process than less productive groups.
> 4. Residual disagreement is high when there is disagreement as to goals, a good deal of self-oriented need behavior, and a feeling of inadequate power to deal with the problem on the part of participants. In low residual disagreement groups the members communicate more adequately and show greater sensitivity to group process.

SUMMARY

The project has for the past three years been engaged in exploratory work, both in the area of methodology and theory construction. From the results of field and experimental studies, a basic methodology has been developed for the description of groups by means of trained observers, participant questionnaires, and interviews. The current analysis of results of a field study of seventy-two conferences, collated and integrated with results of laboratory studies, is beginning to reveal the crucial dimensions of group process as far as certain criteria of conference effectiveness are concerned. The present objective is to determine the major determinants of a number of such criteria, since it seems unlikely that all practitioners and social scientists will at present agree on a single criterion in terms of which a conference should be judged. If, however, we are able to find some of the factors which are related to several more or less accepted sub-criteria, these findings will have immediate usefulness. The practitioner or social scientist may select what is for him *the* criterion.

BIBLIOGRAPHY

1. Fouriezos, N. T., Hutt, M. L., and Guetzkow, H. Measurement of self-oriented needs in discussion groups. *J. abnorm. soc. Psychol.*, 1950, *45*, 682–690.
2. Guetzkow, H. Interagency committee usage. *Pub. Adm. Rev.*, 1950, *10*, 190–196.
3. ———. Unitizing and categorizing problems in coding qualitative data. *J. clin. Psychol.*, 1950, *16*, 47–58.
4. Guetzkow, H. and Kriesberg, M. Executive use of the administrative conference. *Personnel*, 1950, *26*, 318–323.
5. Henry, W. E. and Guetzkow, H. Group projection sketches for the study of small groups. *J. soc. Psychol.*, 1951 (in press).
6. Kriesberg, M. Executives evaluate administrative conferences. *Advanced Mgmt.*, 1950, *15*, 15–17.
7. Kriesberg, M. and Guetzkow, H. The use of conferences in the administrative process. *Pub. Adm. Rev.*, 1950, *10*, 93–98.

SURVEY RESEARCH CENTER: AN OVERVIEW OF THE HUMAN RELATIONS PROGRAM

DANIEL KATZ

Department of Psychology
University of Michigan

APPROACH TO THE PROBLEM

GENERAL OBJECTIVES OF THE PROGRAM

The program is designed to discover the principles governing group performance and group motivation, with specific reference to organizational structure and leadership practices. Specifically, the objectives have to do with the conditions making for a high level of group functioning and a high level of individual satisfaction of the group members. An additional goal of the program is to learn the most effective ways of applying the research findings which it yields.

GENERAL PROCEDURE

The original plan envisaged a ten-year period in which the initial stages would consist of exploratory studies during the first two or three years. The later phases of the program would be devoted to experimental studies, largely of a field character, to test the hypotheses derived from the exploratory studies. The program is now in its third year of operation. Five exploratory studies have been completed; two additional exploratory studies are in process; one large experimental program has been underway for over a year and one minor experimental project is in its initial stages. In addition, one of the exploratory studies completed has been extended to develop hypotheses about the utilization of research results, *i.e.*, about the principles of social change.

From a methodological point of view it was thought that major advances could be made by the following procedures:

1. *By the use of the survey method to give thorough coverage in the study of organizations.* Social organization and group functioning are generally described on the basis of organizational charts, or of the impressions of people who are familiar with the situation, or of expert opinion. In the study of organizations there has been a tendency to accept global descriptions of their functioning from official sources and to neglect the fact that social organization is carried in the interactions of human beings. There have been some studies of segments of total organizations. These have generally involved the people at the lowest level, namely, the rank and file membership. The survey method, however, opens up the possibilities of a thorough coverage of all levels within the organization as well as the relationship of the organization with other social structures. Prior to this research program, in spite of the advances in social science, no organization had ever been studied with the individual as the unit of measurement in terms of all its parts and of all its hierarchical levels.

2. *By obtaining measures of performance which could be related to measures of motivation, attitudes, and morale.* The whole field of social psychology, as well as social science in general, is singularly lacking in research studies which show the relationship of people's perceptions, values, ideas and expressed motivation to behavioral outcome. Thus, one reason for selecting industry for some of the initial studies was the fact that industry, in some cases, has records on the performance and productivity of its people.

3. *By obtaining independent measures of the psychological variables among which relationships are hypothesized.* Frequently, the relationships that appear when attitudinal data are analyzed may be a reflection of some halo factor of the response to the questionnaire form or to the interview schedule. So many of the studies that have been made in the past derive their information about a social relationship from one party to the relationship. We assume that we have measures of effective leadership from studies of leaders alone. Or, we assume that studies of the morale of followers in themselves will give adequate information about leadership. One phase of this problem concerns the matter of a criterion measure. Measures of leadership practice and of organizational policy should be related to some criterion of functioning such as the morale of the followers or their performance. It was felt that a major advance could be made by the use

of such a criterion measure in relation to measures of leadership. Moreover, the use of independent measures made possible the comparison of differential perceptions of the same problems by foremen and union stewards, by workers and supervisors, by workers and stewards.

4. *By a repetition of the same study design in a number of varying situations.* A single study is suggestive rather than conclusive and the findings from a single situation are not generalizable. It was thought that genuine progress could be made by studying a wide variety of institutional settings in the hope that common findings would emerge which would have some degree of generality.

5. *Finally, by designing field experiments to test original findings.* Experiments in field situations lack the precise controls of the laboratory, but they offer real advantages in the manipulation of the significant variables involved. It is extremely difficult to generalize from laboratory experiments to social situations, and it is also difficult to reproduce the important variables in a laboratory setting. By introducing experimental changes into an organization and taking *before* and *after* measures on experimental and control groups it was believed that knowledge in the field could be considerably advanced.

SPECIFIC STUDIES UNDERTAKEN TO DATE

1. *A study of clerical workers in an insurance company.* The first study was begun in the home office of a large insurance company in August of 1947. This company is so organized that it has parallel work groups performing the same functions under the same general technological work conditions and, moreover, it has productivity records on these groups. This setting would have been ideal for an institutional study of social-psychological factors associated with productivity if the productivity differences between work groups had been of a considerable order of magnitude. Though a number of these differences were statistically significant, they were not large in actual magnitude. This meant that a study limited to a productivity design ran a large risk of not coming up with any significant findings. The study was therefore broadened to include (1) a consideration of the interrelations of the dimensions of morale and (2) the relations of morale to other factors such as supervision and type of work.

After extensive pretesting during August, the full-scale study proceeded in September and October of 1947. In all, intensive interviews were conducted with 742 rank-and-file employees and with 73 first-line supervisors and managerial personnel. These interviews were coded; Hollerith cards were punched according to the codes developed, and the material was analyzed during the winter of 1947–48 and the spring of 1948. The main findings were presented to the company in a conference session, and a plan was developed with them during the summer and fall of 1948 for an experimental program as suggested by the findings.

2. *An experiment involving clerical workers.* An experimental program has been initiated at the same insurance company in an attempt to verify suggestions implicit in the findings of the first study. The organizational structure of two divisions has been modified in the direction of shifting the locus of regulation and control down the hierarchical levels to permit more local autonomy. Two parallel divisions are being given different courses of training which are moving in opposite directions.

The spring and summer of 1949 were devoted to the training of the upper levels of managerial personnel and to a mutual working out of the details of the program. The program was formally launched at the lower levels in September 1949 and is still in process.

Productivity records will be used as one measure of the effectiveness of the two programs, and continuing behavioral observations are being made to give data about the nature of the change process taking place. In addition, measures of morale were made at the inception of the program and will be duplicated toward the end of the experimental process.

In many ways this is the largest field experimentation so far attempted in changing organizational structure and the character of leadership under controlled conditions. Moreover, it emphasizes systematic measures of productivity, of worker and supervisory attitudes and perceptions, and of behavioral observations by trained observers. The scope of the program, the significance of the changes attempted, and the locus of the operation in a real-life situation have made the project time-consuming and costly in terms of the usual research standards in the field.

3. *The Pensacola air base study.* During the summer of 1947, while the insurance study was getting underway, the Naval Air Training Command at the Pensacola Naval Air Station was interested in a study of the effective utilization of its personnel resources. Two staff members of the Survey Research Center attended conferences at Pensacola during August 1947. The outcome was a study of the morale of

the Ground School instructional staff at the Pensacola Naval Air Station. A confidential report has been submitted to the command at Pensacola.

4. *A study in a public utility.* The second series of industrial studies has been conducted in a public utility servicing an important part of the state of Michigan. Written questionnaires were administered to all of the 8,075 non-supervisory employees in the company after an extensive pretest of the questionnaire through personal interviews. On the basis of the returns from these written questionnaires, approximately forty work units with the highest morale and forty work units with the lowest morale were selected for further, intensive study. The 750 employees in these work units were interviewed in depth interviews. In addition, all supervisory and managerial personnel of the company were interviewed in sessions lasting from one to three hours. Interviewing ranged from the first-line supervisors to the vice-presidents and president, and included 750 first-line supervisors, 150 second-line supervisors, 200 upper-level personnel and 20 Council members and vice-presidents.

This is the first time a large industrial company has been so completely studied. The information obtained from interviewing the whole supervisory and managerial structure will yield hypotheses about the relationships between levels of management and about the entire management process.

5. *The utilization of research findings.* The objectives of the program include the discovery of the principles of social change which have to do with the utilization of research results for solving organizational and human relations problems. In the public utility already mentioned, several exploratory studies on the process of social change are being conducted, building on the survey results. The method of utilizing research results represents a new point of departure in this field. The results of the research have been used as a means of involving line officials, from the top of the company down, in a consideration of their own problems, the causes of these problems and the remedial measures to be used. The technique has been to present comparative results by department or major units within the company which show relative strong and weak spots in the various dimensions of morale, and to enlist the participation of the line officials in further analysis of the data. These meetings have started at the top of the company and each meeting includes organizational families of at least two levels in the organizational hierarchy. Over two hundred meetings

and conferences between the Survey Research Center and the utility company managerial and supervisory people have already taken place.

The examination of objective data on human relations problems by line officers and their involvement in the program has been a training process in and of itself, and a re-survey is planned to evaluate the effects.

6. *An experimental evaluation of a training program.* The public utility is putting into effect a new human relations training program for its supervisory personnel, a program designed and directed by Dr. N. R. F. Maier. The Survey Research Center is making an evaluation of this program by taking before and after measurements of twenty-five pairs of matched groups. Twenty-five supervisors are receiving the training program, whereas their twenty-five matched counterparts are not. Surveys of the morale of the groups and of the attitudes and leadership philosophy of their supervisors were made during the fall of 1949. The after measurements will be taken in the fall of 1950 in order to discover the effects of the training program both on supervisors and rank-and-file employees.

7. *A study of railroad workers.* Productivity measures were not available in the utility situation, and it was considered necessary to conduct other productivity studies to check on the findings of the original insurance company project. Accordingly, matched groups of maintenance-of-way section crews on a railroad were selected for study. These matched groups were rated high and low in productivity by track supervisors. All of the workers in thirty-six pairs of matched sections were interviewed, as were their immediate foremen. The interviewing took place between November 11, 1948, and January 13, 1949.

Since this study was conducted among a radically different type of worker, in a radically different working environment, it furnishes some degree of check on the generality of the findings among clerical workers.

8. *A study in the automobile industry.* Since the initial studies in the program were being conducted in industrial situations, it seemed important to begin to take account of union-management relations. Not only is this necessary for an understanding of industrial studies in general but the problem of membership in overlapping groups is a special one, worthy of study in itself. A project was therefore launched in an automotive corporation in the spring of 1948 with the

cooperation of the management and of the officials of the United Automobile Workers, C.I.O.

The design of this study utilized the reciprocal attitudes and perceptions of different groups within the company. Three separate groups were set up; one consisted of all the foremen in the production departments, the second was made up of the foremen's counterparts among the union stewards, and the third consisted of a sample of rank-and-file workers in the production departments. A specific objective of the study was an examination of the similarities and differences in the way in which stewards, foremen, and men perceived the same problems; in addition, the study was designed to analyze the relationship between the communication and participation practices of foremen and stewards toward their men and the attitudes of the employees. Finally, the study attempted to discover the degree to which the men identified with the company and with the union, and the correlates of such identification.

The interviewing on this study was completed in July of 1948, and totalled 1,148 interviews. In addition to the interviews at lower levels, nine top union officials and twenty-eight members of top management were questioned.

Besides the major study in the production departments, a written questionnaire was administered to a sample of 388 white collar employees. The questionnaire was similar to the one used in the public utility and covered some of the same material as did the insurance interview. The data from this questionnaire will add material for a comparative study of morale across companies based upon the same measurement instrument.

9. *A study in heavy industry.* The most recent industrial study has been carried on in a corporation manufacturing tractors and earth-moving machinery, which represents a different type of industrial situation than those previously studied. The other studies concerned with productivity were compelled to deal with group records of performance, whereas the tractor company has extensive records on all its employees who are on direct labor cost. All twenty thousand non-supervisory employees of the company filled out written questionnaires during December 1949 and January 1950. Similarly, all the one thousand first-level supervisors have filled out written questionnaires.

This study is giving much more emphasis to the standards that workers have for job performance than was possible in previous studies. So much of the social system at the company revolves around the productivity records and the productivity norms that morale relationships will have to take account of this central area. The study also includes a methodological comparison of written questionnaires and personal interviews. The automotive study contains interesting comparisons of the perception of the role of foremen and stewards held by workers, foremen, and stewards. The tractor study is continuing this investigation of the commonly perceived role of foremen held by men and foremen.

10. *The study of morale and human relations in the Office of Naval Research.* This study was suggested by ONR as the first step in the utilization of the methodology and findings of this program of research in improving organizational and personnel practices within Naval bureaus. Planning on this study began in the fall of 1949 and continued through the winter months of 1950. The objectives of this study are to provide ONR with information about: the individual's concept of his job; understanding of and motivation toward the accomplishment of the major goals of ONR; communication within the organization; sources of satisfaction and frustration on the job; supervisor-subordinate relationships.

PROGRESS TO DATE

The program has assumed three major directions to date. The first direction has been the identification of the dependent variables in organizational functioning. We have assumed from the start that productivity is only one of the major criteria of group effectiveness. The gratifications which individuals derive, directly or indirectly, from their membership in an organization are also very significant criteria of organizational functioning. This is particularly true in large scale organizations of a non-voluntary sort where the performance goals may be set by a few people in the top levels of the organization. It is not only a problem of the efficiency of the organization in moving toward these goals but of the psychological costs and rewards to the entire membership of the organization.

A second direction has been a consideration of psychological, dependent variables from another frame of reference, namely, as intervening variables that affect performance. We have considered the satisfactions or morale dimensions, then, both as dependent variables to be predicted from other factors and as a reflection of intervening variables which could help to predict productivity.

A third direction has been identification of independent variables and their relationship to morale dimensions and to productivity.

In our efforts to identify the dependent morale variables we have moved away from a global concept of morale to the different types of satisfactions that the individuals derive from the industrial situation. We started with the assumption of five such classes of dependent variables, namely:

(1) Intrinsic job satisfaction, that is, the gratifications to the worker from performing a job which challenges his abilities, which gives him a chance to show what he is worth, which allows him to do the things he likes to do.

(2) Involvement in the immediate work group—satisfactions from membership in the sub-system of the organization known as the immediate work group. Here would be included feelings of "group belongingness" and feelings toward fellow workers.

(3) Identification with the company—satisfactions from membership in the larger social system of the total organization. This would include both identification with the organization and liking for the many parts of the structure which are direct or indirect routes to the organizational goals; for example, personnel policies, rules and regulations, recreational programs, etc. Included here, too, is a consideration of the differential allegiance to the company as a system and to the union as a possible competing system. This latter variable is the cross-pressure phenomenon with which Lazarsfeld and Stouffer have been concerned.

(4) Satisfactions deriving from interpersonal relations with the supervisor as a personality.

(5) The indirect satisfactions of the individual's needs which membership in the organization makes possible, namely, the satisfactions which arise because the individual can satisfy his needs outside the company through the wages he gets and the prestige of his job in the outside community. It is becoming fairly common practice to overlook the fact that most people enter and remain in industrial organizations because they have to earn a living.

We made no allowance, originally, for still another component of morale, the satisfactions that derive from being part of an occupational system. Apart from satisfactions arising from the nature of the work and from identification with a specific organization is the identification with an occupational system. For example, a railroader, no matter whether a clerical or manual worker, is often attached to railroading as an occupation and this can be independent of the specific company he is working for.

In our study of the psychological dependent variables—namely, the different systems of satisfactions—our results suggest the validity of breaking away from the blanket concept of morale. The basis for this conclusion is the differential reaction of the various dependent variables. By and large, intrinsic job satisfaction seems to be a function of the work itself. It is influenced by other factors but it is derived much less from working for a company with a good pension system and good recreational facilities than it is from the skill level of the job or the variety and interest of the work content. On the other hand, satisfaction with the company as a social system is not necessarily found among those in the higher level jobs. The people who like the company as a social system are those who participate in its extra-curricular activities, who are proud of working for it, who plan to stay on with the company for a long period. Thus, intrinsic job satisfaction is not necessarily related to satisfaction with the company nor to the factors affecting company identification.

In the same fashion, satisfaction with the primary work group is tied much more closely to supervision than are the dependent variables of intrinsic job satisfaction and company identification. In the insurance study, workers reported more involvement with their group under supervisors following a given type of supervisory philosophy. The supervisors who were more "employee-oriented" headed sections with much more group pride than did the supervisors who were less "employee-oriented." Supervisors in high pride sections were regarded as much more reasonable in their expectations of the work required of employees than the supervisors in the low pride sections. There were more frequent reports of people helping out when necessary in the high pride sections than in the low pride sections. Supervisors reported better interpersonal relations in the sections in which people derived greater satisfaction from their membership in the group.

The satisfactions which the organization indirectly furnishes through wages and status follow different patterns of relationship. In one company, for example, satisfaction with wages was negatively related to length of service. Those with the lower wages presumably were more satisfied because they had lower wage expectations, a characteristic of employees who had been with the company a shorter time. In other words, satisfaction with status and salary is a function of the expectations in terms of training and experience. This was also true in another company with respect to the retirement benefits. The longer the people had been in the company the greater their dissatisfaction with retirement benefits. Moreover, the professional people were more dissatisfied than white collar workers; and the skilled, manual workers were more dissatisfied than the unskilled workers. Satisfactions with the rewards furnished by the organization are related to the individual's expectations. Wages and job level are related to satisfaction only as they are interpreted by the individual in the light of his training and experience.

Satisfaction with wages and status is not necessarily related to other types of gratification. It is true that there is a very definite coloring effect for those who stand high on this index. People who are very satisfied with their wages and with their status also like the company and all parts of its policy. They also like their fellow employees and their jobs. There is some evidence that there is a critical point on any one morale dimension beyond which there is a general halo or coloring effect that extends to other dimensions.

Another type of dependent variable with which we have been concerned is the cross-pressure phenomenon—the effect of being in organizational structures making competing demands. We have only one study in this area, that of workers in automotive production who are also members of the C.I.O. In this company there is clear cut evidence that the perceived incompatibility was much clearer at the leadership level than at the rank and file level. Both foremen and union stewards felt that the company and union were after different goals much more than did rank and file workers. In general, leaders who are competing for the same following are probably more aware of conflict than are the people whom they are attempting to align with them. In this particular situation, moreover, perception of the incompatibility of company and union goals was greater among the foremen than among the union stewards.

Among rank and file workers the perceived incompatibility of goals was greater for those more highly identified with management than for those highly identified with the union. In other words, high identification with the union did not mean rejection of company goals as much as identification with the company meant rejection of union goals. For workers who identified with both groups there was a tendency to minimize the conflict of goals and to perceive the mutual interdependence of the two groups.

In part, the perceived incompatibility of union and management goals is related to the power struggle between the foreman and steward in a particular department. In departments where either foreman or steward seemed to have clear cut power there was less perception of conflict. In departments where there was a struggle for power between foreman and steward there was more perception of the conflict between union and management. It seems probable that labor-management conflict is perceived by the rank and file only if it is translated into the local situation in some fashion.

It must be remembered that the particular company studied represents an unusual situation in the industry. The company, while an important part of the automobile industry, is not as large in size or resources as the "Big Three." The major conflicts of management and labor are fought in Detroit between the U.A.W. and one of the larger companies. Thus, the larger companies tend to set the pace for wages and employee benefits, and the type of relationships worked out at the company studied must be understood in this larger context. The opportunities for cooperation may be greater for this company than for some others in the industry. Within this framework, however, it does not necessarily follow that skillful interpersonal relationships will develop to bring about a high degree of cooperation between management and union. Hence, the specific patterns of interaction at this company have real significance.

As the program has proceeded we have attempted to improve our measures of morale variables in three areas. (1) We have asked questions getting at the involvement of the individual in the primary work group situation. Though our original questions included items on "group belongingness," on group unity and on feelings toward deviant members, we had been weak in questions getting at the perceptions of group norms. (2) We have tried to differentiate more on the company satisfaction level between identification with company goals and involvement in the policies and practices which are supplemental to these goals. (3) Our greatest problem has been the measurement of satisfaction in relation to need. To know that people derive gratification from a system in which they are involved, or that they have a favorable affect toward it, or even that they perceive it in a certain manner, is not enough. When we shift our frame of reference and attempt to use these measures of satisfaction as indications of need or motivation (that is, as intervening variables), we must also have some indication of the importance of the system to the individual. Two men, both satisfied with the content of their jobs, may vary considerably in their motivation. In one case the man may be satisfying an active and deep need, whereas the other is satisfied because he has very little need or want. Therefore, it is necessary to relate the satisfaction measures to people's wants and aspirations. There is no infallible technique for getting at the activity level of needs, but we have recognized the problem and have found some degree of answer in questions getting at aspirations and expectations.

MORALE DIMENSIONS AS INTERVENING VARIABLES

In considering the dimensions of morale as intervening variables, we have thus far found few relationships. The two main findings are the relationship between productivity and (a) identification with one's own sub-group and (b) greater need for progress within the company. This is of interest in that the only objective differences between the matched groups were in the area of supervision and interpersonal relationships. The groups that were compared on productivity were similar in wages and type of work and were under the same general company practices and policies. It was still possible that there could be differential perceptions of the situation and correspondingly differential attitudes. The findings, however, tended to emphasize the importance of the objective situation in that the morale dimensions varied not so much on differences in perception as on differences in the situation itself. Thus, the higher producing groups had greater pride and greater identification with their groups but they did not differ in satisfaction with company benefits, in acceptance of company goals, in satisfaction with wages or in intrinsic job satisfaction.

Job satisfaction, however, did vary with the actual nature of the work. Favorable affect was shown toward company benefits and privileges by those who used them. Satisfaction with wages was related to length of service and education. In other words, where there was an objective basis for differential perceptions they tended to be in evidence. But since our comparison between high and low producing groups was based upon a matching of such factors as type of work, wages, and company policy, there was no differentiation in the corresponding attitudes. Our findings, then, on productivity are limited to a situation in which the major independent variable is supervision. This does not mean that if all other factors could be held constant a difference in wages, for example, would not affect productivity and morale. Thus far we have not been able to make across-company comparisons in which everything would remain constant save a major, objective factor.

INDEPENDENT VARIABLES AND THEIR RELATIONSHIP
TO MORALE AND PRODUCTIVITY

Some reference to the relationships of the independent variables to morale and productivity has already appeared in the discussion of the nature of the dependent variables, but a more complete statement of this relationship is necessary. We have consistently found that the type of work or the level of skill which the job requires is an important independent variable that is related to intrinsic job satisfaction. In our study designs, so far, we have not attempted to relate level of job to productivity because we have not been willing to accept time standards as a measuring device which gives equal units of productive effort for various types of tasks.

A second major independent variable which has assumed importance in at least one of our studies is the size of the immediate work group. In our public utility study it was a correlate of most aspects of morale, that is, the larger work groups were lower in morale than the smaller work groups. This was true even when type of work, union membership, sex of the worker, and age of the worker were held constant.

Our major attention on the side of the independent variable has been given to supervision, both in terms of the personal characteristics of the leader and in terms of supervision as an organizational pattern. Examples of our findings to date can be summarized as follows:

(1) The supervisor with the better productive record plays a more differentiated role than the supervisor with the poor productive record, that is, he does not perform the same functions as a rank and file worker but assumes more of the functions traditionally associated with leadership.

(a) Specifically, in the railroad study the supervisors with better production records gave more attention to the long-range direction of their groups. Instead of operating on a day-to-day basis, they planned the work and anticipated problems and organized their programs accordingly. This ability, involving a temporal frame of reference embracing the future and anticipating problems, has perhaps not been given enough attention in leadership studies.

(b) In general, the supervisors with the better production records gave more time to their supervisory functions, specifically to problems of motivating people. The supervisors of the lower production sections gave more of their time to routine activities which the workers themselves could perform.

(2) The higher producing groups were under section heads who supervised less closely and who, in turn, were under less close supervision from their superiors. A plausible interpretation is that there was more effective motivation of employees where the organizational structure permitted greater freedom in minor decision-making to both the employee and to his supervisor.

(3) Similarly, in terms of some of the morale dimensions, the

more effective supervisor gave more attention to problems of motivation than to problems of institutional routine.

(a) Questions such as the amount of personal interest the supervisor shows in his employees did not always give positive results. More critical items, however, had to do with whether the supervisor built up his people for better jobs, backed them up for these positions, kept them informed on how well they were doing, kept them informed on what was going on in the company. In one study these items differentiated work groups on some of the morale dimensions in a very discriminating fashion, whereas other items which were getting at routine foreman functions of an institutional sort (such as enforcing the rules, keeping the men supplied with materials) showed no differentiation whatsoever. In another study the same groups of items were given to workers and they were asked what their foremen generally did and what they would really like to see him do. Again, the discrepancy between what the worker said his foreman did and what he wanted him to do was greatest on the motivational items and showed no differences on the routine, institutional functions. In this latter study we have not, as yet, taken the further step of comparing the perception of the foreman's behavior with the various morale dimensions.

(b) Another aspect of this motivational problem is the participation dimension. There was evidence from some of our studies that participation practices on the part of the supervisor made for higher productivity. On the morale side, the most striking demonstration of this point came from the automotive study. In departments in which the foremen called their men in to discuss problems there was greater satisfaction with the foreman. Moreover, identification with the union or with the management tended to go with differential practices by foremen or by stewards. Where foremen consulted the men and stewards did not, there was high identification with management. In departments where both foremen and stewards involved the men in decision-making, there was greater liking for the job as a whole. In departments where neither stewards nor foremen involved the men there was less liking for the company than in departments where either steward or foreman involved the men. In either case, the foremen and stewards seemed to be playing similar roles in raising the level of satisfaction with the company. Though the variable of participation and consultation in supervisory practice tended to show a positive relationship to some of the dimensions of morale, this was not true in all situations. Among the railroad employees there was little positive evidence of this effect. In the railroad situation the technical competence and experience of the foreman had a chance to affect performance because of the amount of freedom enjoyed by the section unit. Hence, the foremen who made decisions on the basis of superior know-how could effect productivity, even though the lack of involvement of their groups may have produced some motivational loss.

(4) The same supervisory practices and attitudes did not yield the same results among all groups. In the public utility there were important differences in the way in which supervisory practices were received by small and large work groups, especially among the white collar workers. In the small work groups supervisors following consultation practices had employees with more favorable attitudes toward the supervisor, with more pride in their group, better liking for their jobs, and stronger feeling that the company recognized good work. Among large white collar groups and among blue collar workers these results were not duplicated. Unless there are special institutional arrangements, it is difficult for the formal leader to involve a large group successfully. And the data also indicated a different type of problem with the blue collar worker. In this company it is apparently easier for the white collar worker to identify with his supervisor than it is for the blue collar worker. We found that the white collar worker was more sensitive to and reacted favorably toward the leader who was "employee-oriented," whereas this "employee orientation" of the supervisor made no difference to the blue collar worker. For the worker on the factory floor it took some gross behavioral demonstration of the foreman's interest in his men before there was any favorable reaction toward the foreman.

HYPOTHESES AND FIELD EXPERIMENTATION

In general, our interpretation is that participation and involvement of the men cannot be explained primarily in terms of the personality characteristics of the leader and group effects. Rather, participation and involvement are conditioned by the general situational and organizational context. The evidence for this comes from a number of sources. In the insurance company the better productivity from supervisors following less detailed supervision was a double finding, in that supervisors giving employees more leeway were themselves enjoying more freedom to act. Similarly, in the automobile company the relationship appeared more clearly between supervisory practice and worker attitude when departments were compared than when individual foremen and workers were compared.

On the basis of our early findings, of our observations of the organizational structure of the various companies, and of our interpretations, we decided that the most important variable to examine was the dimension of organizational structure having to do with the locus of control and decision making. Accordingly, we set up a field experiment in the insurance company in which two divisions are operating under a loosened control pattern with actual delegation of power down the line. In other words, the area of freedom for decision-making at the divisional level embraces the area formerly reserved for the departmental head; the area of freedom for decision-making at the sectional level now covers divisional matters and the rank and file employees now take over many of the functions of the section heads. In two other divisions there is a tightening of control with more centralization of decision-making at the top level, more precise definition of job functions, and increased man-to-man accountability down the line. Survey techniques employed before and after these changes, and continuous observation of the experimental groups, will measure the effect of these organizational changes on the criteria of productivity and worker satisfaction.

Part of the theory behind this field experiment can be summarized briefly. Changes in an organization or a social structure imply changes in the accepted role prescriptions for the different levels in the hierarchy and changes in the reciprocal expectations of the many members. A given individual's behavior in the organization is less a function of his deep-lying personality trends and more a function of the expectations of his superiors, his colleagues, and his subordinates. These expectations are based upon the commonly accepted patterns of behavior, whether formally or informally institutionalized, and in addition are enforced by the sanctions of superiors. To put foremen into a training course and then to put them back into their old jobs produces minimal change. They are still perceived in the same way by both the people under them and the people over them. Their institutionalized roles, moreover, have not changed. The authority permitted them has not been increased. Since so many factors in the situation remain constant, it is not realistic to expect radical change.

Experiments on social change must, therefore, take into account the social structures in which change is to take place and must manipulate the variables which control the institutional patterns.

UTILIZATION OF RESEARCH RESULTS

We anticipated at the start that we would have to give considerable time and effort to the problem of utilizing the results of our research. For one thing, it is difficult to obtain continuing cooperation of organizations with an ongoing job to do without making available to them the findings which their earlier cooperation has made possible. For another thing, one of the most effective ways for verifying research findings and for sharpening hypotheses about their meaning is through the application of these results in field experiments. Our program for the utilization of research results has taken two directions. One direction is the field experiment in which we try to test hypotheses through before and after measures on controlled, experimental groups and through behavioral observation of the processes intervening. The second direction is preliminary to the first type. It consists in a large-scale feedback process in which the results of the research are introduced into the company through the line organization in such a way as to give major responsibility for the interpretation and utilization of findings to the line organization itself.

This process utilizes the organizational structure of the company, and starts at the top of the hierarchy. As research materials move down the line, organizational families involving at least two hierarchical levels in the various departments discuss findings in small group meetings and function both as research and as action units. This procedure for utilizing research results has the advantages of (1) maximizing involvement of the line organization in the interpretation of research findings and (2) shifting from a personal, subjective point of view toward morale and organizational functioning to a factual, objective approach.

CONCLUSION

It might be appropriate to conclude by emphasizing our conviction that the research program, as contrasted to isolated research projects, represents a particularly fruitful way of approaching the broad problems of organizational structure. The more detailed examples of our research described in the following papers illustrate some of the ways in which it has been possible to refine measurement techniques and to extend hypotheses by means of a sequence of related studies.

In this description of the Human Relations Program of the Survey Research Center, inadequate attention has been given to the public utility study. Floyd C. Mann, who has directed that work, has been prevented by severe illness from reporting it here.

AN ANALYSIS OF SUPERVISORY PRACTICES
AND COMPONENTS OF MORALE

ROBERT L. KAHN

Survey Research Center
University of Michigan

THE STUDY AT THE TRACTOR company can be used to illustrate two developments in our thinking, one involving the "independent variable" of supervisory practices and the other the "dependent variable" of morale.

Dr. Katz has described our interest in the cross-pressures phenomenon, the situation in which a person perceives himself as the target of demands of conflicting groups. Some of the material from our earlier studies suggested that the supervisor is more often prey to such conflicting forces than is the rank and file worker. We were interested in investigating this phenomenon more methodically, and in tackling the problem of predicting the perceptions and behavior of persons in this cross-pressures situation. Moreover, it seemed to us that the constellation of variables we have called supervisory practices or supervision, and that we have been treating as independent variables affecting productivity and morale, might profitably be looked at also as dependent variables, primarily functions of the requirements of management and the requirements of the workers.

With this general background we arrived at the following hypotheses regarding the perceptions of the foreman:

> When the foreman perceives the expectations of the men as being the same as those of management, he will see his role as congruent with those expectations.
> When the foreman perceives a conflict between the expectations

of the men and those of management, his perceptions of his own role will depend upon:

1. his sensitivity to the attitudes of workers,
2. his concern for the problems of persons under his supervision,
3. his awareness of what factors are responsible for worker motivation,
4. his perception of the job of foreman as defined by management,
5. his perceptions of the demands of his own supervisors, and
6. his perception of the degree of consensus among the men in their demands of him.

In order to test these hypotheses, we questioned foremen about a number of functions which our observations and scouting interviews had led us to think might be important. We included such functions as: enforcing the rules; hearing complaints and grievances; keeping the men posted on how well they are doing; planning the work and making work assignments; making recommendations for promotions, transfers and pay increases; training new employees; training old employees for better jobs; keeping the men informed on what is going on in the company, and the like. For each of these functions we asked the foreman whether he did it, whether the men wanted a foreman to do it, and whether the company wanted a foreman to do it. We asked the men whether their foremen performed each of these functions, whether they wanted him to, and whether the work group as a whole wanted him to.

We are now in a position to determine whether the foreman's perception of his role and his behavior (as perceived by the men in his work group) conforms more closely to his perception of the requirements of management or the demands of the men. Subsidiary analyses will ascertain the congruence between the foreman's perceptions of his own behavior and those of the men he supervises. Ratings of the foreman's behavior in terms of its conformity to the norms of management or to those of the work group then become the major dependent variables in this part of our analysis.

The independent variables listed above dealt with the foreman's perceptions of management and the workers, and with the clarity of the demands which are made of him. There are a number of measures of the foreman's past experience in the company which seem relevant here. We can look on them as operational definitions of "management-oriented" or "worker-oriented" experience. The major measures include:

1. the ratio of the number of months of rank-and-file experience to the number of months of supervisory experience,
2. union membership or non-membership during rank-and-file experience, and
3. presence or absence of apprentice training, a program perceived as the management school for supervisors-to-be.

The clarity of the demands of the men will be measured by the dispersion of the men's perceptions about the mean for each function of the foreman in which their judgments were obtained. We have yet to derive a comparable measure of the clarity of the management's demands on the foreman. The results of this analysis are still ahead of us, and the research is described here primarily for the methodological interest which the approach may have.

Another aspect of our research at the tractor company has to do with some findings on the nature of morale. As Dr. Katz has stated, we began with the idea that morale has several dimensions. The results of our first studies tended to confirm this judgment, and led us to attempt some specifications of the dimensions of morale. The evidence for thinking in terms of these components was primarily the fact that, in interrelating background factors, supervisory practices, and other variables to expressions of specific satisfaction or dissatisfaction, certain clusters of responses had appeared as the reflection of distinct dimensions of morale.

In the tractor company study we tackled the problem of morale in a somewhat different way. We included in the questionnaire some seventy satisfaction items, trying to make the list as inclusive as possible of items used in previous surveys. Some items, of course, failed to discriminate satisfactorily. For the rest, we prepared a correlation matrix, and then did a factor analysis.

The results of the factor analysis reveal very clearly the presence of four factors in the concept of morale as we have used it. The first of these can be described as satisfactions with immediate supervision. Responses regarding technical competence of supervisors, amount of communication, effectiveness with which complaints are handled, and the like are very largely accounted for by this *supervision* factor.

The second factor is bound up with the job itself—including both intrinsic job satisfaction and some of the prestige satisfactions which the job affords.

The third factor seems to consist of what Dr. Katz called satisfaction with the organization as a system. It loads heavily questions which show affect for the company as a whole—for example, whether conditions are getting better or worse; how the company compares with others as a place to work; and how well it is run. This factor is reflected in a greater number of responses than any other.

The fourth morale factor which we have identified is a bit harder to name than the others. It is an indirect satisfaction measure. Wage satisfactions are in it, as are promotions. But there seems to be reflected in it also a more general need for mobility than simply moving up the pay scale. Opportunity for horizontal transfer and chances to learn new things are also present, although satisfaction with wages, present and potential, is dominant.

In short, this analysis provides some confirmation of our use of the morale components which have already been described. In addition, it suggests that satisfaction with immediate supervision may be differentiated quite sharply from satisfaction with the organization as a system, and that the men distinguish also between the human relations skills and the technical competence of the supervisors.

The next steps in this analysis will be to determine the relationship of these morale components and of individual productivity to the independent variables of supervisory practices, type of work, departmental administrative policy, and a number of personal characteristics. We will also test again for relationships between morale and productivity, an area where our findings are very sparse. We have some hope that objective, individual productivity scores and a large population may make this line of attack more rewarding in this study.

FOREMAN AND STEWARD, REPRESENTATIVES OF MANAGEMENT AND THE UNION

EUGENE JACOBSON

Survey Research Center
University of Michigan

THE CONTINUING RESEARCH INTEREST of the Human Relations Program of the Survey Research Center is directed toward an understanding of how the productivity and satisfaction of individual workers and the over-all effectiveness of organizations are related to the ways in which these organizations operate.

As a point of departure for the investigation, in the initial studies in the program, we have taken as a focus for study the relationship between the first-level supervisor and the group of persons immediately under him. We chose this relationship because it is commonly found in most large organizations; it includes the largest number of individuals in most large organizations and promises great reward if understood. Moreover, it is a traditionally manipulatable relationship, that is, the notion of supervisory training programs and changes in supervision is acceptable to organization management, and the possibility of experimental testing of findings therefore exists. Finally, there is a body of literature, both scientific and popular, to furnish guidance for research hypotheses in this area. As our studies have developed, our interest in this relationship has extended to the consideration of the function of the supervisor as part of the larger organizational structure. This emphasis will be demonstrated in Dr. Morse's description of the insurance company experiment.

In the study of an automobile manufacturing company, we explored several ways of using the supervisor-supervised relationship as a means of understanding how the individual worker relates to a large industrial organization.

In addition to the core group of dependent variables which we have measured in all of our studies (attitudes toward the content of the job, the work group, opportunities for getting ahead in the organization, the company, supervision, and the other variables Mr. Kahn has described), in the automobile plant we had an opportunity to study relative loyalty to the company and to an industrial labor union. We could, then, examine the ways in which company foremen and union stewards interacted with the workers as a means of understanding differential loyalty to company and union.

All twelve thousand productive workers in the plant belonged to one local of the United Automobile, Aircraft and Agricultural Implement Workers of America (U.A.W.), a C.I.O. union. In the history of relationships between the plant workers and the company management, there is relatively little evidence of overt hostility. When an A.F.L. Auto Workers Union was organized in 1933, it was accepted by the company without friction and it converted to C.I.O. in 1937 with a minimum of stress. There have been no strikes at the plant that have been sanctioned by the official union organization, although there have been unauthorized work stoppages that have involved union workers in the plant. One occurred during the collecting of data for this study.

The union makes strong appeals to the workers' loyalty, and the company, both before and after the advent of the union, has been concerned with maintaining its reputation in the community as a good place to work and with maintaining a kind of craft pride in workmanship among its employees. Our hunch was that we could, by investigating the way in which the foremen and the union stewards related to the workers, find out something about how the individual worker responded to what Lazarsfeld would call the cross-pressures on him for loyalty to two almost completely overlapping membership groups: the company and the union.

To accumulate data bearing on this question, we had a staff of twenty trained interviewers interview all of the foremen and all of the stewards in some seventy work departments (about 350 foremen and about 350 stewards) and a random sample of workers in the same departments (about 450). Interviews were conducted in the respondents' homes at their convenience. The interviews took from one to three hours, and included questions designed to get at satisfactions, perceptions, expectations and aspirations about their jobs, their supervisors, the company, the union, union-management relations and a variety of related topics. Verbatim transcripts of answers to standard lists of questions in these areas were converted by Survey Research Center content analysis techniques into quantitative data and transcribed on Hollerith cards.

In the area of supervision, we asked the foremen whether they called their men in to help in making decisions about the shop. On the basis of answers to this question, we assigned ratings to each of the seventy work departments. These ratings allowed us to rank the departments from those in which foremen were most likely to report that they involved their men in joint decision-making to those in which they were least likely to report this. Correspondingly, we asked the workers to report on the participation practices of the foremen and, again, we were able to rank the departments in the order of worker report. We asked similar questions of the steward about his involving workers in decisions about the union, and of the worker about his steward's behavior. And, in addition, we asked the workers if they wanted the foreman and steward to involve them in decision-making.

Among our seventy departments we have some in which the report on participation is uniformly high from workers, foremen, and stewards; some in which the report is uniformly low; and others that represent all of the permutations of the three kind of reports.

Comparing workers in high participation departments with those in low participation departments allows us to formulate some hypotheses about the relationship between participation and worker attitudes toward the company and the union. To obtain a measure of relative identification with the company and the union we gave each worker two scores, each based on coded interview responses to a set of five questions. One score was a five-position index of the degree to which he accepted union goals as his own; the other was a five-position index of the degree to which he accepted management goals as his own. The indexes were developed by Dr. Benjamin Willerman of the University of Minnesota, when he was associated with this project. Some workers rated high on management and low on union; some rated high on union and low on management; and some were high on both or low on both. They were arbitrarily divided into three groups on the basis of these combined scores: one group labeled high management-low union, another high union-low management, and the third labeled neutral. The schematic diagram in Figure 1 shows how this was worked out. The relative number of persons in the three groups is a function of the way in which the indexes were constructed rather than any absolute evaluation.

Figure 1

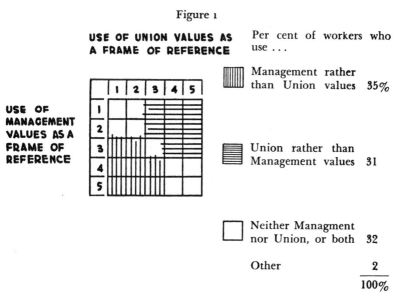

USE OF UNION VALUES AS A FRAME OF REFERENCE

Per cent of workers who use . . .

Management rather than Union values 35%

Union rather than Management values 31

Neither Managment nor Union, or both 32

Other 2

100%

Although analysis of the relationships between these two measures—participation and union-management polarity—is not complete, some regularities in the data are appearing. Uniformly, in departments where the foreman is active in involving the men and the steward is not, the workers are more likely to be high on the management index and low on the union index. In departments where the steward is active in involving the men in working out union matters and the foreman does not involve them, the men are high on the union index and relatively low on the management measure. Where both foreman and steward are active, the men are somewhat higher on the management index. These relationships hold on the basis of the workers' report, the foremen's report, and the stewards' report, and are particularly marked in those departments where there is a consensus of report. Additional analysis is proceeding in two ways: (1) departments will be regrouped in a more detailed categorizing, that is, instead of a simple high participation–low participation grouping they will be ordered on a five-step continuum and the data re-examined; (2) as a second step, more attention will be paid to departments in which there is no consensus to develop hypotheses about the reasons for discrepancy in report.

As background for understanding these relationships we have these additional data on the over-all pattern of participation report and expectation in all of the departments studied:

1. About half as many foremen as stewards report that they make an active effort to involve their men in joint decision processes.
2. About half as many workers report that the foremen call them in for joint decision-making as report that their stewards do.
3. Most workers feel that both the foreman and the steward should involve them in decision-making. Seven in ten say that the foreman should and eight in ten say that the steward should.
4. Among those who say that the foreman and steward should involve them, about twice as many men feel strongly that the steward should enlist their assistance as feel strongly that the foreman should.
5. It is less likely that a worker who reports that his foreman does not call him in will say that he should than it is that a worker who reports that his steward does not call him in will say that the steward should.
6. Men report that they want the foreman to get their help in making decisions because they know how the work should be done and are capable of making suggestions that would add to the productive efficiency of the shop.
7. Men report that they want the steward to get their help in making decisions because the steward is only an agent of the men and has to know what the men want before he can be an effective representative.

In general, the workers expect a closer relationship with their union stewards than with the foremen, but they feel that both the foremen and the steward should make use of their counsel. When the foreman or steward fails to meet the expectations of the worker, there is evidence that worker attitudes toward the company and the union are affected.

Additional data on the power relationships between the foreman and the steward are being analyzed in comparable fashion to determine whether workers' perception of union-management dealings is related to their experience of how the foreman and steward get along.

A third analysis, dealing with the role of foremen who have been union stewards, is also underway as a further exploration of the determinants of worker orientation. In all of these analyses, it is recognized that other factors, apart from the role of the foreman and the steward in their interaction with the worker, have an important bearing on worker attitudes toward the company and the union, and data were collected on some of these additional factors in this study. This presentation is intended to illustrate how survey methods can lead to hypotheses about the ways in which supervisor-worker inter-action is reflected in worker attitudes toward the large organization represented by the supervisor.

AN EXPERIMENTAL STUDY IN AN
INDUSTRIAL ORGANIZATION

NANCY C. MORSE

Survey Research Center
University of Michigan

OUR SEARCH FOR THE CAUSES of group productivity and morale in social organizations began with a series of surveys of industrial organizations. The pattern of correlations found in these surveys led to hypotheses about certain causal relations. A change experiment in an industrial setting seemed the appropriate next step to test some of these hypotheses.

This experiment is designed to test the relationship which one dimension of social organization bears to productivity and morale. The dimension of organization which is the independent variable has to do with the levels at which the major functions of the organization are controlled and regulated, that is, the levels at which decisions are made, administered and enforced. We believe that it is possible to assign a rating to an organization which reflects its position on a continuum of locus of control and regulation. At one end of this continuum would be an organization in which decisions were made and functions controlled entirely by those individuals who were affected most directly by the controls and regulations. At the other extreme we would find an organization in which the ongoing functions were completely controlled by the top level of a supervisory hierarchy.

Operationally, then, the independent variable in this experiment is an index number reflecting the degree to which the functions of an organization are controlled and regulated by the functional units most affected, or by a hierarchy of administrative authority.

The experiment involves four parallel divisions in one department of a large clerical organization. Clerks, supervisors, managers and the general management of the department are involved in the experimental design—all together, about five hundred people. All four divisions have the same type of work, the same work methods and equipment, and approximately the same volume of work. Each division is made up of five sub-units or sections whose work exactly parallels that of the sections in the other divisions. The personnel for the divisions is centrally recruited and assigned. At the beginning of the experiment, the four divisions were divided into two matched groups of two divisions each. These groups were rated on the continuum of control and regulation described above, and on productivity. Measures of job satisfaction were obtained from their members. The two groups did not differ significantly on any of these characteristics.

The two groups of divisions are receiving two different experimental programs. One is designed to increase substantially the amount of control and regulation by the employee work groups and decrease the amount of control and regulation by the upper hierarchy. In this program, employee groups will make decisions about many of the things which affect them and will see that these decisions are carried out and conformed to. The other program is designed to increase the amount of control and regulation by the hierarchy and decrease the amount of control and regulation by the employees. In this latter program, upper management will make all major decisions and see that they are carried out and conformed to.

Both programs started with a training period for the supervisory personnel of the divisions.

In the program where the locus of regulation and control is being lowered, the supervisors included in the program met separately with a member of the company's training department to find out what the general outline of the program was and to plan out what such a program would mean in terms of their roles and functions—in other words, to plan their new jobs. After this preparation phase, the supervisory groups began to apply in their normal operations the plans they had developed. The employees were introduced to the program and began to make and carry out their own decisions in running their sectional work groups. The first line supervisors of a division began to work with their manager to handle the problems of the division. The managers and assistants from both divisions began to meet with the departmental manager to handle problems at the departmental level.

In the program where the locus of control and regulation is being raised, the training period also involved information and instruction sessions for the supervisors. During this period, with the cooperation of line supervision, staff experts studied the operations of the divisions to discover means for increasing employee efficiency and satisfaction. Out of these investigations various projects were developed and were then introduced into the divisions. One of the projects introduced to increase efficiency was the measurement of individual productivity.

Both of these programs are still developing. Although the programs were introduced a year ago, neither set of divisions is yet a well-integrated, well-rounded social organization of the type planned. They are moving to the point where one can be called a miniature social organization characterized by self-regulation and control by the functional units most affected, and the other a miniature social organization characterized by regulation and control by an upper hierarchy. It is difficult to say how soon these organizations will mature, and therefore how soon the differences in productivity and morale can be interpreted in terms of the results of the two programs.

The measurement of the growth, development, and effects of these two types of structures is quite an extensive task. Our measurements should answer the following questions:

1. Were there actual shifts in the control and regulation index in the direction expected?
2. If so, why did these occur?
3. What effects did the control and regulation variable have on such dependent variables as productivity and morale?
4. What factors account for the relationships between the control and regulation variable and the dependent variables, if any relationships exist? In other words, what are the intervening variables?
5. What are the ways in which the two types of organizations are alike?
6. What accounts for these constancies?

To answer these questions, the clerks will be given questionnaires. Supervisors and managers will be intensively interviewed. We also plan to interview intensively a sample of clerks. We are measuring personality by an especially constructed questionnaire. We have observers in all the meetings and in the employee work space. This direct observation will be particularly useful in providing us with a dynamic picture of the two programs. In addition, we have records of most of the "behind the scene" conferences, the planning conferences before the introduction of the programs to the divisions and the succeeding conferences between upper level company personnel and members of our staff.

It is too early to make a thorough evaluation of this study. Our experience indicates that a field experiment of this type is difficult and time consuming. Significant change in part of an ongoing organization is resisted because it disturbs existing uniformities and interrelationships and because it creates precedents. The maintenance of controls is difficult because changes in other parts of the organization seem to require changes in the experimental divisions. Furthermore, the requirements of measurement interfere with the objective of having changes perceived as part of the real life situation by members of the experimental group. While these problems are difficult, our experience shows that they are not insoluble. It is our belief that such studies as this will move us much closer to an adequate understanding of the functioning of social organizations.

DEVELOPMENT AND FUTURE PLANS
OF THE HUMAN RELATIONS PROGRAM

ANGUS CAMPBELL

Director, Survey Research Center
University of Michigan

MY PURPOSE IS TO SUMMARIZE some of the things that have been reported by my associates and to make some general remarks regarding the present status of the Human Relations Program and its likely future.

I would like to call to your mind three facts about this program which I think are important. In the first place, it should be noted that all of these studies were conducted in natural settings. They have all been concerned with ongoing industrial organizations. About half of the budget of this program has been carried by the cooperating companies themselves.

I think it must be clear that this program is a comparatively large-scale enterprise. Dr. Katz has been supervising for the last three years a working group numbering between twenty and twenty-five professional people and probably as many more assistants of one kind or another, not including interviewers, coders, and various other part-time assistants. This has been group research in the full sense of the term.

It is evident from our experience that group research, as applied in the field of social science, has both strengths and shortcomings. It is apparent, of course, that a working group of a dozen or two dozen people, all having specialized skills, can carry through projects of a scope that no single researcher, no matter how enterprising, can possibly hope to undertake. We also find that the presence of a number of different people in the same area results in a great deal of intellectual cross-fertilization, stimulation of ideas, and general corrective feedback. There is no doubt at all that in these two respects group research has returned valuable dividends.

There is, however, one aspect of group research which has given us difficulty during the three years of this particular project. When a group as large as this attempts to make common progress, there is almost inevitably some loss of communication across the lines of the various projects. We have, at present, four separate teams in this program carrying on research undertakings in different situations, different places, all of them within a common research area but not oriented toward the same specific research objective. One of our most persistent difficulties is the problem of keeping these teams intimately aware of each other's activities so that they receive maximum profit from one another's experience. I mention this not as a peculiarity of the particular work teams at the Survey Research Center, but as a characteristic difficulty of research programs undertaken by sizeable groups.

The third fact I should like to mention is that this series of studies was originally conceived as a *program* of research. The original statement which Dr. Likert wrote in 1947 was called "A Program of Research on the Fundamental Problems of Organizing Human Behavior." The general objective of this research program was originally stated as: "To discover the underlying principles applicable to the problems of organizing and managing human activity." The program was initially conceived as a ten-year undertaking. We have completed the third year. I think it is apparent that ten years will not be an adequate time to answer this very broad objective, but we, of course, expect that in ten years some considerable achievement will have been reached.

In the three years that we have been active, we have been mainly concerned with four problems: (1) to devise a system of theory and hypotheses relevant to our basic research objective; (2) to figure out the categories of data which would be relevant to these hypotheses; (3) to consider appropriate research designs through which these data could be obtained; and (4) to develop measurement techniques by which these data could actually be gathered. These problems have all required considerable developmental study.

Our original approach to the problem of conceptualizing theory in the area of our interest has been, I should say, of a broad, exploratory nature. We began, psychologist-wise, looking for correlations of various factors with morale and productivity. We have gradually sharpened our objectives as we have proceeded. It would be most pretentious to represent our activities as conforming closely to an ideal model of programmatic research. On the one side it has not always been possible to program a sequence of studies so that we could exploit it fully in the design of those that followed. On the other side, we are almost never able to arrange our individual studies precisely as we would like them. The practical problems of working with live organizations often compel us to trim our sails to some degree.

In the delineation of categories of data we began with rather general statements of data in the field of productivity and morale. You have seen that we have had to spend a good deal of energy in the breaking down of the term "morale," for example, to a number of categories of satisfactions. You have seen from Mr. Jacobson's presentation that we have begun to think in the general area of *perceptions* as an important variable in this field. We are now developing a conceptual frame work to guide further research in the area of organizational variables.

The problem of study design is made quite difficult, not only by the general difficulties of arranging the best suitable design, but also by the realistic problems of creating acceptable research projects in the local situation—in this case, in industry. We have, as you have seen, conducted all of our studies in ongoing industrial situations, and of course no such research undertaking can move at all without the cooperation of the industry itself. This has made us more sensitive to the applied aspects of our research than we might otherwise be.

The question of research techniques has been of continuing importance. We came into this field, of course, with some experience in the general problem of gathering psychological data. We have modified our accustomed approaches in a great many ways. At present we have underway a number of methodological studies comparing the various procedures which we are using, particularly the paper-and-pencil questionnaire and the free-answer interview. We find that various procedures are suitable for different situations. We have been engaged in rather extensive studies of analysis techniques—the ways in which these voluminous data taken from, in some cases, ten or twenty thousand workers can be organized most effectively, both from the point of view of extracting the greatest proportion of the content of the interview and also from the point of view of making the presentation most intelligible.

The specific problems involved in the experimental study which we have underway have been mentioned by Dr. Morse. I think they might well deserve considerable elaboration. Suffice it to say at the moment that we have found from this single but very intensive experience that the difficulties of introducing an experimental design, even where top management locally is friendly toward the experiment, are extensive and difficult to foresee in full. We discover that it is not simply a matter of creating situations A and B on the day the experiment starts, that A develops over time and B develops over time, and A and B gradually assume the features which the original design proposed.

I should not fail to mention that one of the phases of technique which has been of great importance throughout this program is the development of skills in integrating our work with these ongoing social structures with which we have been cooperating. The importance of creating a satisfactory working relationship between the research team and both management and labor can scarcely be overemphasized. This is true not only for the development of the original research plan but it is equally true for the post-research phase of reporting the research findings back to the interested groups in the industry.

The actual achievements of the program during these three years have been presented by Dr. Katz and the others, and I think I should not take time to enumerate them. We regard them as provisional and we certainly all regard the program as having completed only its introductory phases.

Our plans for the future are already indicated in the directions the program now takes. It was originally proposed by Dr. Likert that as the program developed we would place increasing emphasis on studies of higher management. This is already becoming a feature of the series of studies with rather detailed research now underway both in the public utility project and in the study in the home office of a Federal research agency.

We also expect to go forward with additional experimental designs. Our experience in the insurance study which Dr. Morse has described has equipped us, we feel, to develop studies of this kind with greater effectiveness and with a greater appreciation of the practical problems which are inevitably involved.

Finally, we feel that we are now prepared to move into a specific program of research on the problem of utilization of research data by the ongoing agency. We have made a great many qualitative observations, especially in the public utility study, and Floyd Mann, who has been directing this project, has made his particular interest this general problem of data utilization. We hope now that in our subsequent efforts in this area of the field we will be able to set up research designs in which we can specifically measure the effects of Technique A as opposed to Technique B. We are all very much concerned with the techniques for introducing research findings into ongoing organizations. We are generally inclined to feel that social scientists typically have failed to give sufficient consideration to this ultimate phase of the total research problem. We hope not only to make this an area of considerably more attention than it has been typically given, but to make it an area of research investigation.

We are concerned that we have not, perhaps, given enough attention to two kinds of data which have doubtless occurred to you. We are interested on the one side in knowing more about the general character of the organization in which our work is being done. We have obviously been aware that one company might be thought paternalistic and another impersonal, let us say, but we have not up to this moment given great attention to these atmospheric measurements in the companies where we have studies. We are presently thinking along these lines. We also want to gather more data than we presently have regarding so-called "personality characteristics" of the individual workers. We do not feel that our attention to this set of information has been sufficient. We gather a basketful of data on the individual's age, education, number of children and the like, and the size of our populations has permitted us, in some cases, to analyze these variables independently. There are, however, obviously other more personal attributes of our respondents that we are neglecting and we would feel better if our interviews included this type of information. It cannot be doubted that the personality of the individual worker mediates between the external work situation and his own reactions to it. Up to this point in our work we have had to disregard these intervening variables.

BIBLIOGRAPHY

1. Katz, D. The attitude survey approach to labor-management relations. *Psychology of Labor-Management Relations,* A. Kornhauser, Ed. Publication No. 3 of Industrial Relations Research Assn., 1949, 63–70.
2. ———. Employee groups: what motivates them and how they perform. Advanc. Mgmt., 1949, *14* (1), 1–6.
3. ———. Good and bad practices in attitude surveys in industrial relations. *Proceedings of Second Annual Meeting of Industrial Relations Assn.,* 1949, 212–221.
4. ———. Morale and motivation in industry. *Current Trends in Industrial Psychology.* Pittsburgh: Univ. of Pitt. Press, 1949, 145–171.

5. Likert, R. and Katz, D. Supervisory practices and organizational structure as they affect employee productivity and morale. *Executive Personality and Job Success.* Personnel Series 120, American Management Association, New York, 1948.
6. Maccoby, N. A quantitative comparison of certain psychological conditions related to group productivity in two widely different industrial situations. Unpublished Doctor's Thesis, Univ. Mich., 1950.
7. Mann, F. C. Putting human relations research findings to work. *Michigan Business Rev.*, 1950, 2 (2), 16–20.
8. Willerman, B. Group identification in industry. Unpublished Doctor's Thesis, M.I.T., 1949.
9. Productivity, supervision and employee morale. Survey Research Center, Univ. Mich., 1948.

RESEARCH IN CONTEMPORARY CULTURES

MARGARET MEAD

Columbia University

COLUMBIA UNIVERSITY RESEARCH IN Contemporary Cultures was inaugurated in 1947, under the direction of the late Professor Ruth Benedict, to study a series of contemporary cultures which either were represented by large immigrant populations in the United States or were strategically important in the international scene. It was planned: (1) to use the methods which had been developed by anthropologists in World War II for studying cultures inaccessible to immediate observation; (2) to test these methods by combining them with work on living communities, both in the United States and in the home countries; and (3) to combine the methods with those of members of other disciplines—historians in the case of cultures of societies of the past, psychologists and psychiatrists where living representatives were available in sufficiently large numbers for testing and interviewing. The goals were threefold: (1) to explore and refine the methods of studying inaccessible cultures; (2) to develop a body of systematic descriptive materials on a selected series of cultures; and (3) to train a group of graduate students and more senior members of the various cooperating disciplines in this approach.

RESEARCH DESIGN

At the height of the research activity the project had a membership of about seventy-five workers and altogether some 120 people took part in the program. The project was built as a series of research seminars, each working on a separate culture, a number of seminars which cross-cut the cultural seminars and drew on part of their membership, and a project seminar which all the members of the project attended. Each seminar had a convener who was a senior anthropologist. The personnel of each seminar was diversified in terms of discipline and status so that later comparison would provide materials on the advantages and disadvantages of various types of group composition. The French seminar, for instance, consisted of a group with a rather even level of methodological sophistication while some of the other seminars presented a much wider spread of experience, training, and sophistication. The seminar groups were also varied in terms of the number of nationalities represented and the type of interdisciplinary composition. While many of these variations were dictated by the exigencies of available personnel, the results of the variations could be systematically recorded and compared. The work of each of the cultural seminars was presented in related ways in the general seminar so that, by reports on the different cultures, the optimum degree of cross-cultural comparison could be obtained. Anthropology is a science which depends for its results upon an opportunity to compare the ways in which human capacities are used or neglected in different cultures. (For example, some of the relationships which may be found in the personality structure of persons reared in societies with small biological families can be recognized when individuals from such societies are compared with individuals from societies in which the cultural expectation is for a large extended family.)

Although the approach was interdisciplinary, anthropology provided the organizing conceptual scheme: (1) It is useful to study the totality of the learned behavior of individuals who share, by birth or later entry, a common tradition. (2) This common shared tradition may be expected to be systematic, its systematic nature being based upon the common properties of human beings, *e.g.*, the central nervous system, the patterns of human reproduction and growth, the structure of the receptors, *etc.* (The most striking example of this systematic nature of culture can be found in language. All languages which have been studied have been found to have a grammatical pattern and a systematic arrangement of sounds which, in turn, may be related to the sound-producing and sound-discriminating capacities of human beings.) (3) The systematic nature of any culture can be most efficiently and rapidly ordered by one or more minds which deal with all the material collected, as any segmenting of the material by a division of labor in which observations are not progressively shared and cross-compared brings about actual interference in the integrative process. (This is the particular anthropological form of the recognition that, in the human sciences, the observer must be included as *part* of any set of observations, not so that his individuality may be discounted, but so that it may be accurately included in any later interpretation.) This meant, for instance, that all materials were processed in a form to be available to all the members of a research seminar. The minutes of the seminars, for the most part verbatim reports, reveal the extent to which each observation reported was taken account of in terms of the member of the research team who had made it. (4) Single individuals, outside their own society, may be used as informants to obtain the systematic aspects of the culture which they represent. This is the methodological counterpart of the need to use the *total* personality of the anthropological observer as a systematizing instrument through which the culture may be perceived and ordered.

The research was further directed to those aspects of a culture which could be referred to common membership in a nation (for example, aspects of culture which might be said to be *French,* in contradistinction to those behaviors which could be characterized as Breton or Provençal). This choice was deliberate and was related to the specifically applied character of the research, which, while it aimed to increase our knowledge of human cultures—particularly of complex contemporary cultures and the appropriateness of methods of studying them—was also designed to throw light on problems of relations between nations and problems of special ethnic groups in the United States. (For example, how would the circumstance that the chairman of a committee for cross-national negotiation was a Frenchman or a Chinese be expected to affect the conduct of committee proceedings? Or, for purposes of a domestic program, in what ways would one have to take account of the ethnic composition of part of a city or of the personnel of an entire occupational group?) Circumstances peculiar to each of the cultures selected dictated the particular emphasis in the research. (For example, in the case of Russia, we laid our principal emphasis upon the study of Great Russians rather than upon Ukrainians, Byelo Russians, *etc.,* because Soviet *national* activities are predominantly Great Russian. In the study of Chinese culture, on the other hand, special attention was given to "Cantonese" culture since the Chinese community in New York City is largely from Kwantung Province.)

Working with members of contemporary societies, many of which are at present torn by political schisms, it was particularly necessary to preserve the complete anonymity of informants and to develop ways of characterizing a culture which were acceptable to its own members. This latter requirement was met systematically by the inclusion in each seminar of members of varying degrees of sophistication from the culture being studied and also by the inclusion of representatives of at least one other culture besides that of the United States, to reduce the danger of the results being expressed as a hyphenated American sub-culture, such as Chinese-American or Syrian-American. This meant that each seminar included members of at least three cultures.

SPECIFIC RESULTS OF RESEARCH

The results may be summarized under three main headings: (1) the characterization of the seven cultures studied: pre-Soviet Great Russians, Czech, Polish, Eastern European Jewish, French, Syrian, and Chinese; (2) follow-up and extensions of these studies in work on culture contact situations involving the same groups in the United States; and (3) laying the groundwork for further research, under other auspices, in Czechoslovakia and Poland, and for subsequent work on the interpretation of contemporary Soviet culture on the basis of systematic statements about pre-Soviet culture.

In the study of pre-Soviet Great Russian culture, the informants were all adults; there was no possibility of studying children or of checking observations against the contemporary situation, for pre-Soviet Great Russian society has ceased to exist. The research was, therefore, limited to interviews with adults, analyses of various types of documents, and the schematization of the results in a form which would lend itself best to an analysis of contemporary Soviet culture. Under these circumstances emphasis was laid upon one of the methods now available for delineating character structure—the culture as represented in the organization of the individual personality—rather than upon any attempt to reconstruct the society, which could never be available for observation. This method consists in a cross-integration of adult productions—verbal reminiscences, autobiographies, literature, patterns of gesture while lecturing, arrangements of furniture in rooms, memories of houses formerly lived in, etc.—with accounts of the ways in which children were cared for, reared, and educated at the period when these adults were growing up. From such an analysis, which owes much to comparative observations of primitive cultures and also to the findings of dynamic psychology and studies of child development, it is possible to describe the pattern of the culturally regular character and to express this in terms of the impact of the society upon the growing child at periods of development whose properties are known.

Such an analysis of Great Russian character structure, particularly of the background of the intelligentsia and of observations by intelligentsia on the peasantry, made it possible to construct a schematic picture of pre-Soviet Great Russian character based upon the proportional importance of learning during the first two years of life, the elaboration and perpetuation of this emphasis in later developmental periods, and the marked persistence of this prefigurative model in the character structure of adults, who in turn would re-express these same emphases in their own handling of children.

So the traditional Great Russian character can be related to the kinds of thinking and feeling which have been identified in the psychology of young childhood. Among these early childhood characteristics, we may distinguish a tendency to accept the coexistence of very rapid alternations of feelings of love and hate towards the same person, a tendency to view temporal sequences as reversible, and vividness of bodily imagery; there is a tendency to confuse thoughts, acts, and deeds, and to treat them all as equally real. These characteristics may be attributed not only to the developmental period traditionally and unconsciously stressed in Russian character formation, but also to specific Great Russian institutions pertinent to child rearing: a peculiarly confining and long period of swaddling; the gratification of the child's needs for food and warmth and affection during periods of unswaddling; the continuation of swaddling through teething with no possibility of the child using its hands; the care of the child by a nurse, grandmother, or elder sibling in contexts in which the child was subjected to continuous auditory stimulation from the conversation of many persons; and a belief—expressed in these practices—that the child was very strong and needed to be confined lest it destroy itself. The character structure which developed under these circumstances was distinguished by great powers of endurance and a rather low capacity for self-initiated activity, with a tendency towards extreme mood swings from optimism to despair, a pervasive sense of sinfulness and very little confidence in own capacity for ethical self-regulation, a combined hatred for, belief in the necessity for, and capacity to tolerate restrictive external authority, a capacity to invest a distant leader figure with an aura of complete goodness combined with a persistent dislike of all bureaucratic intermediaries between the leader and the self [1].

Against this pre-Soviet character, it is possible to place the character of the Bolshevik—the product of the emerging intelligentsia class with its western orientation, smaller family, and emphasis upon internal ethical controls—and to trace the way in which the Bolsheviks, who themselves had only a special version of the traditional character structure, attempted to alter themselves and simultaneously to mould the entire population of the Soviet Union into a new personality type which would be purposeful and would have an internalized conscience structure, a regard for time and for materials, and a capacity for continuous optimistic pursuit of long term goals. The schematic understanding of pre-Soviet character structure made it possible to give a systematic account of such contemporary aspects of Bolshevik behavior as the desire for complete control over every detail of life, paralleled by an emerging Soviet character in which belief in the omniscience of the political police is an essential element; the lack of modulation in Bolshevik response to details of quite differing size and importance (when viewed from a Western point of view); and the extreme emphasis upon focus and upon the definition of the individual's will by "swimming against the current."

The studies of Polish and Czech culture were centered upon the contrasts in the way in which Poles and Czechs, from the same area of Europe and sharing in past and contemporary political relationships with East and West, handled similar problems. These studies worked out the background in early learning of the *Czech* tendency to resist the pressure of authority and superordination by an unyielding withdrawal, and of the *Polish* capacity to transcend threats and suffering by acts of individual bravery. While both the Czech and Polish cultures emphasize modes of behavior prefigured in the period between two and four years, the Czech emphasis is upon meeting a never-defined standard, while the Polish emphasis is upon the attainment of complete autonomy vis-à-vis a challenging world. This Polish emphasis on autonomy reveals itself in later life, for instance, in the tendency so to divide work that each individual is responsible for an operation which is regarded as a whole. Other implications of the differences in Polish and Czech behavior in cross-national situations may be found, on the one hand, in the Polish intolerance of any open insult or spoken derogation and in their dependence on subjectively defined challenges to action, and, on the other hand, in the Czech craving for recognition from the outside together with an inability to find the type of approving external authority from whom such approval could be obtained.

The Czech and Polish researches were preliminary and exploratory. The original conveners of both groups have been able, under other auspices, to do field work in these countries [2] subsequent to the Communist seizure of power. It is therefore possible to coordinate the original hypotheses with observations of the behavior of the Polish and Czech peoples in their home countries under changing political conditions.

A third part of the research has been a reconstruction of the culture of the small Eastern European Jewish community called the *shtetl,* which was characteristic for those Jews who lived within the pale of settlement in the Old Russian empire and in adjacent national territories. This exploration of Eastern European Jewish culture was begun as a device for interpreting material provided on different Eastern European national cultures by Jewish informants, since it had been found that there was no systematic basis for analyzing responses which contained characteristic Jewish components, as compared with responses which might be, for instance, Russian, Polish or Hungarian. In the course of delineating these special Jewish cultural elements, with the help of historical documentation and because of the presence in the project of a *shtetl*-reared but western-trained anthropologist, it became possible to treat this Eastern European Jewish tradition as a culture in itself, even though the people who shared the culture were members of different national societies [3]. This development is an example of the value of following the dictates of the material rather than in imposing any fixed, preconceived pattern upon it. In this study, special emphasis has been laid upon patterns of interdependence and responsibility between rich and poor, healthy and sick, learned and unlearned, upon the educational devices by which the rational tradition and love of learning were inculcated, and upon the complexities connected with the place of the Jewish community in societies where they had bargaining powers but no powers of control. This analysis now makes it possible to use information provided by highly articulate Jewish informants on Eastern Europe with a high degree of precision; it also provides a coherent background for the study of cultural change among the very large number of Americans of Eastern European Jewish origin.

A study of French culture was included in the project for two reasons: (1) It seemed most desirable that the methods which had been

used and would be used to work out the culture of inaccessible societies should also be applied—at least on a small scale—to the culture
of one society which is completely accessible and which also is an integral part of the Western European scientific tradition. It was hoped
that by this means the results of studies of French communities by
French research workers could be compared with the hypotheses developed by work with isolated individual informants outside the
country. (2) French culture has been of such importance in the development of cross-national diplomatic and political forms that it
seemed important to include it. At the same time it was recognized
that it was unjustifiable to expend a great amount of effort applying a method which, while it yielded valuable results when exercised
across barriers of time or uncrossable space, is much less rewarding
than firsthand studies in living communities. The French study is,
therefore, a series of hypotheses, carefully constructed so that they
can be tested on the spot; it is a statement about method rather than
a statement about French culture as such [4].

The Middle East is an area which, while of increasing political
importance in the world today, has been subjected to very little of this
modern type of anthropological study, so it was planned to include
one middle Eastern culture in the project. Syria was chosen because a
large number of middle Eastern nationals in the United States are
from Syria. The results are of interest in illuminating (1) the nature
of a culture which has developed for many hundred years in adaptation to alien rulers, with an expectation on the part of many of its
members that they might live and trade in any part of the world; (2)
the type of Americanization which occurs among a people already accustomed to adapt to alien demands; (3) the behavior of Christians as
a minority group in relation to Mohammedans—which is in many
ways reminiscent of the position of the trading Jewish minorities in
the Christian West; (4) the mechanisms by which a culture is maintained which embodies a balance between a very low but very secure
position of women and a much higher but far less secure position
of men. The Christian Syrian culture can be seen to have institutionalized many adaptive devices in ways comparable to those embodied
in Jewish culture in the West, and provides us with material on the
conditions under which culture contact can be prolonged and cultural identity can still be preserved.

The largest research group and the longest period of research was
devoted to an exploratory study of Chinese culture [5], using the en-
clave of "Cantonese" in New York's Chinatown, individual infor-

mants from other parts of China and a variety of literary, artistic, and other types of documentation. Attention was focused upon the way in which the Chinese develop, manifest, and teach their children a system of human relationships which emphasizes mutual dependence and the autonomy of the individual person within a system of rigidly prescribed role relationships, which rewards conformity with a sense of security and goodness, but which also develops unfulfilled needs for intimacy, for understanding and for being understood. Studies of interpersonal relationships and child rearing practices reveal significant aspects of the ways in which the young child is reared by a human being who listens and attends to its needs, who teaches it to look with its eyes but never to reach with its hands or to question, who attends it constantly and yet preserves its autonomy—even small infants are wrapped in the separate cocoon-like quilts in which the members of a Chinese family habitually share the same bed in safe, interconnected separateness. This continuous human attention interpenetrates with the child's own desire for food or sleep or elimination, so that willing becomes a matter of acting in complementary unison with an adult and this develops into a fragile harmony between internal needs and external demands. During later years the security and spontaneity so developed are subjected to exacting demands made on the child to learn in wholes, to learn before understanding, to learn without questioning or explanation. These early and later learning experiences are combined in a view of truth as multi-faceted, a tolerance for many different truths which the West would find contradictory, and a limited personal commitment to any given cause or goal. There is a demand that the individual be able to conform to prescribed roles and yet preserve sincerity of feeling on matters of conviction—a demand that one must actually harmonize one's feelings with the system of externally imposed demands. Within the wide but encompassing circle of the extended family in which a man's self-respect is enhanced to the extent to which the father himself bows to the ancestors, within the wide limits of clan membership where the relationship of each to each is known and obligations and privileges are defined, the approved character type both for men and for women is a mild, unaggressive, gentle, succoring one; deviant types—the soldierly male, the proud defiant woman—are recognized but disapproved and disallowed. Congruent with this disallowance, while there is great acceptance of the cycles of life concerned with food and succorance, including procreation, sexual passion is definitely regarded as dangerous and likely to disrupt the cycle of orderly sustenance, arranged marriage, and the correct discharge of family duties, which have a timeless wholistic quality, resisting change.

Against this analysis of traditional Chinese national character, which has been found to be highly consistent (most of the differences which are phrased as regional, being ways in which temperamental differences in *any* Chinese group are expressed), it is possible to place the picture of change under the impact of Western ideas and to make systematic predictions as to the probable impact of Soviet ideals and practices upon Chinese life.

FINDINGS IN THE FIELD OF PURE RESEARCH

First, the research has increased our knowledge of the limitations and possibilities of interviewing and studying isolated individuals outside their societies, in an attempt to construct a diagram of the culture and to understand the culturally regular dynamics of personalities reared within that culture. The possibilities of such a method may be exemplified again by consideration of what we know when we know the grammar and phonetic pattern of a language, with only the vocabulary of the particular set of texts from which that grammar was worked out. While such knowledge does not permit us to extrapolate from known to unknown words, we can say with enormous chances of correctness what the formal properties of the unknown words would be. This must still be contrasted with field work, during which a complete vocabulary and detailed examples of every sort of usage—formal and informal, secular and sacred, intimate and distant—have been collected and checked by observation. From field work it would be possible to compose a new folk tale, a new harangue to a patron, or a diatribe against a political opponent which would be approximately correct, since it would be based on experience and observation as well as upon formal knowledge of structure, and since one would use as vocabulary words which retained their historical particularity and idiomatic correctness as well as the properties of structure and the sounds which could be formally derived.

In current practice, the historian and the political scientist are often in the position of having the knowledge which can be obtained only by long experiential contact, but who have never made their knowledge explicit by stating it in terms of formal pattern, while the anthropologist, working rapidly and at a distance, is in the position of knowing only the pattern. For purposes of prediction, it is sometimes possible to combine these two approaches [6], so that the anthropologist makes a formal prediction and the historian or political scientist corrects it by detailed knowledge and experience of the whole society.

Second, during the course of the research it has been possible to work out a much more systematic approach to the problem of cultural character and the ways in which proportional stress or neglect of the potentialities of different developmental periods may be recognized both in the child rearing practices in a culture and in the personality structure of the adults who rear the next generation [7]. It is now possible to identify the nature of the clues provided by a study of child rearing and to place the whole problem in a firmer perspective; this is a step beyond that taken when psychoanalytical theory, with its focus on the life history of the single individual, was brought into anthropological work and resulted in attempts to treat child rearing as causal rather than as one self-perpetuating mechanism of an ongoing social system. Detailed study of the way a culture is learned provides a method of analysis of the personalities who embody it, and a way of integrating formal institutional analysis, identified historical sequences, and psychological theory.

Third, the systematic use of films, literature, children's drawings, and projective tests has highlighted problems of thought, which have been obscured by the contemporary emphasis of depth psychology on the mechanisms of defense. By exploring the relationship between those aspects of thought which are inner oriented and the way in which a culture mediates these processes in relation to the external environment, the necessary systematic groundwork has now been laid for delineating the *cultural* factors in scientific thought, engineering skills, artistic creativity, *etc.* [8].

NEXT STEPS

It is possible to outline four stages in this type of research on cultures at a distance. *Stage one*: The construction of the preliminary hypotheses, which are equivalent to an outline of the grammar and phonetic pattern of a language. *Stage two*: The testing and amplification of these hypotheses with systematic bodies of material of a variety of types, such as a complete coverage of a periodical or a set of films, analysis of changes of laws, reports of parliamentary debates, *etc. Stage three*: Placing this formal knowledge of the culture within the living society by field studies on the spot, combined—in the case of complex modern cultures—with various types of sampling. *Stage four*: Experimental verification of the formal cultural pattern which has been hypothesized, by the construction of experimental situations within which the performances of representatives of one culture can be compared with those of representatives of another culture. Research in Contemporary Cultures has concerned itself mainly with *Stage one*, with only occasional pieces of work of the *Stage two* type. For the Soviet Union, *Stage two* has been developed under another project. On Czechoslovakia, *Stage three* has been worked out for certain aspects of the culture. In those instances where increased understanding is crucial and access to the countries in question—either for field studies or for surveys—is not feasible, it is possible that *Stage four* may be substituted if a few nationals of the particular country are available. Such a sequence of research would, however, be dictated by the exigencies of a practical situation; it would not be an optimum procedure scientifically.

The question has been raised whether it is legitimate to use the time of trained research workers constructing hypotheses in New York City about the cultures of inaccessible societies and whether—if practical considerations of national and international applicability were put aside—all such workers would not be better employed in studying the whole fabric of living societies *in situ*. This research on national character was begun, and owes its principal continuing impetus to the problems which confront us in dealing—either across the conference table or in combat—with peoples about whom we have too little information. Further, the interdisciplinary character of this type of research is possible only if situations can be created where members of disciplines other than anthropology have an opportunity to work with anthropologists on living material. This method is also providing a series of transformations, which will make it possible for anthropologists and historians to integrate their results, which should very considerably advance our systematic knowledge and capacity to predict within contemporary complex societies.

BIBLIOGRAPHY

1. Gorer, Geoffrey. "Some Aspects of the Psychology of the People of Great Russia." *The American Slavic and East European Review*, Vol. VIII, October 1949, 155–166.
   Gorer, Geoffrey, and Rickman, John. *The People of Great Russia. A Psychological Study.* London: Cresset Press, 1949. New York: The Chanticleer Press, 1950.
2. Benet, Sula. *Not by Bread Alone.* Denuis, Dobson, Ltd. and Roy Company. (In press.)
   Garvin, Paul L. "Standard Average European and Czech." *Studia Linguistica*, Vol. III, No. 2, 1950.

Rodnick, David. "Czechs, Slovaks and Communism." (MS prepared for publication.)

3. Joffe, Natalie F. "The Dynamics of Benefice among East European Jews." *Social Forces,* Vol. 27, No. 3, March 1949, 238–247.

Zborowski, Mark, "The Place of Book Learning in Traditional Jewish Culture." *Harvard Educational Review,* Vol. 19, No. 2, Spring 1949, 87–109.

———— "Children of the Covenant." *Social Forces.* (In press.)

Zborowski, Mark, and Landes, Ruth, and others. "Hypotheses Concerning the Eastern European Jewish Family." *Psychiatry.* (In press.)

Zborowski, Mark, and Herzog, Elizabeth, and others. "It Was In Our Town." (MS prepared for publication.)

4. "Some Hypotheses about French Culture." Edited by Rhoda Métraux. (MS prepared for publication.)

5. Abel, Theodora M., and Hsu, Francis L. K. "Some Aspects of Personality of Chinese as Revealed by the Rorschach Test." *Rorschach Research Exchange and Journal of Projective Techniques,* Vol. XIII, No. 3, 1949, 285–301.

Bunzel, Ruth. "Explorations in Chinese Culture." (MS prepared for publication.)

Muensterberger, Warner. "Some Prevalent Characteristics of Southern Chinese Orality and Passivity." *Psychoanalysis and the Social Sciences,* Vol. III. (In press.)

Weakland, John H. "The Organization of Action in Chinese Culture." *Psychiatry,* Vol. 13, No. 3, August 1950, 361–370.

6. Sturmthal, Adolf. "National Patterns of Union Behavior." *The Journal of Political Economy,* Vol. LVI, No. 6, December 1948, 515–526.

7. Benedict, Ruth. "Child Rearing in Certain European Countries." *The American Journal of Orthopsychiatry,* Vol. XIX, No. 2. April 1949, 342–350.

Wolfenstein, Martha. "Some Variants in Moral Training of Children." *Psychoanalytic Study of the Child,* Vol. V. New York, International Universities Press, 1950.

8. Abel, Theodora M. "The Rorschach Test in the Study of Culture." *Rorschach Research Exchange and Journal of Projective Techniques,* Vol. XII, No. 2, 1948, 79–93.

Mead, Margaret. "Some Relationships Between Social Anthropology and Psychiatry." *Dynamic Psychiatry,* edited by Franz Alexander. Chicago: University of Chicago Press. (In press.)

STUDIES IN NAVAL LEADERSHIP

Part I

CARROLL L. SHARTLE

Personnel Research Board
The Ohio State University

DR. STOGDILL AND I WILL JOINTLY describe the Studies in Naval Leadership. I shall give a statement on the background of the research, and Dr. Stogdill will cover the Navy studies in greater detail.

The Ohio State studies were designed as a ten-year program to develop research methods, and to obtain facts which might have value in better understanding leadership and which might aid later in the education, selection, training, and assignment of persons for leadership roles in our society.

Our studies have been largely limited to business, military, and educational organizations. We have deliberately chosen these types of organizations, for we feel it gives us sufficient range of leader phenomena, and yet limits our scope so that reasonable progress can be made. The Navy is thus a partner in a larger research program which is supported by other sources, including the Rockefeller Foundation and the Human Resources Research Laboratory of the Air Force.

Thus far the studies have been cross-sectional rather than longitudinal. It is hoped that in the cross-sectional studies variables can be identified and measuring instruments standardized for use in longitudinal and experimental approaches.

The approach to leadership which we shall outline had its beginnings in a large occupational study conducted by the Federal Government beginning in 1934. It was originally called the Occupational

Research Program and was supported by foundations, as well as by the Government.

The program of research was outlined to discover for the first time what the occupations were in the United States, and what were the aptitudes, abilities, education, experience, and other requirements necessary for success in these occupations. In the course of the studies *The Dictionary of Occupational Titles* was developed, descriptions of occupations were prepared, and measures of aptitude and abilities were tried out in industrial, business, and educational situations. This work is still in progress as a part of the United States Employment Service program.

In making studies of some twenty thousand occupations, it was noticed that a large proportion of occupations, about 70 per cent, were of a relatively simple nature. Little formal education was required to perform the tasks. Half of these occupations had a training period of one week or less. For the bulk of the jobs in our economy formal education fell low in importance as compared to other factors. One factor which seemed to be nearly universal was the ability to work under the supervision one finds as a part of the job and to adjust to the conditions of work, both in terms of physical surroundings and human beings in the work environment.

Occupational studies such as these have revealed many important facts about our occupational life. It is interesting to note, however, that as we approach higher-level occupations, and particularly those with administrative duties, relatively little research had been done. There are, perhaps, several reasons for this. Since most of the population is employed in the less complex pursuits, the simpler occupations deserve more study. Also, it appears that higher-level occupations, being more complex, require greater research ingenuity and longer research study in order to discover facts which may be useful. Further, there appears to be a kind of reluctancy to study higher-level jobs because of the status of the persons in the occupations as compared to the status of the investigators.

About four years ago the Personnel Research Board of the Ohio State University took up the matter of studying higher-level positions. After a series of planning conferences, it was decided to emphasize the leadership aspects of occupational behavior since it appeared that these aspects were of high importance and were ones which would be of particular interest to institutions of higher learning where, it is assumed, future leaders are receiving their education. Likewise, throughout the entire occupational hierarchy the matter of leadership and interpersonal relations seemed worthy of study, particularly if one were to begin his studies at the top levels of an organization where leadership should surely exist.

Before undertaking a series of investigations of such magnitude, certain decisions were made at the planning stage. Some of these are as follows:

1. The studies of leadership should yield a greater return if the resources of several sciences are brought into play rather than one.
2. The social sciences are the most applicable to the problem, for leadership is predominantly a social phenomenon.
3. Concept formation and research methodology will need to be developed. Therefore, the sciences selected should be those which have unique methodologies. They should be sciences which are not limited in their scope to research in any one organizational area. History, anthropology, sociology, economics and psychology meet this criterion.
4. In the course of the investigation, methodology and results should be reviewed critically by representatives from disciplines whose areas of investigation and professional practice are in the organizational fields being studied. Disciplines meeting this criterion are education, business administration, military science, political science, and engineering.
5. Not only should the various sciences learn from each other in terms of theory, methods, and results, but likewise the disciplines which have interests in the several organizational areas should learn from each other. Thus the military executive should profit from a knowledge of the leadership phenomena and administrative practices in business and educational organizations as well as from a knowledge of such phenomena and practices in his own setting.

I should like now to tell you something of the methods we have applied in studying so-called leaders and the groups or staffs of which they are a part. First, I should like to discuss the performance of the leader himself.

Who Is a Leader

Naturally, in selecting persons for study one must apply a definition or have specific criteria. We may define a leader in several ways, such as the following:

1. An individual who exercises positive influence acts upon others.
2. An individual who exercises more important positive influ-

ence acts than any other member of the group or organization
he is in.
3. An individual who exercises most influence in goal-setting or
   goal-achievement of the group or organization.
4. An individual elected by a group as leader.
5. An individual in a given office or position of apparently high
   influence potential.

Since we are studying organizations in business, industry, education, and government, we have chosen initially to select on the basis
of the last definition, namely, persons in high office. Later on we may
select persons on the basis of other definitions.

We began our studies in industry and took as our subjects persons
in high office, such as presidents, managers, vice-presidents, department heads and the like. Analyses were made of their activities by
interview, observation, and questionnaire. We were interested in
"what" they did and with whom they worked. It was merely description of activities without any attempt to appraise the quality of performance. We found that the various activities performed could be
classified into categories and we received self-estimates of the percentage of time spent on these activities.

1. *Inspection of the Organization.* Direct observation and personal inspection of installations, buildings, equipment facilities, operations, services, or personnel—for the purpose of
   determining conditions and keeping informed.
2. *Investigation and Research.* Acts involving the accumulation
   and preparation of information and data. (Usually prepared
   and presented in the form of written reports.)
3. *Planning.* Preparing for and making decisions which will affect the aims of the organization as to volume or quality of
   business or service (including thinking, reflection, and reading, as well as consultations and conferences with persons
   relative to short-term and long-range plans).
4. *Preparation of Procedures and Methods.* Acts involving the
   mapping of procedures and methods for putting new plans
   into effect, as well as devising new methods for the performance of operations under existing plans.
5. *Coordination.* Acts and decisions designed to integrate and
   coordinate the activities of units within the organization or
   of persons within units, so as to achieve maximal over-all
   efficiency, economy, and control of operations.
6. *Evaluation.* Acts involving the consideration and evaluation
   of reports, correspondence, data, plans, decisions, or performances in relation to the aims, policies, and standards of
   the organization.

7. *Interpretation of Plans and Procedures.* Acts involving the interpretation and clarification for assistants and other staff personnel of directives, regulations, practices, and procedures.

8. *Supervision of Technical Operations.* Acts involving the direct supervision of personnel in the performance of duties.

9. *Personnel Activities.* Acts involving the selection, training, evaluation, motivation, or disciplining of individuals, as well as acts designed to affect the morale, motivation, loyalty, or harmonious cooperation of personnel.

10. *Public Relations.* Acts designed to inform outside persons regarding the program and functions of the organization, to obtain information regarding public sentiment, or to create a favorable attitude toward the organization.

11. *Professional Consultation.* Giving professional advice and specialized assistance on problems of a specific or technical nature to persons within or outside the organization (other than technical supervision and guidance of own staff personnel).

12. *Negotiations.* Purchasing, selling, negotiating contracts or agreements, settling claims, *etc.*

13. *Scheduling, Routing and Dispatching.* Initiating action on determining the time, place, and sequence of operations.

14. *Technical and Professional Operations.* The performance of duties specific to a specialized profession (*e.g.,* practice of medicine, auditing records, operating mechanics or equipment.)

A pattern was prepared for each executive showing the proportion of time spent on the various activities. It would seem that in an organization there are certain patterns of activity which go together for organizational effectiveness and harmonious working relationship. When we find the interrelations between patterns, it appears that a top person in selecting a principal assistant tends to choose someone with a pattern dissimilar to his own. We have developed patterns for six hundred executives and administrators in industry and the navy. We will soon have them for fifty school administrators. We also plan to compare patterns for persons who change positions. It is our hypothesis that an administrator probably takes his pattern with him when he moves to a new administrative post.

A second kind of instrument we have developed for studying leader behavior is concerned with estimating the degree of responsibility, authority, and delegation practiced by the administrator. Scales have been prepared which are specific statements of behavior [1, 5]. The items have been weighted so that a score can be given for responsibility, for authority, and for delegation. The scales seem to be useful in showing differences among business executives and naval officers.

A third approach to leader behavior has been an attempt to determine "how" the leader performs his role as contrasted to what activities he performs. We have developed a number of dimensions of leader behavior. In one study we collected eighteen hundred specific statements of leader behavior. On the basis of our knowledge of leader performance and what we considered important to know about it, we set up nine dimensions of leader behavior. These were as follows:

> *Initiation*—the frequency with which a leader originates, facilitates, or resists new ideas and new practices.
>
> *Membership*—the frequency with which a leader mixes with the group, stresses informal interaction between himself and members, or interchanges personal services with members.
>
> *Representation*—the frequency with which a leader defends his group against attack, advances the interests of his group, and acts in behalf of his group.
>
> *Integration*—the frequency with which a leader subordinates individual behavior, encourages pleasant group atmosphere, reduces conflicts between members, or promotes individual adjustment to the group.
>
> *Organization*—the frequency with which a leader defines or structures his own work, the work of other members, or the relationships among members in the performance of their work.
>
> *Domination*—the frequency with which the leader restricts the behavior of individuals or the group in action, decision-making, or expression of opinion.
>
> *Communication*—the frequency with which a leader provides information to members, seeks information from them, facilitates exchange of information, or shows awareness of affairs pertaining to the group.
>
> *Recognition*—the frequency with which a leader engages in behavior which expresses approval or disapproval of the behavior of group members.
>
> *Production*—the frequency with which a leader sets levels of effort or achievement or prods members for greater effort or achievement.

The items of behavior were re-evaluated and the most suitable items were arranged according to the nine dimensions, comprising a list of 150 items. The items were set up to be checked according to frequency, as the following examples:

(Initiation)
HE TRIES OUT NEW IDEAS ON THE GROUP
Always   Often   Occasionally   Seldom   Never
(Membership)
HE CALLS MEMBERS BY THEIR FIRST NAMES
Always   Often   Occasionally   Seldom   Never
(Communication)
HE CALLS THE GROUP TOGETHER TO DISCUSS THE WORK
Always   Often   Occasionally   Seldom   Never

There were from ten to twenty items for each dimension.

The leader behavior description was then given to 357 persons. Two hundred five described a leader of a group in which they had been members, or had recently been members, while 152 described themselves as leaders.

I shall not dwell on the detailed statistical analysis which was made on this instrument, but mention only a few of the results. We found that many of the dimensions of leader behavior were not unique and were highly related to each other. A factor analysis showed that we had perhaps three dimensions, or factors, rather than nine. These were as follows:

1. A maintenance of membership factor—behavior that increases a leader's acceptability to the group. It is heavily loaded with low domination and high membership dimension.
2. Objective attainment—behavior high in the production and organization dimensions.
3. Group interaction facilitation—behavior or acts stressing the mechanics of effective interaction of group members. Loadings high were organization and communication.

Thus our nine armchair dimensions when put to the empirical test did not maintain their uniqueness as well as we had hoped. Leader behavior dimensions seem to stand out more distinctly when developed and applied on one type of administrative organization.

We asked the respondents, after describing the leader, to give an over-all rating of leadership quality. We found that eight of the nine dimension scores were related significantly to the over-all evaluation when the subordinate did the describing and evaluating. However, when leaders described and evaluated themselves, the relations were significant for only four dimensions.

The subordinates associated good leadership with low domination, but with high amounts of all the other dimensions except production, which showed no significant relationship to evaluation.

The leaders who described themselves associated higher evaluations with integration, organization, and communications down.

In educational groups we found less domination, less representation, less organization, and less communications down reported than in other types of groups, particularly military and industrial.

One very interesting application of the leader behavior description is to compare the dimension scores of self-descriptions with those of descriptions made by superiors and subordinates. The superiors and the subordinates agree more closely with each other than with the self-description of the leader they describe.

Another application is to have half of the subordinates describe a leader and the other half describe the ideal leader for that job. We believe the extent of discrepancy scores between the ideal person in the job and the actual person can give important clues for leadership training.

The Group or Staff

As I indicated earlier, the study of the leader himself is incomplete without a knowledge of the environment in which the leader performs. One kind of environment is the organization, or the group of which the leader is a part. A second kind of environment is the larger society or culture of which both the leader and his group are a part. Regarding the former type, we have been very much interested in how to describe a group as objectively as possible. We have been using several methods:

1. *Formal organization chart.* What written material, diagrams, reports and other data are available which describe how the organization works, or perhaps better, how it is supposed to work?
2. *Sociometric ratings.* With whom do the members of the organization work? This is sometimes called the informal organization or interpersonal chart.
3. *Group morale and effectiveness.*
4. *Group dimensions.* What are the basic dimensions of the group? How do groups differ in these dimensions?

I should like to tell you about the group dimensions, for I think they afford a very interesting approach to the study of an organization.

Hemphill and Westie [3] of our staff have recently published a method of describing groups which was based on an earlier study by Hemphill [2] at the University of Maryland. Hemphill and Westie have developed scales for fourteen dimensions whereby a group can be described by its members or by outside observers.

The group dimensions are as follows:

1. *Autonomy* is the degree to which a group functions independently of other groups and occupies an independent position in society. It is reflected by the degree to which a group determines its own activities, by its absence of allegiance, deference and/or dependence relative to other groups.
2. *Control* is the degree to which a group regulates the behavior of individuals while they are functioning as group members. It is reflected by the modifications which group membership imposes on complete freedom of individual behavior and by the amount or intensity of group-derived government.
3. *Flexibility* is the degree to which a group's activities are marked by informal procedures rather than by adherence to established procedures. It is reflected by the extent to which duties of members are free from specification through custom, tradition, written rules, regulations, codes of procedure, or even unwritten but clearly prescribed ways of behaving.
4. *Hedonic Tone* is the degree to which group membership is accompanied by a general feeling of pleasantness or agreeableness. It is reflected by the frequency of laughter, conviviality, pleasant anticipation of group meetings, and by the absence of griping and complaining.
5. *Homogeneity* is the degree to which members of a group are similar with respect to socially relevant characteristics. It is reflected by relative uniformity of members with respect to age, sex, race, socio-economic status, interests, attitudes, and habits.
6. *Intimacy* is the degree to which members of a group are mutually acquainted with one another and are familiar with the most personal details of one another's lives. It is reflected by the nature of topics discussed by members, by modes of greeting, forms of address, and by interactions which presuppose a knowledge of the probable reaction of others under widely differing circumstances, as well as by the extent and type of knowledge each member has about other members of the group.
7. *Participation* is the degree to which members of a group apply time and effort to group activities. It is reflected by the number and kinds of duties members perform, by voluntary assumption of nonassigned duties and by the amount of time spent in group activities.
8. *Permeability* is the degree to which a group permits ready access to membership. It is reflected by absence of entrance re-

quirements of any kind, and by the degree to which membership is solicited.

9. *Polarization* is the degree to which a group is oriented and
works toward a single goal which is clear and specific to all
members.

10. *Potency* is the degree to which a group has primary significance for its members. It is reflected by the kind of needs
which a group is satisfying or has the potentiality of satisfying, by the extent of readjustment which would be required
of members should the group fail, and by the degree to which
a group has meaning to the members with reference to their
central values.

11. *Size* is the number of members regarded as being in the group.

12. *Stability* is the degree to which a group persists over a period
of time with essentially the same characteristics. It is reflected
by the rate of membership turnover, by frequency of reorgani-
zations, and by constancy of group size.

13. *Stratification* is the degree to which a group orders its members into status hierarchies. It is reflected by differential distribution of power privileges, obligations, and duties and by
asymmetrical patterns of differential behavior among members.

14. *Viscidity* is the degree to which members of the group function as a unit. It is reflected by absence of dissension and personal conflict among members, by absence of activities serving
to advance only the interests of individual group members,
by the ability of the group to resist disrupting forces, and by
the belief on the part of the members that the group does
function as a unit.

The scales for describing the dimensions were developed from approximately eleven hundred items or statements. Items selected
were those judged by experts as relative to the particular dimension
and independent of all other dimensions.

The final set of items numbered 355. Each relevant item describing a group asks the respondent to indicate on a five-point scale how
true he considered the item for the group. For example, three of the
items for the dimension of intimacy were:

1. Members of the group do small favors for one another.
2. All members know each other very well.
3. Members address each other by their first names.

I shall not describe the technical steps which Hemphill and Westie
followed in determining the reliability of the scales and the relative
independence of the various dimensions. In general, the scales were
quite satisfactory in regard to both these standards. The scales are
easy to administer and it is possible for any or all members of a group

or of a staff to indicate how they perceive it. A profile for each staff or group can be made to show similarities and differences among organizations.

We have been using a group description scale in a number of college departments described by their members. I can assure you that there are significant differences among groups in higher education.

STATUS FACTORS

In regard to the broader cultural framework I should like to mention the status attitudes and status perception. Seeman [4] of our group, who has been exploring these sociological concepts, subscribes to the tenet that "leadership-followership patterns of a given institution are related to or are in part functions of the status systems and status ideologies which characterize the larger society in which the given institution functions." Status is defined as the relative position within a hierarchy, the hierarchy involving ordering of individuals on an inferiority-superiority scale. In measurement it may be in terms of (1) subjective status or how a given subject views his own position in a given hierarchy; (2) accorded status indicated by the position assigned to him by others; and (3) objective status in terms of a selected criterion assumed by the observer, such as income in dollars as an indicator of economic position.

In psychology I am sure we are aware that status differences affect behavior. If we define leadership in terms of influence, it is certainly important to observe the role of status in these behavior patterns.

We have been measuring status position largely as the respondent sees himself in terms of occupational prestige and social position in the community. The respondent describes his occupational status, for example, by comparing it to other occupations in the North-Hatt Scale [6].

For measuring status perceptions, items have been developed to which the subject responds in terms of a five-point scale. These items are not designed to measure attitudes, but rather the respondent's perception of the amount of status difference in society. Examples of these items are as follows:

1. Most people in the United States are able to classify others in their own community as to their social standing.
2. In our society the possibility of moving from one social or economic level to a higher level has decreased a great deal.
3. Most people in the United States pick their friends and associates from among those who have the same social standing as they have.

Concluding Statements

Another set of items attempts to get at the respondent's status attitudes, his preferences as to how much status difference there should be on a variety of hierarchies.

I should now like to present several statements concerning the studies just described. The statements have been substantiated in one or more of the studies, and have not been found untrue in any of the research. I should like also to point out certain implications of these findings.

Leadership behavior can be described reliably and in such terms that behavior differences can be shown in quantitative terms.

Group or staff behavior can be described in quantitative terms reliably with dimensions which are quite independent of each other.

The fact that leader behavior and group behavior can be reliably described is encouraging for future investigations. One can approach problems descriptively without involving oneself or one's subjects in commitments concerning whose behavior or what behavior is good or poor. The investigator simply wishes descriptions of what takes place. The matter of criteria can be taken up separately and at another time. Later, after patterns of dimensions have been related to various criteria, the descriptions can be used as tools in selection, training, transfer and other problems.

There are stereotypes of ideal leader behavior in organizational settings as perceived by group or staff members. The dimensions suggest that the ideal leader in most instances is one who places few demands upon the persons he leads, he does not interfere with their freedom, and he is a group member and "one of the boys." However, at the same time, he is perceived as ideally not a part of the group, as one who can do things for the group that the group cannot do, and as one who gets things done. There seems to be a basic conflict in our ideologies of leaders. We want persons in leadership roles, and yet we do not want to place limitations upon ourselves to submit to leadership.

In regard to group behavior, stereotypes no doubt exist but they are less pronounced than those of leader behavior. In other words, subordinates are much more agreed about what the ideal leader should be than they are about what the ideal group should be.

Subordinates' descriptions of their leader are directly related to their evaluations of him. However, attitudes of relative goodness of groups are related less to the descriptions of the dimensions of groups.

In other words, members of organizations seem to describe groups with less bias than they describe leaders. This may be related to the matter of stereotypes just mentioned.

Stereotypes present interesting problems in the study of human relations. Suppose we find that the stereotype of a "good" administrator or executive, as described by subordinates, turns out to be, according to other criteria, the less successful administrator. This can well be in some organizations, at least, and it may result in efforts to train staff members to see administrative behavior in a different light. On the other hand, one may attempt to train supervisory personnel to fit the stereotype. In training supervisory personnel and in inducting new staff members in an organization, both methods are used. But how much of each remains an unsolved question.

When a given administrator describes himself as a leader, this self-description is nearer to the subordinates' description of the *ideal* leader than it is to the description of him by his staff. In other words, the subordinates perceive him less in terms of their ideal than he perceives himself in terms of their ideal.

In a hierarchy an intermediate supervisor is described by his superior more like the descriptions of his subordinates than like his description of himself. Thus, the superior and the subordinates are more in agreement regarding the description of the intermediate supervisor than is the supervisor agreed with his superior or his subordinates about his own behavior.

This means that administrators, in terms of our leader behavior dimensions, perceive themselves quite inaccurately if one uses their superiors' and subordinates' descriptions as criteria. It will be interesting to discover if there are other behavioral differences when one compares administrators who give more accurate descriptions with those who are at considerable variance with the descriptions of their superiors and subordinates. It will be interesting to note if other measures of social perception are related, and if certain kinds of training will produce significant changes in self-perception. It will be very much worthwhile to discover what and how much change in administrative behavior will reflect significant changes in perceived behavior by superiors and subordinates.

We find that those leaders who delegate more authority tend to have assistants who in turn delegate more to their assistants. It appears that the granting of freedom for decision and action tends to result in a chain reaction down the line. If one assumes, and there is evidence for it, that the top person in the chain has the most influence in establishing and maintaining the degree of delegation down the line, it is obviously very important to know the behavior of the top person. It is also apparent that when one attempts through training or other means to change behavior within the chain, his results may be fruitless unless changes in behavior of the top person also occur.

Communications appear to be one of the most important factors in administrative behavior. Where more communications are reported present, there is less discrepancy between descriptions of the administrator and descriptions of ideal behavior as reported by subordinates. Communications are certainly procedures which can be studied, evaluated, and improved. Lack of communications may be one reason why administrators' self-descriptions are inaccurate when compared to descriptions by subordinates.

Status attitudes of an administrator are related to his leader behavior. In other words, how the administrator perceives the ordering of individuals in our society, and his attitudes toward that ordering, are related to certain phases of leader behavior as perceived by his subordinates.

This has important implications for the training of administrators and officers if one is to change leader behavior to make it more ideal in the eyes of subordinates. Technique training in so-called human relations skills appears inadequate without a concern for the broader social framework of our society. Thus the man who believes in wide differences in status in our society or vice-versa may show limited progress in changing certain dimensions of his supervisory behavior so long as these status attitudes remain fixed. In other words, the training of administrators and officers in leader behavior must be examined much more broadly than we in psychology have been accustomed to do.

In this paper I have attempted to present an approach to the study of leadership as an aspect of administrative behavior. The methods of investigation include the study of the individual, the study of the group or staff, and the study of the culture in which the individual and the staff are found. I have also attempted to present briefly some of the findings which may be relevant to certain problems of mutual interest. In the paper that follows, Dr. Stogdill will continue a discussion of these studies particularly as they are related to the Navy ʻ project.

BIBLIOGRAPHY

1. Browne, C. G. Study of executive leadership in business. I. The R, A, and D scales. *J. appl. Psychol.*, 1949, *33*, 521–526.
2. Hemphill, John K. Situational factors in leadership. Ohio State University, *Bureau of Educational Research Monographs, 32*, 1950, 136 pp.
3. ———— and Westie, Charles M. The measurement of group dimensions. *J. Psychol.*, 1950, *29*, 325–342.
4. Seeman, Melvin. Some status correlates of leadership. Paper given in Chicago, July 11, 1950, at the Cooperative Conference for Administrative Officers of Public and Private Schools, sponsored by the University of Chicago and Northwestern University.
5. Stogdill, Ralph M. and Shartle, Carroll L. Methods for determining patterns of leadership in an organization structure. *J. appl. Psychol.*, 1948, *32*, 286–291.
6. Wilson, Logan and Kalb, William L. *Sociological Analysis.* New York: Harcourt, Brace and Co., 1949, Chapt. 13.

STUDIES IN NAVAL LEADERSHIP

Part II

RALPH M. STOGDILL

Department of Psychology
The Ohio State University

DR. SHARTLE HAS DESCRIBED SEVERAL of the studies in progress at Ohio State, and has outlined the areas in which integration of the projects has been attempted. The present discussion will be concerned with one of these projects: The Studies in Naval Leadership.

The studies are aimed at discovering general principles concerning administrative leadership, as well as practical applications. The practical objectives have been stated as follows: (1) to determine the value of various methods of appraising leadership performance, (2) to develop facts and methods for use in the selection, assignment, and transfer of persons in positions of leadership, and (3) to derive basic principles and methods which may be applied by Naval officers in evaluating the leadership requirements of various group situations. Although these objectives are stated in practical terms, the task is not conceived as one of problem solving, but as one in basic research.

The methods of the study include a modified job analysis of leadership positions, and an analysis of organization structures in relation to the purposes and functions of the organizations. Data are obtained by direct observation, by interviews, by a study of published charts and manuals, by the use of scales and inventories, and by modified sociometric techniques. This approach to the problem is based on the assumptions that a study of leadership may be properly concerned with persons who occupy positions which presumably involve leadership performance, and that the first task in such a study is to discover what leaders do and how their work is performed. For sampling purposes, a leader is defined in these studies as a person who occupies an administrative position, either line or staff. However, it is not assumed that all administrators in an organization will exert equal influence as leaders.

Several methodological objectives were formulated at the beginning of the project in order to give guidance to the conduct of the research. These decisions were (1) to develop methods of a generalized nature (that is, applicable to civilian as well as military organizations) in order that comparable data might be obtained from a wide variety of organizations, (2) to reduce time limits of the research instruments to a minimum in order that the studies might be conducted in operating organizations with the least possible interference with activities, (3) to concentrate on the intensive analysis of data from each organization studied with the aim of discovering relationships, rather than to analyze superficially the data from a large sample of individuals or groups, and (4) to strive for simplicity in theoretical formulations. Each of these decisions has exerted marked influence in determining the nature of the research.

Theoretical Considerations

An application of the principle of theoretical simplicity may be illustrated in an analysis of the concept of leadership. If the concept is reduced to its simplest and most fundamental terms, it is found first that leadership appears only in a social group. That is, leadership appears only where people are interacting and perceiving themselves as members of a social aggregate. Second, the members will be working together on some sort of task. Working together again implies interactions. The task may be vaguely or clearly defined. Third, the members will have assumed some degree of differentiation of responsibility for the accomplishment of the common task. Leadership implies role differentiations. These appear to be the minimal conditions which permit the emergence or existence of leadership. This analysis leaves out of consideration the multiplicity of factors which determine the qualitative aspects of leadership.

We begin with a social group. But we are interested in a particular kind of group, that is, one in which the members are working together on a task and in which they are differentiated as to responsibility for the execution of the task. In other words, we are working with organized groups, with organizations. What I wish to point out here is that the minimal conditions that permit the existence of leadership are exactly the same variables that define an organization. We feel that it is very important to the progress of our research to incorporate, even at this very simple level, the concept of leadership and the concept of organization in the same theoretical framework. It provides a basis for deriving increasingly more detailed concepts and formulations, and permits us to study leadership and organization in terms of the same variables and with the same instruments.

For example, the condition of working together on a task suggests that leadership and organization may be studied as aspects of work performance, with job analysis as a possible methodological approach. The differentiation of responsibility carries the same and an additional implication. It implies, first, differentiation as to kinds of task performance, as evidenced in functional specialization. And second, it implies differentiation as to levels of performance, as evidenced in structural hierarchies of authority, accountability, and the like. If we add to this the concept of working together, working interactions, we find first, some sort of formal model of specified and expected working relationships, as exemplified by an organization chart or manual. (But we note that many organizations do not have well defined models.) Second, we find working relationships and informal interactions which may or may not correspond with the organization model. That is, members may not be working with the people with whom they were originally expected to work.

This breakdown suggests that leadership may be regarded as a function of the working relationships among group members who are coordinating their efforts for the accomplishment of a common task. It also suggests that leadership may be studied as an integral aspect of work performance and organizational functioning. The methods that have been developed for the Navy project are designed to study leadership from this point of view.

METHODS

The following methods have been employed in the Navy project:
1. *Interview with commissioned officers.* This includes questions pertaining to the history and aims of the organization and its various subdivisions, the responsibilities of the executive, and his methods of communications and working with staff.
2. *A study of organization charts and manuals.* These sources provide data as to the formal structure of the organization, its goals, functions and responsibilities.

3. *Sociometric Methods.* The executive's list of the persons with whom he spends the most time in getting work done permits the charting of informal organization. The test-retest correlation with a two year interval for one sample is .9.

4. *Time expenditure logs and check lists.* These check lists require the executive to estimate or log the time he spends in various kinds of work performance. The test-retest correlations with a two-year interval range from .0 to .9 for self-estimates of various kinds of work performance.

5. *RAD Scales.* These rating scales require the executive to estimate the level of his own authority, responsibility, and the authority he delegates to others. Split half reliabilities of these scales range from .6 to .8.

6. *Leader Behavior Descriptions.* Scales which can be used for self-descriptions or for descriptions by others. The behaviors to be described are Communications, Production, Representation, Domination, Recognition, Initiation, Systematization, Membership, and Integration. Split half reliabilities range from .6 to .9.

7. *Rating Scales.* Morale ballots, estimates of group opinion forms, decision-making scales, and other devices.

8. *Production records.* Performance records, reenlistment records, disciplinary records, and other records indicative of performance and morale.

These methods have been employed in the study of a rather wide variety of Naval organizations. Approximately twenty ships and twenty shore establishments have been studied.

LEVELS OF ANALYSIS

The first organizations studied served the purpose primarily of testing and revising methods. Nevertheless, they yielded information which has been subjected to several levels of analysis. First, it is possible to construct a profile of the responses of a single individual. Second, it is possible to obtain a profile of the average of the responses of several individuals in the same professional specialty, thus yielding some idea as to what variables are specific to various technical and professional positions. In the same way it is possible to obtain a profile of the average responses of individuals in different echelons in the organization, thus yielding an index of variables that are characteristic of performance at different administrative levels. Third, it is possible to compare the average scores of all members of the organization with average scores of all members of another organization on the same variable. This level of analysis permits us to determine what aspects of performance are specific to a particular organization. Fourth, it is possible to compare the responses of an individual with those of his superiors and subordinates. This permits us to study relationships at a very simple level. Fifth, through the use of sociometric charts it is possible to study the working relationships among all members of an organization. Sixth, through the correlation of each variable with every other variable it is possible to gain some conception of an organization as a constellation of interacting variables, and to isolate some of the factors which appear to describe the organization as a going concern.

I should like to present briefly some of the results that have been obtained at each of these levels of analysis. First, the construction of a profile of a single individual is useful primarily as source material for other levels of analysis. The second level involves the construction of an average profile for the members of a given professional specialty, or level of organization. For example, the work profile of personnel officers shows time spent in Personnel Activities, Planning, Coordination, and Interpretation; while public information officers are shown to spend time in Public Relations, Planning, and Evaluation. If we inspect the profiles of the members of an organization when classified as to echelon, we find that top level administrators spend major proportions of their time in Planning and Public Relations. Second echelon administrators spend large proportions of their time in Evaluation and Planning. Third echelon administrators spend major portions of their time in Planning and Coordination, while fourth echelon administrators spend more of their time in Planning, Evaluation, Supervision, and Interpretation than in other responsibilities. It can be observed that work becomes more diversified at the fourth echelon in the organization hierarchy. Analysis reveals increasing diversification of function at successively lower echelons, but not to a statistically significant degree.

The third level of analysis, which permits a determination of the factors that are common to all the organizations studied and those that are unique for specific organizations, yields a large body of information. These results may be illustrated by describing the findings from an analysis of data from four Naval and four business organizations. This analysis, done by Mr. E. A. Fleishman, indicates that there are no significant differences among the eight organizations in average amount of time spent by administrators and executives in Inspection, Interpretation, Research, Personnel Activities, and acting as Professional Consultant. Significant differences are observed among Naval organizations, among business organizations, and between Naval and business organizations in Coordination and Reading and Answering Mail. Naval and business organizations differ significantly in the average amounts of time spent with Assistants and with Outside Persons, as well as in Thinking and Examining Reports. Naval officers differ significantly from business executives in self-estimates of level of Responsibility and Delegation of Authority to subordinates, but no significant differences are found between Naval officers and business executives in self-estimates as to level of Authority.

The fourth level of analysis permits us to determine certain relationships between the performance of superiors and subordinates. It is observed, for example, that persons who describe themselves as delegating more authority to their subordinates have subordinates who in turn describe themselves as possessing a higher degree of responsibility and authority and who delegate more to their assistants than do their associates whose superiors do not delegate so freely. The superiors who tend to delegate more also tend to receive a larger number of nominations as work partners than do those who delegate less freely.

The fifth level of analysis permits us to chart the working relationships among all members of the organization. When the sociometric chart is superimposed upon the formal organization chart, discrepancies between formal organization and informal organization become readily apparent. It has been found in all Naval as well as business organizations studied, that some discrepancies appear. Reference to interview data, however, reveals that most of these discrepancies are related to the demands of short-term objectives and work requirements. There are, of course, some instances in which discrepancies appear to be related to personal factors. Those persons who are revealed as having the greatest number of working relationships within the organization are usually those who are at the focal point of activities necessary for the attainment of the immediate primary objectives of the organization. Those individuals who bypass one or two superiors in order to work with an individual who is in a still higher echelon, are found to be technical specialists such as public information officers, public works officers, and legal officers who possess technical information that cannot be readily transmitted through their immediate superiors.

The sixth level of analysis permits us to study an organization as a complex of selected variables in interaction. The basic method is that of constructing a table of intercorrelations among all the vari-

ables. Cluster analysis and factor analysis are probably the most efficient methods for isolating the combinations of variables that describe
the operations of an organization as revealed through a table of intercorrelations. Using factor analysis, it is possible to rotate the factors
in such a manner as to determine which are common to all the organizations for which data on the same variables are available. Such a
factor analysis was performed by Dr. Robert H. Wherry on tables of
intercorrelations obtained from a study of three Naval organizations.
The following factors were found in common in the three organizations: (1) high level administration, (2) high level policy making,
(3) methods planning, and (4) personnel functions. Two other factors, each specific to a single organization, were found. These were
(1) technical consulting and (2) investigation-report writing. These
are not characteristics of persons, but of organizational functioning
as measured by the performances of persons.

THE RELATION OF ESTIMATED TIME TO LOGGED TIME

A large portion of the data we collect consists of self-descriptions,
self-estimates, self-perceptions. One of the troublesome questions
we always have in mind is whether administrators can with any high
degree of accuracy estimate the way they spend their time. If we are
to place reliance upon our data it is necessary to have an answer to
this question. In order to obtain data on this point, a restudy was
made in 1949 of a Naval Air Station that had been previously studied
in 1947. Mr. Charles F. Elton assisted in the study. Forty officers were
asked to keep daily work logs. The logs could be simply executed by
checking the beginning and end of a task on a chart subdivided into
one-minute intervals, and by entering on the chart a code letter to
indicate the kind of work performed. Because of emergency conditions caused by heavy snowstorms and interruption of operating
schedules, it was possible to keep the log for only a period of three
days. At the end of this period, the logs were collected and forms
were distributed requiring the officer to estimate the amount of time
spent in various kinds of work performance during the period over
which the log was kept. Analysis of the results indicates that there is
a fairly high correspondence between logged time and estimated time
in such performances as Writing Reports, Reading Mail, Talking
with Other Persons, Operating Machines and Attending Meetings.
The correlations between logged time and estimated time on these
variables range from .4 to .8. However, the correlation between
logged time and estimated time for Thinking is .3 and for Planning

.o. Some of the correlations are lowered by the fact that very small amounts of time were logged or estimated for the performances in question. These tentative results suggest that self-estimates of objectively observable kinds of work performance have some correspondence with logged time in the same performances.

A CRITERION STUDY

An experiment was designed, in collaboration with Dr. Donald T. Campbell, for testing the previously described variables against as many criteria of leadership as we could devise. A squadron of ten submarines was selected for study. Since submarines are very similar as to organization structure, number of personnel aboard, and type of operations performed, these ships seemed appropriate for testing differences that might be found among them due to the influence of leadership. Commissioned officers were interviewed individually and were asked to fill out a large set of forms. Enlisted men were tested in groups in which they were asked to give the same kinds of information requested from the officers. Among the variables which we thought might serve as criteria of leadership are the following: morale ballots, ratings of ships, departments, and department heads by squadron command officers; departmental effectiveness ratings by commanding officer and executive officer, leader behavior descriptions by subordinates, leadership ratings by superiors; nominations for command of the ship in peacetime, command in wartime; nominations for best all-round leader; nomination for worst leader. These nominations permitted enlisted men to mention both officers and enlisted men. On a test of group opinion, each officer and enlisted man was asked to estimate what per cent of enlisted men on the ship would answer yes to each of thirty questions relating to morale and conditions aboard the ship. In addition, disciplinary records, reenlistment records, and various ship and departmental performance records were obtained.

Several months have been required to process the data obtained from the submarine study. We have just completed several tables which contain fifteen thousand correlation coefficients. We have not had time to examine these in any detail. However, I should like to mention a few features that appear upon superficial examination of a table of intercorrelations among variables for the ship "in port." The highest correlations on the chart are between Military Rank and Level in the organization hierarchy and between nomination for leader in Wartime and nomination for leader in Peacetime. These two correlation coefficients are above .9. Both Military Rank and Level are correlated with nominations for Wartime and Peacetime leader to the extent of .6.

A set of rather highly intercorrelated items consists of leader behavior descriptions of officers as seen by their enlisted subordinates. The dimensions: Communication, Recognition, Organization, Initiation, Membership, Integration and Representation are intercorrelated to the extent of .5 to .6. These leader behavior dimensions are correlated with nominations for Wartime leader, Peacetime leader and All-Round leader to the extent of .5 to .6. Leader behavior self-descriptions are less highly intercorrelated than are descriptions by others. The average intercorrelation among dimensions for self-descriptions is approximately .2. Self-descriptions and descriptions by others are not highly correlated. The average correlation between self-descriptions and descriptions by others is approximately .2.

Nominations for Wartime and Peacetime leader are correlated to the extent of .6 with Military Rank and Level in the organization. They are also correlated to the extent of about .4 with sociometric score. In general, it may be said that nominations for Wartime and Peacetime leader are correlated with high Military Rank and Level in the organization, with nominations for working partner, with Delegation of Authority to subordinates and with being perceived by others as engaging frequently in such behaviors as knowing what is going on in the organizaton, giving punishment and praise, organizing work, starting new ideas and practices, associating on rather intimate terms with other members of the organization, keeping subordinates informed, integrating subordinates into a working team, and representing the group as spokesman.

Comparison of two separate tables, one showing intercorrelations among variables for the ship "in port," the other showing intercorrelations among variables for the ship "at sea," reveals only a few marked differences. We shall discuss here only the intercorrelations among variables representing estimates or time spent in various kinds of work performance. Time spent in conferring with superior officers is correlated with time spent in Personnel Activities in port, but not with time spent as Technical Consultant when the ship is at sea. These findings correspond with conditions as revealed by the interview. When the ship is in port there are many problems relating to personnel releases, transfers, leaves and liberty, discipline and the like which must be taken up with superior officers. However, when the ship is at sea these problems abate, and when an officer spends time with a superior it is usually in relation to some technical problem that arises. Time spent in making Speeches or talking to groups in port is correlated with Attending Conferences and Examining Reports, while making Speeches at sea is correlated with Teaching and Coordination. These findings also make sense. When the ship arrives in port, large quantities of mail, directives, and reports are received, and the officers attend conferences ashore. The information received from these sources is passed on to others in group meetings. When the ship is at sea, instruction becomes very important and is sometimes carried on in groups; also groups of men are called together to receive instructions for purposes of coordinating plans and operations. With the ship in port, time spent in Public Relations is correlated with time spent in Professional and Technical Operations and acting as Technical Consultant. However, time spent in Public Relations is not highly correlated with any other variable with the ship at sea. Acting as Professional or Technical Consultant is not highly correlated with other variables with the ship in port, but is correlated with time spent in Scheduling with the ship at sea. The magnitude of the correlation coefficients under discussion ranges from .3 to .6. It is very much regretted that time has not been available for further examination of the data obtained from the submarine studies.

Job Versus Man

One of the questions in which we have been very much interested may be stated somewhat as follows: Does an administrator develop certain patterns of work performance which he carries into a new position, no matter what its nature, or is his pattern of work performance determined by the requirements of the job? Our restudy of a Naval Air Station after a lapse of two years, permitted us to acquire tentative information on this question. In the restudy we found a number of officers who occupied the same position as two years previously. We found that a number of officers had been transferred to different positions within the organization. A number of positions were occupied by officers who had not been on the station two years previously. This enabled us to study Same Man in Same Position; Same Man in Different Position; Different Man in Same Position. It was possible to construct three tables of intercorrelation, correlating data found in 1947 with those obtained in 1949. The variables that appeared to be characteristic of the *man* rather than the position are Delegation practices, time spent in Public Relations, Evaluation, Reading and Answering Mail, Reading technical publications, and time spent with Outside Persons. Variables that appeared to be characteristics of the *position* rather than of the man are Level in the organization structure, Military Rank, time spent in Personal Contacts, time spent with Assistants, time spent witth Superiors, time spent in Supervision, Coordination, and Writing Reports, as well as number of nominations received for working partner. That these results are not entirely unrealistic is indicated by the fact that Military Rank for Same Man—Same Position is correlated .9 even though a two year period elapsed between the data collections. The correlation for Level in the organization is .8. Both of these correlation coefficients dropped to .0 for Same Man—Different Position, but were raised to .9 and .6 for Different Man in Same Position. The very fact that these findings reveal a characteristic condition of an organization, namely that the same position is likely to remain approximately at the same echelon level over a period of time and is likely to be filled by a person of the same military rank, suggests that the other results obtained may have some validity also.

In addition to obtaining general information, we feel that our methods should be tested to determine what practical applications they may have. As one step in this direction, we designed what might be called a clinical prediction study, in which we shall attempt to follow up officers who have been transferred to new positions. The plan requires us to study an officer in his present position immediately before his transfer to a new position. Then, before he arrives in his new postion, we shall study the present occupant of that position. On the basis of the information accumulated from the transferee, his superiors and his subordinates, and from the occupant of the job to which he is to be transferred and that person's superiors and subordinates, we shall make a prediction as to what changes will occur after he has become established in his new position. The prediction is then to be checked by a follow-up study six or eight months later of the officer in his new position. All data including interview data, observations and impressions, in addition to the quantitative data, will be utilized in making a recorded prediction on each of the variables for which quantitative data are obtained for an individual. In addition, the reason will be written out, justifying the prediction on each variable. These predictions, which are made by several researchers, are then to be sealed and put away until after the follow-up data have been collected. We have just completed a pilot study in which we interviewed ten officers who are to be transferred, as well as their superiors and subordinates and other members of their organizations. We have also interviewed the officers whom they are to replace and other members of their organizations. The data have been transferred to special forms devised by Dr. David Bakan in order to facilitate the recordings of our predictions, but since we have just returned from this field trip, it has not been possible as yet to record our predictions. The trial study indicates that it is at least possible and feasible to collect data for such purposes. It is planned to obtain data on fifty or sixty transferees and on the officers whom they are to replace as the next phase of our data collection program. Whether we succeed in our attempts to predict an officer's future behavior in the new position is perhaps not of as great an importance as that we have made the attempt, and have been willing to subject our methods to a rigorous and realistic type of test.

BIBLIOGRAPHY

1. Stogdill, Ralph M. Personal factors associated with leadership: A survey of the literature. *J. Psychol.*, 1948, *25*, 35–71.
2. ———— and Shartle, Carroll L. Methods for determining patterns of leadership behavior in relation to organization structure and objectives *J. appl. Psychol.*, 1948, *32*, 286–291.
3. Shartle, Carroll L. Leadership and executive performance. *Personnel*, 1949, *25*, 370–380.
4. ————. Organization structure. *Current Trends in Industrial Psychology.* Pittsburgh: Univ. of Pitt. Press, 1949, 14–31.
5. Stogdill, Ralph M. The sociometry of working relationships in formal organizations. *Sociometry*, 1949, *12*, 276–286.
6. ————. Leadership, membership, and organization. *Psychol. Bull.*, 1950, *47*, 1–14.

SOME RESEARCH ON LEADERSHIP IN SMALL GROUPS

LAUNOR CARTER

Department of Psychology
University of Rochester

SINCE THIS REPORT WILL BE largely concerned with research results, the theoretical position on which the work is based will be indicated only very briefly. In considering the functioning of small groups it is convenient for purposes of research and analysis to think in terms of three major determining factors. These three factors are:

1) the leadership and other abilities of each member of the group relative to the particular task toward which the group is oriented,
2) the personality characteristics and goal orientations of the individual members of the group and the interaction of these characteristics with the similar characteristics of other members of the group, and
3) group characteristics, that is, those characteristics tending to to be typical of groups of a particular size and structure.

It seems apparent on theoretical grounds that these three determinants of group behavior are not independent but interact. Thus while it is possible to determine the dimensions of generalized groups, it will probably be found that for any given group these dimensions are fundamentally determined by the goals and personality characteristics of the individuals composing the group and the leadership and other abilities required by the particular task toward which the group is oriented.

The first point emphasizes that individuals probably differ in their leadership ability relative to the task toward which the group is oriented. Two problems are implicit in this statement: 1) how is a person's leadership ability to be determined, and 2) to what extent are different kinds of leadership ability required as the task toward which the group is oriented changes.

CRITERIA FOR JUDGING LEADERSHIP ABILITY

Before we can determine how successful a leader has been in a given situation we need to know what constitutes our criterion of successful leadership. In the final analysis the labeling of an individual as a successful leader involves an act of judgment regarding both what function a leader should fulfill and how well he has fulfilled or is capable of fulfilling that function. In our research we have been attempting to determine the extent to which various judgments regarding a person's leadership ability agree. In doing this, the following five commonly recognized methods of assessing leadership potential have been used:

1) *Situational tests.* In situational testing the basic method is the setting up of miniature work-tasks similar to actual problems which might be faced later. Several individuals are introduced into the situations, often without a formal leader being designated, and careful note is made of the group interaction and leadership behavior of those involved. It is hoped that those demonstrating leadership behavior in such "artificial" miniature situations will later perform similarly when faced with real leadership problems. Harris [4] gives an extensive account of the use of this technique by the British War Office Selection Boards, and Jennings [5] has recently summarized its use.

2) *Nominations.* Several studies have demonstrated the usefulness of asking members of the group to nominate individuals for positions of leadership. Williams and Leavitt [7] report nominations to be their most successful measure in picking Marine combat leaders, and Wherry and Freyer [6] consider it one of their "purest" measures of leadership.

3) *Faculty Ratings.* Faculty members are all familiar with attempts to rate students. Prospective employers and graduate departments ask for ratings of leadership.

4) *Friends' Ratings.* Traditionally the judgment of friends is sought when evaluations are desired.

5) *Activity Ratings.* One method of assessing a subject's ability is to determine the extent to which he has been a leader in past activities.

These criteria are described in greater detail in previous publications [1, 3] where it is shown that the reliability of assessments based on each of these criteria are adequate except for the friends' ratings and faculty ratings on college students. In one study [1] a hundred high school boys were assessed by collecting information from four of the sources listed above; in another study [3] using thirty-six college students as subjects all five criteria were obtained. The tables of intercorrelations between the different criteria (given in the above articles) show that the situational test assessments are only slightly related to any of the other criteria. In the high school study the nominating scores have some relationship to faculty ratings and activity scores, while in the college study the relationships are lower. Faculty ratings and friends' ratings are not significantly related to other criteria except for several of the relationships in the high school study. For the high school students, activity scores have a moderate relationship to some nominating scores and to the faculty ratings, but such a relationship disappears in the college study. The general conclusion drawn from these intercorrelations is that while there is some positive relationship between the different criteria of leadership, it is so low as to throw doubt on the adequacy of the definition and uniqueness of the concept of leadership and certainly makes studies based on any one criterion of limited generality.

A "VALIDATION" OF SITUATIONAL TESTS. It can be objected that most of the measures so far considered are not really criteria but simply predictors of future leadership performance. It may be argued that the situational tests afford an opportunity to assess an individual's performance so that a prediction can be made regarding his later performance in more "real" situations. During the past school year the forty men in one of the Naval ROTC classes at the University of Rochester were studied through the use of situational tests. They were formed in groups of eight and were run in a leaderless situation on reasoning, mechanical-assembly and discussion tasks. Later they were run in groups of four in leaderless situations and also in situations where one of them served as the appointed leader.

Members of the project have spent much of the summer following some of these students on their summer training cruise in an effort to obtain criterion data against which to "validate" the situational tests. In the end, only twenty-six men went on cruises, the remainder were either eliminated from training, chose Marine Corps training, or received aviation training. Five men went on one ship, ten on another, and eleven on a third. All of the cruises were not the same because of different training regimes, different type of ships; and one cruise was cut short because of the immediate need of the ship for other purposes. On each ship assessments of the studied midshipmen were obtained from commissioned officers and from midshipmen from other universities. As a preliminary treatment the subjects have been divided into two groups: those falling in the upper and lower half in the judgment of the commissioned officers, and those falling in the upper and lower half as viewed by the midshipmen from other universities. The subjects' performance in both the leaderless and appointed situational tests have been compared with these summer cruise assessments. The following tetrachoric correlations were obtained:

Assessment by commissioned officers and leaderless situational tests .52
Assessment by commissioned officers and appointed leader situational tests .58
Assessment by other midshipmen and leaderless situational tests .60
Assessment by other midshipmen and appointed leader situational tests .00
Commissioned officer assessments and midshipmen assessments .24
Ratings in leaderless situational tests and in appointed leader situational tests .60

While these correlations give a general picture of the results, a more intimate feeling for the problem may be obtained from a detailed consideration of the data for five of the subjects on one ship. The ratings and ranks shown under Situational Tests in Table 1 indicate these subjects' performance in the leaderless situations and when serving as the appointed leader. On this summer cruise, the midshipmen were organized into divisions composed of a commissioned officer, about ten senior midshipmen, and about thirty sophomore midshipmen. Each senior had a one-week assignment or tour of duty as either the midshipmen junior division officer or as boatswain's mate. At the end of this tour of duty he was assessed by at least four other midshipmen with whom he had worked and by the division commissioned officer. At the end of the six-week cruise each division commissioned officer and each senior midshipman from the other universities made an assessment of the subjects by making a paired comparison of the leadership ability of our subject and each of the other seniors in that division.

TABLE 1

A Comparison of Summer Training Cruise Performance with
Ratings Obtained on Situational Tests

Subject	Situational Tests				Summer Training Cruise					
	Leaderless Tests		Appointed Leader		Tour of Duty		Paired Comparisons			
							Comm. Officers		Other Seniors	
	Ratings	Rank	Ratings	Rank	Ratings	Rank	%	Rank	%	Rank
A	2.5	1	2.0	1	2.2	1.5	53	3	61	3
B	2.9	2	2.8	3	3.0	4	30	4	64	1
C	3.3	3	3.0	4	2.2	1.5	64	2	62	2
D	4.0	4	2.5	2	2.6	3	78	1	44	5
E	5.0	5	3.3	5	4.0	5	14	5	49	4

It is instructive to consider the ratings each man received. Subject A received the highest ratings in the situational tests. He tied for highest rating on his tour of duty and was rated very high by the other seniors. But the commissioned officer's ranking places him in the middle of our group. One wonders if this may not be the result of A's previous status as an enlisted man in the Navy and his resultant ambiguous attitude toward officers and vice versa. Subject B ranked high on the situational tests but received quite low ratings for his tour of duty and in the paired comparisons made by the commissioned officer. Subject B is a quiet, hardworking, conscientious, slightly withdrawn individual. It was remarked that, "He would be a swell leader in civilian life but not in the Navy." His peers, the seniors, valued him very highly. The commissioned officer pointed out that while he was a good worker, he didn't know how to give commands and actually worked with the men! Here is a case where a marked discrepancy in the ratings is caused by disagreement as to the definition and concept of leadership. The picture for subject C is fairly consistent, with the tests rating him somewhat under his performance on the cruise. He has been described as the "strong, silent type." Subject D was a very interesting individual. In the leaderless situation he ranked at about the middle, while in the appointed situation he was quite high. On the summer cruise, the commissioned officer rated him very high while the seniors rated him very low. This is quite consistent—in positions of authority he grasps his power, he tries very hard to please those superior to him, he keeps his men working but often inefficiently. On the other hand he is officious, always giving advice and information which is often wrong and not wanted. One senior confided that he was one of the most disliked men in the NROTC unit. Subject E was low all the way through. He is a pleasant easy-going, unmotivated individual who just does not do anything. The impression is gained that he might be quite capable if he could be motivated. The point of this individual consideration of each record is to suggest that while, when viewed statistically, the data appear to have some consistency, when viewed broadly with the personality characteristics of the subjects and the frame of reference of the raters in mind, the data becomes even more consistent and belief in the validity of situational testing is enhanced.

At the same time, it must not be forgotten that these results are based on only twenty-six cases; the need for additional data is obvious. It should also be mentioned that in addition to the leadership ratings there are available for each of the men a number of other ratings such as cooperativeness, prestige, initiative, and friendliness. It may well be that some combination or ratio of these other ratings with the leadership rating will yield closer approximations to the material gathered on the cruise.

ON THE DEFINITION OF LEADERSHIP. The foregoing material points up the difficulty of defining what the concept of leadership means. To one person it means "democratic group interaction," to another, high group productivity however achieved, and to a third, being able to command and order. Thus there is no one definition of leadership. In our studies we have been attempting to determine what we mean by leadership. One could try writing out a formal definition—but how much would this simply reflect rationalization and an attempt to achieve "logical" coherence?

During 1948-49 each subject run in leaderless group situations was rated on eleven different characteristics such as cooperation, insight, leadership, etc. The ratings on these characteristics were intercorrelated and then factor analyzed. The results are complicated, since separate ratings were made by task and by size of group. As a very tentative statement, the following two factors seem to appear:

Factor I	Factor II
Insight	Cooperation
Initiative	Friendliness
Leadership	Insight
Interest	Efficiency
Activity	Loquacity

Thus our raters seem to think of leadership as involving essentially insight and initiative, but friendliness, loquacity, etc., do not seem to be involved.

This year similar data have been collected with ratings made on nineteen characteristics and in situations where the leader was appointed and where he emerged in leaderless tests. By comparing the factorial composition of these two situations, it should be possible to make a more exact definition of the leadership requirements in each.

LEADERSHIP ABILITY AS A FUNCTION OF THE TASK

The first section emphasized the extent to which leadership was dependent on the particular criterion used in its assessment. In this section it will be pointed out that different leadership abilities are required, depending on the particular task toward which a group is oriented. In work with high school subjects [1] three tasks were used and with college subjects [3] six different tasks were employed. Since leadership ratings were made at the end of each task, we can determine which tasks seem to require common abilities. The detailed correlations are shown in the publications mentioned above. From these correlations it would be noted that only one of the thirty correlations is negative and that that one is not statistically significant. The general positive nature of the correlations indicates that leadership performance is not completely specific but rather, from knowing that a person was a leader in one of the tasks, we can predict that he will tend to be a leader in other tasks. At the same time, it is apparent that there are certain tasks for which leadership performances seem to be significantly interrelated into groups. Thus, while there is a certain generality of leadership, there is also a tendency for some people to show leadership more specifically in certain families of tasks than in others.

To investigate these relationships more closely a centroid factor analysis was completed for the correlation matrices showing the

TABLE 2

Rotated Factor Loadings for the Leadership Ratings on Six Tasks

	First Factor		Second Factor	
	Fours	Pairs	Fours	Pairs
Reasoning	.60	.73	.00	−.04
Intellectual Construction	.53	.60	.04	.46
Clerical	.49	.34	.23	.60
Discussion	.02	.53	.55	.04
Motor Cooperation	.10	.06	.50	.50
Mechanical Assembly	−.04	.07	.43	.64

relationship between the different tasks. Table 2 shows the rotated factor loadings derived from these matrices.

The loadings on the first factor are highest on Reasoning, Intellectual Construction, the Clerical task, and for the pair sessions, on Discussion. In our previous study [1] the Clerical task was closely related to the Intellectual task. From these loadings it would seem that there are those people who tend to be leaders in that constellation of situations which might be characterized as "intellectual." The second factor is not orthogonal to the first factor; the angle between the two factors for the "four" situations is 57°, and for the pair sessions it is 81°. The highest loadings on the second factor are on Mechanical Assembly, Motor Cooperation, and the Clerical task. Intellectual Construction for pairs and Discussion for fours also seem to be involved. The Discussion loading is hard to reconcile with the other loadings. With this exception, all the other loadings seem to suggest a "doing things with one's hands" factor.

Thus it seems that there are different families of leadership situations. The two sets of tasks identified here are the result of the particular tasks originally used and additional information is needed to determine the number of families of situations which exist.

PERSONALITY CHARACTERISTICS AND LEADERSHIP PHENOMENA

In the introduction the importance of the personality characteristics and the interaction of the members of the group was mentioned.

While the type of task on which the group is working is important in influencing a person's leadership standing, his goals and personality characteristics as they relate to the other members of the group are of equal or greater importance. A person who might make an effective leader with one group of individuals might do very poorly with another group, or two groups of equal ability may perform very differently depending on the extent to which the members' personalities conflict or fit harmoniously.

AN ILLUSTRATION OF THE PROBLEM. An illustration of this comes from some of our work with leaderless groups. One of our groups was made up of four quite capable individuals. One of the participants, called Green, was described by an observer as follows: "Green is very rapid in movement, restless, makes himself at home in strange situations, displays a great deal of friendliness, appears insensitive to others' reactions to him, incessant talker, seems to articulate every thought or observation which may occur to him, very aggressive, very self-assertive, tries to dominate every situation, superior intellectually, gives evidence of great interest in work at hand, shows rapid insight into intellectual tasks." This is a surface personality description but is the way Green probably appeared to the other members of the group. How effective was the group composed of Green and three other capable individuals? A group observer reports regarding the first leaderless group meeting: "For the first few minutes of the group work, Green attained the leadership role, very rapidly saw the results to be achieved by the group and loudly and boisterously pointed out end-goals. After a very brief period of such group work, the other three individuals showed evidence of rejecting such leadership. Green became an 'isolate,' and the other three individuals tended to ignore his comments and suggestions although they were frequently valuable. Even though Green's leadership was to a large extent abortive, he continued to dominate most situations and exerted influence because of his very aggressive behavior. . . . The isolation of the dominant individual had a negative effect on group work and achievement." Even after the group had worked together about twenty hours in seven different sessions, another observer says of the last session: "This group was a rather inefficient one, with evidence of antagonism between members and the almost complete rejection of Green by the others." Here we have four capable individuals who make a group which functions inefficiently because of conflicting individual personality characteristics. In contrast we have had other groups composed of somewhat less capable individuals who worked together harmoniously with high group productivity. As an illustration we had another group where the participants' scores on the Primary Mental Abilities Tests were slightly inferior to those of Green and his co-workers. But in this group there were no apparent personality conflicts. An observer describes their final session as follows: "The group as a whole was unusually efficient, worked together harmoniously, was very friendly, and seemed to be very highly motivated. The distribution of leadership abilities was fairly broad. All subjects entered actively into the tasks, and all assumed responsibility for getting work done. The group seemed to have developed a strong team spirit."

The problem is to be able to understand which people will work well together and which will not. We are now exploring a number of leads in this field but have only most tentative results. In 1948-49 we administered to our subjects a long battery of objective personality, ability, and interest measures, gave an individually administered Rorschach (administered and interpreted by Dr. Howard Siple), collected autobiographical data, and held two three-hour interviews with each subject. From the objective test scores, the personal history data, and the interviews, a personality sketch is being written; from the Rorschach results another personality description has been obtained independently. From this material we are going to try to predict how groups composed of the different individuals worked as they performed in the leaderless task situations.

INDIVIDUAL PERSONALITY AND GROUP FUNCTIONING. Mr. William Haythorn has been investigating the extent to which particular individuals exert a facilitator or depressor effect on the functioning of groups. In a leaderless group situation nine groups of four members each were run. Subsequently, the members of any one group were run in all possible pairs, that is, A and B, A and C, A and D, B and C, B and D, and C and D. From the performance ratings the average effectiveness of any group member can be determined. As an example, let us suppose that A and B have fairly high average performances while C and D have low average performances. Then it has been found that when a person of high performance, such as A, works with any other person, he facilitates the performance of the other member of the group even though the other group member (B, for instance) is a high performing member. Likewise, if the individual is a low performing member, such as C, he depresses the performance of the other group members to a level below that of their normal performance. Thus there appear to be people who are typically depressors or facilitators of group functioning in influencing the normal level of performance of the other members of the group. This work is just now being completed and a detailed description will be forthcoming shortly.

FORMAL GROUP STRUCTURE AND LEADERSHIP STATUS

It is clear that in many situations an individual's status on the leadership-followership continuum will depend on factors which are characteristic of the group of which he is a member. Formal determinants such as age, length of membership, sex, election to office, *etc.*, undoubtedly influence leadership performance. Forty subjects have just been run in a small-group laboratory situation where leadership structure was fixed at two levels. The subjects met in groups of four and worked on a reasoning, a mechanical assembly, and a discussion task. At the first meeting the subjects were placed in a leaderless group situation and each subject was given a leadership rating for his performance on each task in this unstructured situation. On subsequent sessions groups were run with a formally appointed leader. Each of the subjects served as the appointed leader of a group working on three tasks similar to those used in the leaderless situation. Again the subject's leadership performance was rated. The correlations between the leadership rating made in the leaderless situation and those made while serving as appointed leader were .48 for the reasoning task, .39 for the mechanical assembly task, and .49 for the discussion task. If the leadership ratings on three leaderless sessions are combined and compared with the total leadership rating for one appointed session, the resulting correlation is .55. If these correlations are corrected for the unreliability of the raters' observations, a relationship of about .65 exists between the excellence of performance in a leaderless situation and performance when acting as an appointed leader.

However, the average leadership ratings received by the appointed leaders while working in the appointed situation with new co-workers, were considerably more favorable than their ratings from the leaderless situation. The ratings were made on a seven point scale with the low end being favorable. In the leaderless situation the average rating was 4.17, while the average rating for these same subjects while working as the appointed leader was 3.25. This difference is significant at well beyond the 1 per cent level, giving a critical ratio of 5.0. From these results, it is clear that a formal change in the position of an individual in the structure of the group results in a very significant change in the individual's level of leadership performance. While the formal designation of an individual as a leader results in his behaving more like a leader, the relative excellence of his behavior in this formal position is to a considerable extent revealed by his performance in the unstructured leaderless situation. But in the leaderless situations behavior is largely determined by the individual's leadership ability, his goals, his personality, and the interaction of these factors with those of the other individuals composing the group. While formal structure may well determine the role an individual takes, his goals and personality characterictics will tend to determine the effectiveness of his performance in that role.

The following persons have worked with me on different aspects of this program: Mary Nixon, Margaret Howell, Beatrice Meirowitz, William Haythorn, and John Lanzetta.

BIBLIOGRAPHY

1. Carter, L. F. and Nixon, M. An investigation of the relationship between four criteria of leadership ability for three different tasks. *J. Psychol.*, 1949, *27*, 245–261.
2. ———. Ability, perceptual, personality, and interest factors associated with different criteria of leadership. *J. Psychol.*, 1949, *27*, 377–388.
3. Carter, L. F., Haythorn, W., and Howell, M. A further investigation of the criteria of leadership. *J. abnorm. soc. Psychol.*, 1950, *45*, 350–358.
4. Harris, H. *The Group Approach to Leadership Training*. London: Routledge–Kegan Paul, 1949.
5. Jennings, H. Military use of sociometry and situation tests in Great Britain, France, Germany and the United States. *Sociometry*, 1949, *12*, 191–202.
6. Wherry, R. J. and Fryer, D. H. Buddy ratings: Popularity contests or leadership criteria? *Personnel Psychol.*, 1949, *2*, 147–159.
7. Williams, S. B. and Leavitt, H. J. Group opinion as a predictor of military leadership. *J. consult. Psychol.*, 1947, *11*, 283–292.

LEADERSHIP IDENTIFICATION AND ACCEPTANCE

FILLMORE H. SANFORD

Institute for Research in Human Relations
Philadelphia

General Approach to Leadership

THIS STUDY, LIKE ANY OTHER BASIC study of leadership, has as its central aim the making of valid general statements about the very general problem of who influences whom under what circumstances. The present research adopts as its means a focus on factors in the *follower which are associated with the acceptance or rejection of leaders and leadership.*

The thinking that lies behind the decision to study leadership by studying the follower starts with the notion that there are three basic and delineable factors in any leadership phenomenon: (a) the leader, (b) the situation, and (c) the follower. If we are to make the most meaningful and general sentences about leadership, the reasoning is, we must ultimately deal—and deal simultaneously—with each of these three general factors. The present project is concerned primarily with the follower as a factor in the acceptance or rejection of leadership. But before describing the work on the follower, it will be well to think for a minute about the other basic factors in leadership events.

There is no need to argue that it is important to study the leader. The leader's behavior will obviously have something to do with the degree to which his followers are willing to follow. But there is good reason to believe that it is not enough to study the leader alone. The personality or pattern of behavior that wins followers in one situation will alienate followers in another. The "natural born" combat

158

skipper will not fare so well, perhaps, if he tries to run an office in the Department of the Navy with the same leadership techniques that paid off well while his submarine was on a ninety day combat patrol. It is important to study the leader, but he must be studied as he relates to other recognizable factors in the leadership event.

One such factor, we have indicated, is the situation. Studying the traits or behaviors of the leader will be more profitable if these traits or behaviors are studied in relation to the definable characteristics of the situation in which the leader is operating.

It can also be strongly argued that the *follower, too, must be studied* if we are to see most clearly what happens in a leadership event. It is the follower as an individual who perceives the leader, who perceives the situation, and who, in the last analysis, accepts or rejects leadership. The follower's persistent motives, points of view, frames of reference or attitudes will have a hand in determining what he perceives and how he reacts to it. These psychological factors in the individual follower cannot be ignored in our search for a science of leadership.

Given the general conviction that the follower has a role which relates to his behavior in the presence of a leader, we can proceed to a number of hypotheses about what discoverable psychological factors have a relevance for the acceptance or rejection of leadership. We can say that for any given culture there is a pattern of basic attitudes toward authority which helps determine the role which leaders in that culture must play. We can say that in any given group of followers there are attitudes, expectancies, or needs which may be common to many members and which have a hand in determining the reaction to the leader or to leadership. These needs or attitudes may be systematically related to the dimensions of the situation. Or they may *determine* the situation, for the individual lives in a psychological world and his motives surely help determine that world. At any rate, it can be argued that if we can understand certain things about the follower we will be a stride ahead (a) in predicting what leaders will be accepted or rejected, and (b) in gaining a comprehensive understanding of leadership.

INSTRUMENTS AND PROCEDURES

THE INTERVIEW

In order to explore the follower's "readinesses" for leadership, an elaborate interview was constructed to tap both surface and deep lying attitudes toward authority in general and toward both specific leaders and leader-behaviors.

The interview included seventy items of various forms. There were direct questions with yes-no answers, sentence-completion items calling for free response answers, "projective" questions and cartoon-like projective devices. In terms of content, the items can be described in terms of the following categories:

1. *Items in the area of "general ideology of leadership."*
   Examples: "The president of the U.S. should be a man who. . . ."
   "In a democracy a leader must . . ."
2. *Items in the area of "functional ideology of leadership."*
   Examples: "The leader who tells people exactly what to do and how to do it will make people. . . ."
   "Followers who disagree with the leader should . . ."
3. *Items relating to Heroes and Villains.*
   Example: "Could you tell me the name of a great person, living or dead, whom you admire the most?"
4. *Items relating to the Advisor-Advisee relationship.*
   Examples: "I prefer that the person I go to for advice be . . ."
   "Whom did you go to the last time you wanted advice from someone?"
5. *Items tapping attitudes about specific leadership roles.*
   Examples: "Our military leaders must be men who . . ."
   "School teachers, as leaders are . . ."
   "As leaders women are generally . . ."
6. *Items pertaining to the nomination and characterization of leaders.*
   Examples: "In your opinion, who are the individuals in this neighborhood who have become the leaders and have been accepted as leaders by the people around here?"
   "Would this person be a very good, fairly good, or poor leader in a large public meeting?"
7. *Personality items.*
   a. Personal Security scale.
   b. Authoritarian-Equalitarian scale.
   c. Miscellaneous items on values, worries, *etc.*
8. *Face data items.*

THE SAMPLE

This interview was administered to a total of 963 people in the city of Philadelphia. The sample was constructed by selecting from census data twenty-four representative four-block areas and interviewing randomly within each of these areas. The plan was to secure forty interviews from each area, giving an N of 960. A comparison of the sample with population data shows it to be representative, within small margins of error, with respect to the usual characteristics of the population.

CODING AND ANALYSIS

The responses to the first two hundred interviews were used to construct the categories for coding the answers to each of the questions. These codes were then used on the total sample. Since the coding had to be done by people relatively untrained in psychology, the coding system involved relatively obvious categories, based on the manifest rather than the latent content of the answers.

After an interval of one month, 201 of the original respondents were reinterviewed for the purpose of examining the reliability of the various parts of the interview schedule.

GENERAL PLAN FOR THE ANALYSIS OF DATA

The data from the interview are being subjected to analyses designed to explore and to test hypotheses in each of the following general areas:

1. *The topography of leadership.* An examination of sociometric data from each of the twenty-four areas. Who nominates whom as a leader in what sort of urban areas?

2. *The American ideology of leadership.* What are the prevailing attitudes toward authority and the prevailing ideas about leaders among the American people? How do these ideas and attitudes vary from group to group?

3. *Attitudes toward specific leaders and specific leadership roles.* What are the prevailing attitudes toward doctors, lawyers, teachers, ministers, *etc.*, as leaders? What are the prevailing attitudes toward Franklin D. Roosevelt, a leader with whom everyone is familiar?

4. *The Advisor-Advisee patterns in urban areas.* Who goes to whom for advice about what?

5. *Personality factors and the orientation to leaders and leadership.*
   What dynamic factors in the follower are associated with his attitude toward authority, his readiness to accept or reject certain sorts of leadership?

6. *Methodological research.* How do simple projective procedures work in field interviewing? What sort of questions yield the highest reliability? What sort of respondent answers with the most psychological consistency?

The present summary must omit many interesting, but lesser, aspects of the data. The material on personality variables affecting the orientation to leaders will be presented in relatively greater detail.

Then we will set down a tentative set of constructs, derived from the personality data, and go on to the presentation and analysis of the descriptive data on existing attitudes toward leaders and leadership.

DATA ON THE "TOPOGRAPHY" OF LEADERSHIP

The major aim of studies under the heading of "topography" of leadership was to relate sociometric data on the nomination of local leaders to sociological aspects of the twenty-four urban areas in which the interviewers worked. The topographical analysis is as yet not complete, but the study yields facts which lend support to the notions (a) that in urban areas the "neighborhood" is of diminished importance in communication or in social action, (b) that the political leader is a very important cohesive force in the urban locality, and (c) most of the effective leadership in the urban area can be found within an eight block area.

PERSONALITY FACTORS IN THE "READINESS FOR LEADERSHIP"

To date, a large portion of our effort on the project has gone into the analysis of "deep" personality factors as they are associated with the orientation to authority and to leaders. The reasoning behind this concentration of effort has been (a) that the follower's "depth" orientation to authority is worth studying in its own right; it has a chance of paying off eventually in terms of useful procedures for selecting and training both followers and leaders, and (b) that the study of the "dynamics" of followership will give us insight into the psychological dimensions of the leader-follower relationship and hence increase our ability to deal systematically with other aspects of our data.

The study of personality variables has focused on two areas. First, we examined the relation between the individual's so-called personal security and his orientation to leadership. Then, we studied the individual's "authoritarianism" as it is associated with his "readiness" for leadership. The present report will be extensively concerned with the material in the latter area; it now appears as the most nutritious segment of the whole study.

AUTHORITARIANISM AND THE ORIENTATION TO LEADERS

Our primary approach to the problem of personality factors in the leader-follower relation involved the broad variable known as "au-

thoritarianism." Our attempt was to devise a feasible scale for meas-
uring this variable and to examine the relation between the scores
on this scale and the individual's feeling for leaders and leadership.
The theory guiding this aspect of the study is that developed by
Fromm [2, 3] and further delineated by Adorno, Frenkel-Brunswik,
Levinson, and Sanford [1].

Authoritarianism is described as a broad syndrome of attitudes
rooted deep in the dynamics of personality. The authoritarian person is one who, because of his learned way of adjusting to parental
authority and to people, is characterized by the following: great con-
ventionality; scorn for the out-group or for any who depart from
standard in-group values and virtues; an open hostility combined
with overt submission to the strong; an opposition to the soft, the
idealistic and the human; a calculating or bargaining orientation to
people; and an intellectual rigidity with a great intolerance for am-
biguity. We can think of this syndrome in terms of a "depth insecur-
ity" (Fromm's "feeling of worthlessness") that finds expression in
the individual's many and varied attempts to cover it up or to overcome it.

Theory would lead us to expect that this broad variable has much
to do with the readiness to react to leaders and leadership. If we can
set up this variable as a continuum and devise a way of describing the
individual's position on this continuum we can expect that those who
fall toward the highly authoritarian end of the scale will, for example, demonstrate a hostility-ladened submission to strong leaders,
avoid group responsibility, emphasize the bargaining orientation to
any leader, etc. Those who score toward the other end of the continuum, the theory goes, should be more rational in their orientation to
leaders, should be willing to accept group responsibility, should emphasize the human and social function of the leader, etc.

In order to test these hypotheses, the procedure was to devise a
scale, suitable for use in a door-step interview, that taps this variable.
Such an instrument is the Authoritarian-Equalitarian scale used in
the study. This scale is, for the most part, an adaptation of the
F-scale developed by the California people [1]. It is composed of
eight items, has a repeat reliability of .78, a split-half reliability of .58,
and the items correlate satisfactorily with the total score. The scale
is admittedly crude but sufficiently adequate for exploratory use and
for group comparison. The eight items used on the scale are listed
below. Respondents were asked whether they agreed or disagreed
with each statement and whether they agreed or disagreed a little,

pretty much, or very much. The scoring was based on an arbitrary assignment of one for the most equalitarian answers (disagree, very much with items 1, 2, 3, 4, 6 and 7; agree, very much with items 5 and 8), six for the most authoritarian answers, and two, three, four, or five for the four intermediate answers.

Items on Authoritarian-Equalitarian (A-E) scale.

1. Human nature being what it is, there must always be war and conflict.
2. The most important thing a child should learn is obedience to his parents.
3. A few strong leaders could make this country better than all the laws and talk.
4. Most people who don't get ahead just don't have enough will-power.
5. Husbands should help their wives with the dishes and care for the children.
6. Women should stay out of politics.
7. People sometimes say that an insult to your honor should not be forgotten. Do you agree or disagree with that?
8. People can be trusted.

The scores on this scale were first related to other items in the interview which seemed to tap deep personality variables. Such a procedure served as a "validation by congruence" by showing that the scores on the scale keep the sort of psychological company that theory dictates they should.

The next procedure was to examine the relation between the scores on the scale and a wide variety of ideas about, and orientation to, leadership.

Table 1 gives a sample of the sort of data this analysis yields.

TABLE 1

Relation of A-E Scores to the
Acceptance or Rejection of Directive Leadership

Data based on responses to cartoon-projective device
depicting a strongly directive leader

Category of Response	N	Mean A-E Score	Categories Compared	Critical Ratio
1. Withdrawing ("I quit," etc.)	36	3.75	2,3	1.60
2. Acceptance ("We'll obey")	149	3.68	2,4	3.37
3. Tentative acceptance ("It depends," etc.)	144	3.52	2,5	3.91
4. Rejection ("You're nuts," "you're too arbitrary")	471	3.41	3,4	1.37
5. Group centered responses ("Let majority decide," "let's talk it over")	98	3.13	3,5	3.25

TABLE 1 (*continued*)

6. Couldn't understand picture	17	3.41	1.5	2.80
7. Don't know	44	3.59		
8. Reject	4			
	963	3.46		

Table 1 presents the coded responses to the cartoon-like projective device. And it gives the mean A-E score for those individuals giving each kind of response. We can see that high scorers on the scale tend either to express withdrawal responses ("I quit," *etc.*), or submitting responses ("Just tell us," or "We'll obey"). The low scorers take a calmer and more group centered stand, either mildly rejecting the dictatorial leadership or adopting a rational, group centered position.

Other items yield psychologically consonant data. High scorers think the president of the U.S. should "pay off" to his followers, that leaders in Washington should be "more American," that the best advisor is a high-status figure who can magically fix things, that followers who disagree with the leader should be "thrown out." They admire great persons who are symbols of power and in-group prestige and when they nominate a local leader they endow him with a halo and perceive him as being good for a wide variety of leadership functions.

By and large, the low scorers are characterized by psychologically opposite tendencies.

The results of this authoritarian-equalitarian analysis can be summarized in terms of the following general headings.

1. *Reaction to power, status, prestige.* Authoritarians tend, generally, to prefer status-ladened leadership, to accept strongly directive leadership, and to talk in terms of "power" words when characterizing "good" leaders. They nominate "power" figures as admired great persons, they accept doctors and teachers as leaders, they prefer prestigeful "fixers" when in need of information or advice. They express a willingness to accept strongly directive leadership on the part of the boss, the group leader, or the "best leader" anywhere. And when talking about leaders in general or leaders they themselves have nominated they emphasize power-flavored attributes—education, popularity, strength. When leaders show signs of weakness or of nonconformity, however, the authoritarians may express thinly disguised hostility. The leader who is not sure of himself "should drop dead," and the openly undemocratic leader tends to provoke the "safe" withdrawal response ("I quit").

The E (low-scoring) people, by contrast, appear able to take power or leave it alone. They are free to reject powerful leaders and strongly directive behavior on the part of a leader. They select humanists and liberals as heroes, they calmly reject doctors and school teachers as leaders. They react with equanimity in the face of a leader's directive behavior. They appear able to accept strong leadership (for example, in an emergency) when the situation demands it, but they have no built-in need for powerful authorities.

2. *Emphasis on material support.* Authoritarians appear to be characterized by something of a "father-feed-me" dependency on leaders. In speaking of either national or local leaders, they frequently focus on what the leader has done for a special group of which he, the follower, is a member. The best local leader is one who "looks out for people" (looks out for me?) and the best national leader is one who "takes care of the little man" (me?). There appears here the "bargaining" orientation to leadership that seems to play so large a role in the reaction to political leadership.

This emphasis is not strong in our low-scoring people.

3. *Emphasis on love support.* Authoritarians do not appear to perceive nor to care for the leader's warmth and responsiveness to people. They appear to judge the leader in terms of down-to-earth pay off. "If he looks out for me and if he is powerful enough, I will follow him." The equalitarian, on the other hand, in answer to "ideological" questions, talks in terms of the leader's responsiveness to his followers. They say that the good leader is one who "likes people" and who is "guided by his followers."

4. *Emphasis on in-group virtues.* The authoritarians demonstrate a concern for the leader's reflection of good solid "character." Their national leaders should be honest, and should be "true Americans," and even their emergency leaders and military leaders should be men of "character." The authoritarians tend toward over-conformity *themselves,* achieving security by adhering rigidly to in-group values and by demanding that all others do likewise.

5. *Emphasis on the leader as a person.* Authoritarians appear to be relatively more aware of the leader as a person while the equalitarians tend to think of the leader as one who has a social function to perform. There is a strong suggestion that the authoritarian is inextricably bound up in his own personal and emotional feeling with the leader and hence cannot back off to see the leader in a social context. In many instances the equalitarians will talk about a leader's ability to get a specific job done and appear relatively objective in selecting

leaders for jobs or observing how a certain behavior will affect the people the leader is leading. The authoritarian rarely gives evidence of either objective thinking about the leader's function or of discriminating comment about the fitness of a given leader for a given job. This tendency is most pronounced in the halo effect operating for authoritarian people in connection with the choice of local leaders.

6. *The need for cognitive structure.* Though the interview did not yield many data relevant to the individual's need for cognitive structure, there is suggestive evidence that cognitive structure is of no great concern to the authoritarian, but is of relatively more concern to the equalitarian. Where the later wants to "listen to all sides," or read the newspaper, the authoritarian listens to the president or the church to get the answers. One has the impression that the authoritarian keeps ready-made authoritative answers. The equalitarian, more tolerant of ambiguities, more inclined to accept personal responsibility, will prefer leaders who help him figure out things for himself.

7. *Relations with fellows.* Authoritarians do not appear concerned, in leadership situations, with the welfare of their fellow followers. They make their own individual peace with the leader and worry not at all about the leader's relation to other people in the group. Followers who disagree with the leader should be suppressed. The good leader is not one who can maintain warm relations with his followers, but one who looks out for "me and mine," who is strong and admirable enough to deserve "my" submission to him.

The equalitarians appear more inclined to empathize warmly with the follower who disagrees with the leader, to trust people, to appraise the leader in terms of his concern for the welfare of all.

8. *Orientation to responsibility.* High scorers do not often join groups, do not become officers in the groups they do join, report unwillingness to do volunteer work for the school or for the community chest. They appear to be willing to accept the leader's role when it is offered on a platter, but appear interested in using the role more to enhance their own status than to achieve group goals. Low scorers, by contrast, are more inclined to join things and to become officers in their groups. They are more willing to do volunteer nonstatus work and when they accept the leader's role they do so in a relatively nondirective and group-centered manner.

We can summarize our findings fairly adequately in terms of these eight general headings. The next step is to back off a way and appraise these results as they fit into more general contexts. We can back

off to two separate but related vantage points. First, we can look at
our results as they relate to personality and personality theory. Then
we can study them for their relevance to the study of leadership. Both
sorts of contemplation are important, but for our purposes here the
implications for leadership demand more attention. We will not here
deal with personality or personality theory except incidentally.

IMPLICATIONS FOR THE STUDY OF LEADERSHIP

The study of authoritarianism has two general kinds of implications for the study of leadership phenomena. First, here is a variable
which, studied in itself, may have direct bearing on the understanding of leadership. Authoritarians, for example, may behave in a distinct way in the presence of a given leader and it may be very useful,
both from a theoretical and practical standpoint, to know about this
distinct way of behaving. In the second place, the examination of this
variable as it relates to the readiness to respond to leaders, points
the way to the formulation of general constructs of possible use in
creating a general theory of leadership.

We have evidence here that those who score high on the A-E
scale are predisposed to react in a distinct way to leaders in general
and to specific leaders or specific attributes of leaders. The scale is not
perfect, the evidence is not overpoweringly clear, and conventional
standards of validity have not been met, but there is little room to
doubt that a reliable scale can be developed for any population, and
that such a scale will relate significantly to expressed attitudes toward
leaders in any situation. And there is at least a basis for believing that
the relating of such a scale to overt social behavior will yield important and practically useful results.

There are many hypotheses that now appear promising and that
are almost immediately testable. For example, we can imagine
actual groups in which the average "authoritarianism," either
through self-selection or selection from above, is high. In such groups
we have clear and testable hypotheses about what sort of leader behavior will be selected or, once selected, how it will be reacted to. It is
easy to imagine the reaction of a group of individuals high in "authoritarianism" to a laissez-faire or non-directive leader. Or imagine
the great discomfort of such a group when the leader operates in a
"sense of the meeting" manner where there is not even the security
and safety of standard parliamentary procedure. On the other hand,
a group of individuals with a low modal score on our variable

might be expected to go into a morale decline under an inescapably rigid and directive leader. Followers who want responsibility and participation can be expected to suffer severe frustration at the hands of a leader who believes that the purposes of democracy are fully met if the group is allowed an occasional vote on rigid, pre-planned alternatives.

On another tack, we can conceive of different socio-economic groups in the population having different modal scores on our ideal scale and that these scores will be related to the sort of leaders a given segment or group will prefer. We can conceive of an instrument that succeeds in comparing not only sub-groups in a given culture, but also cultures within cultures, with respect to basic attitudes toward authority. And we can ask such questions as the following: What is the modal German as compared with the modal American attitude toward authority; and what does this have to do with the sort of leaders that happen in the two cultures? What about Negroes? How authoritarian are they? And how does this relate to their readiness for leadership? What about Catholics or Jews? Or people in the South in comparison to Californians? The study of scores on a scale will not be sufficient to answer these questions, but a thorough study of basic attitudes toward authority can be expected to shed revealing light on the question of who influences whom in these various cultures or classes or groups or situations.

A less high-flown consideration concerns the selection of individuals who will make up a group. In many military and industrial situations we may, when we know more about authoritarianism, want to select for a certain job or type of job only those who score high or only those who score low. Or we may want to exclude extremely high authoritarians from any group situations. On the basis of casual observation one suspects, for example, that those who during the recent war had the most trouble making peace with the military hierarchy were high authoritarians who could not follow leaders they perceived as inferior in some way to themselves. Imagine an authoritarian private who had been a successful insurance salesman taking orders from an ungrammatical sergeant. Perhaps he would defer to rank and become passively happy. But one suspects that his general military effectiveness would be reduced by his conflict over following a leader who, however competent at a particular job, was not a man of conventional power and prestige.

The equalitarian, on the other hand, might be expected to take a relatively rational view of the authority of the sergeant or of a boss. He could be expected to accept authority that was functional, whatever the status of the source of authority, and to react to any authority or hierarchy in a relatively sane and latherless way.

Such notions lead to the crisp hypothesis that there will be a correlation of usefully high proportion between scores on a good test of "authoritarianism" and A.W.O.L. behavior or re-enlistment rate.

A further possible implication of our study for leadership bears on leaders themselves. Who becomes a leader—the equalitarian or the authoritarian? One can make a case, in fantasy, that the extreme authoritarian will rarely be *selected* as a leader in normal American situations where the followers have free choice. And he will rarely become a leader on the basis of his own efforts to do jobs and assume responsibility. He will be found most frequently in leadership positions where appointment has come from above and where his responsibility is primarily to his superiors rather than to his followers.

Once in a leadership position, the authoritarian can be expected to behave in a way quite different from the equalitarian. He may be expected to use his position more for the enhancement of his own status than for the filling of his social function. He may be a constitutional martinet, demanding differential respect and rigid discipline even in situations where such behavior has none but a rationalized connection with the achieving of a job. And he perhaps will have only one way of playing the leadership role—a way that may be adaptive when guns in close proximity are being fired in anger but is sadly ineffective when he is in a position of chair-borne leadership.

By contrast, the equalitarian, possessing more tendency to affiliate with people and less to dominate, might be expected to meet the emotional needs of followers in many standard American situations. Hence he will be widely selected as leader where the followers have both a freedom of choice and an adequate exposure to the leader's personality. He can be expected to assume responsibility gracefully, to accept authority without conflict, to be concerned with his followers at least as much as with his superiors. Perhaps because he has a more rational attitude toward authority, including his own, he can become less interested in his own status, more interested in the job to be done, and adjust his role to the demands of the situation.

All this is at the moment only fairly reasonable fantasy. But one can make a strong hypothetical case that the individual's deep orientation to authority is bound to affect (a) the likelihood of his becoming a leader in free situations, (b) his readiness to assume responsibility, (c) the style of leadership he adopts in meeting the needs of his followers and of his superiors, and (d) his general effectiveness in any leadership situation. Just for the sake of argument, we can state the following clear and testable hypotheses:

1. In a military or industrial situation, the leader who is high in a good test of "authoritarianism" will:
    a. be rejected by relatively many of his followers and
    b. accepted by relatively many of his superiors.
2. The leader who is low on "authoritarianism" will be:
    a. accepted by relatively many of his followers and
    b. rejected by relatively many of his superiors.

Both of these hypotheses assume that both the authoritarian and equalitarian are willing to assume responsibility and authority. There may be some people who are essentially equalitarian but who still are made extremely nervous by the possession of authority. They are so desperately in need of being loved by everybody that they cannot assume a control that might run the risk of stepping on a follower's toes and losing love. Such people will probably be rejected by everybody, above and below, who is at all interested in achieving a structure or in getting a job done.

All these casually stated hypotheses about both followers and leaders are testable—and probably worth the testing. The practical payoff involved is promising. So will be the payoff in terms of meaningful declarative sentences about the general phenomenon of leadership.

THE NEEDS OF THE FOLLOWER

The attempt to conceptualize the authoritarian's needs and the equalitarian's needs leads one almost immediately to wish for a generalized system of constructs in terms of which we can deal with needs of followers *in general*. We can conceive of a set of constructs, each one clearly amenable to definition and to quantitative description, in terms of which we can describe the prevalent needs of any group of followers in any situation. One group of followers in one situation will have a certain profile of needs. A different group in a different situation will have a different profile. Each individual will have his own persisting pattern of authority—relevant needs and each culture its own pattern or profile of predispositions toward leaders and leadership.

Whether such an attempt to conceptualize follower needs will as-

sist in the formulation of the ultimate theory of leadership, remains
to be seen. At this juncture, however, the attempt to deal conceptually with follower needs appears worthwhile. There follows a list of
needs or factors which appear of importance in determining the follower's feeling for the leader. These needs will be simply enumerated
here. There is presently no space for a full discussion of them. The
enumeration and skeletonized definition will suffice here to illustrate
an approach, a line of reasoning, and a big problem.

1. *The Need for Material Support.* The need to be fed, clothed,
   "paid off" by authority.
2. *The Need for Ego Support.* The need to have the leader increase "my" self-esteem, "my" feeling of importance.
3. *The Need for Love Support.* The need to have the leader love
   "me," the need for an atmosphere of approval.
4. *The Need for Affiliation with One's Fellows.* The need to
   have warm relations with other members of the group; this
   need is related to a concern for the welfare of one's fellow-
   members and a desire for the leader to facilitate interpersonal
   relations.
5. *The Need for Submission.* The need to submit to a strong
   leader; tendency to feel safe when authority is very strong,
   protective, directive.
6. *The Need for Structure.* The need to know what is going on,
   what the problem is, where "we" are headed, how to get there.
7. *The Need for Conformity.* The need to stick to in-group
   values and procedures, associated with the need to have others
   do likewise.
8. *The Need to Advance Group Goals.* The need for the group
   with which the individual is identified to succeed in carrying
   out its function.

Such a list of needs has obvious shortcomings, but it still has something to be said in its favor. We can maintain that each of these needs,
whatever its level and whatever its current degree of conceptual fuzz-
iness, has something to do with the acceptance or rejection of
leadership. At an immediate practical level, such a list may assist
materially in dealing with the data, to be summarized later, on American attitudes toward leadership. We can now, if we wish, roughly
profile the needs of the authoritarian. We can probably profile the
needs of the American people or of a given economic class. Such a
profile even now will help materially in predicting what leaders will
be accepted by whom.

In thinking about the use of such an approach to leadership phenomena, several sorts of hypotheses arise. We can set up hypotheses
about the relations of these needs to one another or we can hypothe-

size about the way the needs relate to the characteristics of the situation. We may eventually find that such a road, though currently tortuous and rocky, is the best road to a comprehensive theory of leadership.

The American Orientation to Leaders

One major purpose of the whole project on Leadership Identification and Acceptance was the description of the American follower's orientation to leadership. We wanted to talk about our whole sample in terms of attitudes and ideologies. And we wanted to talk about the orientation to leadership in the various sub-segments of the population. Minimally, we wanted to talk about these things in standard English. Maximally, we wanted to talk in terms of psychological genotypes such as those we have been dealing with.

To date, some progress has been made toward this general goal. But the richness of the data has by no means been completely mined. The present report will present a summary of one completed slice of this total aspect of the data as an example of the sort of analyses now in progress.

The Roosevelt Story

Our 963 respondents were asked (a) whether they thought F. D. Roosevelt was a good leader, and (b) why. Ninety-six per cent of the population thought he was a good leader and gave reasons for their opinions. Forty-two per cent of the population named Roosevelt as the great person, living or dead, they admired most.

Our plan was to use these data to learn about the orientation of the American people to national political leadership. Certainly if we can describe the relation of the population to this one universally known leader we will learn a good deal about the American people in general and their more specific readinesses to respond to other national leaders.

The data on the nomination of FDR as a great person were used as an index of the *amount* of admiration for the man among the segments of the population, while the data on the reasons given for thinking he was a good leader served as an indication of the *flavor* of the feeling for his leadership.

The facts from this study are of the following sort:

1. Roosevelt is admired as a great person with almost equal frequency by all economic groups; women admire him somewhat more than do men; whites more than Negroes, Catholics and Jews more than Protestants. Laborers express admiration

slightly more frequently than do business men and union laborers more than do non-union laborers. He is less appealing to the educated than to the uneducated.

2. For the total population the most frequently mentioned reasons for thinking he was a good leader fall into the following categories:
   a. his personal democracy,
   b. his championing of the "little man,"
   c. his general and personal competence.

3. *Infrequently* mentioned reasons for thinking him a good leader are:
   a. competence or accomplishments in the international area.
   b. "the common touch,"
   c. the personal victory over hardships,
   d. his advancement of democratic ideals.

4. Different segments of the population gave different reasons for thinking he was a good leader. For example, the lower economic classes and the Negroes cite most frequently his championing of the underprivileged, while the middle class puts relatively more emphasis on his personality and his competence.

The conclusions from these facts are that the following three dynamic factors primarily account for the Roosevelt phenomenon:

1. *The follower's need for material support.* Roosevelt's "payoff" in material terms was very important, especially among the lower economic classes.

2. *The follower's need for love support.* Roosevelt was seen as a man who was warm, who liked people, who was personally democratic. His meeting of the people's need for approval and love from above was crucial in determining his tremendous acceptance.

3. *The need to submit to power.* Roosevelt's perceived strength and status was an implicit but still probably a cardinal factor in the people's reaction to him.

METHODOLOGICAL AND "INCIDENTAL" STUDIES

The interview which served as the basic source of information for the study yields data that are relevant to a number of problems other than those relating directly to leadership. The use of a wide variety of items, many dealing with relatively deep personality variables, yielded incidental but nonetheless significant data on such problems as reliability and the meaning of the "Don't Know" response to interview items. Perhaps the most interesting of these incidental studies concerned projective devices on the doorstep. Seven cartoon-like projective devices were used to elicit data on relatively "deep" personality factors. An intensive analysis of the responses to these novel stimuli show them to be feasible and profitable devices for use in field studies.

Plans for Future Research

The original plan for the next year's work called for a program involving the simultaneous study, with improved instruments and sharpened hypotheses, of followers, of leaders, and of the situation in which leadership occurs. This program was to be executed in an organized urban community. The existence of the current emergency, however, has led to the decision to move toward the more practical by taking our instruments and hypotheses into a military situation and seeing if our approach and procedures cannot be turned to practical ends.

Just which one or ones of various alternate procedures will be followed is not now clear. The following possibilities are under consideration.

1. *The development of a personality test for the selection of leaders.* It is pretty clear that the individual's orientation to authority—his own or that exercised by others—his deep-lying feeling for people and his basic orientation to responsibility have much to do with his likelihood of success as a military leader. It is also probable that a sanitary instrument to measure these factors can be devised, standardized and validated in a hard-headed way. If such an instrument can be devised, it will have obvious utility. And research of this sort would not be entirely lacking in basic implications.

2. *The development of an instrument for the selection of followers.* The enlisted man who is taken from civilian life and thrust into a military organization (a) must adjust to authority, (b) must be able to relate successfully to his fellows, (c) must establish some way of meeting responsibility. The potentialities for these adjustments lie deep in his personality. One can at least imagine an instrument that will tap these potentialities and that can be used both in selection and in classification of military personnel. It is not hard to imagine enlistees who do not possess the sort of potentialities that will enable them to make any sort of adjustment to the military. Perhaps an instrument systematically getting at the variables tapped by our follower interview can assist in the screening of such people. But more importantly, some military assignments require unique sorts of adjustment to authority, to group life, to responsibility. We may be able to construct an instrument that would enable us to predict actuarially which

individuals are most likely to fit into military jobs demanding certain sorts of psychological orientation and certain sorts of interpersonal relations. It would be a mistake, for example, to assign the individual who is a chronic rebel and a chronic distruster of people, to a military job demanding intense and intimate cooperation. Nor should the completely passive and compliant soul be put in units where the individual is called on for initiative and ingenuity. At least, at the level of fantasy, it now seems possible to predict who is the rebel and who is the conformist and who can be either if the situation demands it.

3. *The study of followers, leaders, and situation in one frequently occurring kind of military group.* It may be advisable to concentrate on one type of military group and intensively to study in that group the leader-follower relation. For example, if the study were done on submarine crews, the procedure might be to study the characteristics of the social organization and of the psychological situation aboard a submarine, to examine the pressures and requirements exerted upon crew members, to study the needs and expectancies of members of the group, to study the function and personality of officers and to seek for interrelational factors. One would expect that in the submarine situation, where interdependence is great, where interaction is intimate, and where the visibility of the end product and the means of achieving it are high, there will be unique demands made on members of the group. There will be unique leader-oriented needs. And the leader-follower relation will be sufficiently delineable to allow for the eventual selection of both those leaders and followers who are personally equipped to participate comfortably and effectively in it.

Which of these or other alternate plans will be followed will be determined by (a) opportunity and (b) the decision reached when the best obtainable wisdom has been brought to bear on the problem of detailed planning.

This report is a summary of only part of the research that has been done under this project. From its inception, this study of leadership has been a collaborative enterprise. In addition to the author, among the most direct contributors to the present paper have been the following personnel on the staff of the Institute for Research in Human Relations: John N. Patterson, Barney Korchin, Harry J. Older, Emily L. Ehle, Irwin M. Rosenstock and Doris M. Barnett.

BIBLIOGRAPHY

1. Adorno, W., Frenkel-Brunswik, E., Levinson, D., & Sanford, R. N. *The Authoritarian Personality*, New York: Harpers, 1950.
2. Fromm, E. *Escape from Freedom*, New York: Farrar and Rinehart, 1941.
3. ———. *Man for Himself*, New York: Rinehart, 1947.

EFFECTS OF GROUP PRESSURE UPON THE MODIFICATION AND DISTORTION OF JUDGMENTS

S. E. ASCH

Department of Psychology and Education
Swarthmore College

WE SHALL HERE DESCRIBE in summary form the conception and first findings of a program of investigation into the conditions of independence and submission to group pressure. This program is based on a series of earlier studies conducted by the writer while a Fellow of the John Simon Guggenheim Memorial Foundation. The earlier experiments and the theoretical issues which prompted them are discussed in a forthcoming work by the writer on social psychology.

Our immediate object was to study the social and personal conditions that induce individuals to resist or to yield to group pressures when the latter are perceived to be *contrary to fact*. The issues which this problem raises are of obvious consequence for society; it can be of decisive importance whether or not a group will, under certain conditions, submit to existing pressures. Equally direct are the consequences for individuals and our understanding of them, since it is a decisive fact about a person whether he possesses the freedom to act independently, or whether he characteristically submits to group pressures.

The problem under investigation requires the direct observation of certain basic processes in the interaction between individuals, and between individuals and groups. To clarify these seems necessary if we are to make fundamental advances in the understanding of the formation and reorganization of attitudes, of the functioning of public opinion, and of the operation of propaganda. Today we do not possess an adequate theory of these central psycho-social processes. Empirical investigation has been predominantly controlled by general propositions concerning group influence which have as a rule been assumed but not tested. With few exceptions investigation has relied upon descriptive formulations concerning the operation of suggestion and prestige, the inadequacy of which is becoming increasingly obvious, and upon schematic applications of stimulus-response theory.

The bibliography lists articles representative of the current theoretical and empirical situation. Basic to the current approach has been the axiom that group pressures characteristically induce psychological changes *arbitrarily,* in far-reaching disregard of the material properties of the given conditions. This mode of thinking has almost exclusively stressed the slavish submission of individuals to group forces, has neglected to inquire into their possibilities for independence and for productive relations with the human environment, and has virtually denied the capacity of men under certain conditions to rise above group passion and prejudice. It was our aim to contribute to a clarification of these questions, important both for theory and for their human implications, by means of direct observation of the effects of groups upon the decisions and evaluations of individuals.

The Experiment and First Results

To this end we developed an experimental technique which has served as the basis for the present series of studies. We employed the procedure of placing an individual in a relation of radical conflict with all the other members of a group, of measuring its effect upon him in quantitative terms, and of describing its psychological consequences. A group of eight individuals was instructed to judge a series of simple, clearly structured perceptual relations—to match the length of a given line with one of three unequal lines. Each member of the group announced his judgments publicly. In the midst of this monotonous "test" one individual found himself suddenly contradicted by the entire group, and this contradiction was repeated again and again in the course of the experiment. The group in question had, with the exception of one member, previously met with the experimenter and received instructions to respond at certain points with wrong—and unanimous—judgments. The errors of the majority were large (ranging between $\frac{1}{2}''$ and $1\frac{3}{4}''$) and of an order not encountered under control conditions. The outstanding person—the critical subject—whom we had placed in the position of a *minority of one* in the midst of a *unanimous majority*—was the object of investigation. He faced, possibly for the first time in his life, a situation in which a group unanimously contradicted the evidence of his senses.

This procedure was the starting point of the investigation and the point of departure for the study of further problems. Its main features were the following: (1)The critical subject was submitted to two contradictory and irreconcilable forces—the evidence of his own experience of an utterly clear perceptual fact and the unanimous evidence of a group of equals. (2)Both forces were part of the immediate situation; the majority was concretely present, surrounding the subject physically. (3)The critical subject, who was requested together with all others to state his judgments publicly, was obliged to declare himself and to take a definite stand vis-à-vis the group. (4)The situation possessed a self-contained character. The critical subject could not avoid or evade the dilemma by reference to conditions external to the experimental situation. (It may be mentioned at this point that the forces generated by the given conditions acted so quickly upon the critical subjects that instances of suspicion were rare.)

The technique employed permitted a simple quantitative measure of the "majority effect" in terms of the frequency of errors in the direction of the distorted estimates of the majority. At the same time we were concerned from the start to obtain evidence of the ways in which the subjects perceived the group, to establish whether they became doubtful, whether they were tempted to join the majority. Most important, it was our object to establish the grounds of the subject's independence or yielding—whether, for example, the yielding subject was aware of the effect of the majority upon him, whether he abandoned his judgment deliberately or compulsively. To this end we constructed a comprehensive set of questions which served as the basis of an individual interview immediately following the experimental period. Toward the conclusion of the interview each subject was informed fully of the purpose of the experiment, of his role and of that of the majority. The reactions to the disclosure of the purpose of the experiment became in fact an integral part of the procedure. We may state here that the information derived from the interview became an indispensable source of evidence and insight into the psychological structure of the experimental situation, and in particular, of the nature of the individual differences. Also, it is not justified or advisable to allow the subject to leave without giving him a full explanation of the experimental conditions. The experimenter has a responsibility to the subject to clarify his doubts and to state the reasons for placing him in the experimental situation. When this is done most subjects react with interest and many express gratification at having lived through a striking situation which has some bearing on wider human issues.

Both the members of the majority and the critical subjects were male college students. We shall report the results for a total of fifty critical subjects in this experiment. In Table 1 we summarize the successive comparison trials and the majority estimates.

TABLE 1

Lengths of Standard and Comparison Lines

Trials	Length of Standard Line (in inches)	Comparison Lines (in inches)			Correct Response	Group Response	Majority Error (in inches)
		1	2	3			
1	10	8¾	10	8	2	2	—
2	2	2	1	1½	1	1	—
3	3	3¾	4¼	3	3	1*	+ ¾
4	5	5	4	6½	1	2*	−1.0
5	4	3	5	4	3	3	—
6	3	3¾	4¼	3	3	2*	+1¼
7	8	6¼	8	6¾	2	3*	−1¼
8	5	5	4	6½	1	3*	+1½
9	8	6¼	8	6¾	2	1*	−1¾
10	10	8¾	10	8	2	2	—
11	2	2	1	1½	1	1	—
12	3	3¾	4¼	3	3	1*	+ ¾
13	5	5	4	6½	1	2*	−1.0
14	4	3	5	4	3	3	—
15	3	3¾	4¼	3	3	2*	+1¼
16	8	6¼	8	6¾	2	3*	−1¼
17	5	5	4	6½	1	3*	+1½
18	8	6¼	8	6¾	2	1*	−1¾

* Starred figures designate the erroneous estimates by the majority.

The quantitative results are clear and unambiguous.

1. There was a marked movement toward the majority. One-third of all the estimates in the critical group were errors identical with or in the direction of the distorted estimates of the majority. The significance of this finding becomes clear in the light of the virtual absence of errors in control groups the members of which recorded their estimates in writing. The relevant data of the critical and control groups are summarized in Table 2.

TABLE 2

Distribution of Errors in Experimental and Control Groups

Number of Critical Errors	Critical Group* (N = 50)	Control Group (N = 37)
	F	F
0	13	35
1	4	1
2	5	1
3	6	
4	3	
5	4	
6	1	
7	2	
8	5	
9	3	
10	3	
11	1	
12	0	
Total	50	37
Mean	3.84	0.08

* All errors in the critical group were in the direction of the majority estimates.

2. At the same time the effect of the majority was far from complete. The preponderance of estimates in the critical group (68 per cent) was correct despite the pressure of the majority.

3. We found evidence of extreme individual differences. There were in the critical group subjects who remained independent without exception, and there were those who went nearly all the time with the majority. (The maximum possible number of errors was 12, while the actual range of errors was 0–11.) One-fourth of the critical subjects

was completely independent; at the other extreme, one-third of the group displaced the estimates toward the majority in one-half or more of the trials.

The differences between the critical subjects in their reactions to the given conditions were equally striking. There were subjects who remained completely confident throughout. At the other extreme were those who became disoriented, doubt-ridden, and experienced a powerful impulse not to appear different from the majority.

For purposes of illustration we include a brief description of one independent and one yielding subject.

Independent. After a few trials he appeared puzzled, hesitant. He announced all disagreeing answers in the form of "Three, sir; two, sir"; not so with the unanimous answers. At trial 4 he answered immediately after the first member of the group, shook his head, blinked, and whispered to his neighbor: "Can't help it, that's one." His later answers came in a whispered voice, accompanied by a deprecating smile. At one point he grinned embarrassedly, and whispered explosively to his neighbor: "I always disagree—darn it!" During the questioning, this subject's constant refrain was: "I called them as I saw them, sir." He insisted that his estimates were right without, however, committing himself as to whether the others were wrong, remarking that "that's the way I see them and that's the way they see them." If he had to make a practical decision under similar circumstances, he declared, "I would follow my own view, though part of my reason would tell me that I might be wrong." Immediately following the experiment the majority engaged this subject in a brief discussion. When they pressed him to say whether the entire group was wrong and he alone right, he turned upon them defiantly, exclaiming: "You're *probably* right, but you may be wrong!" To the disclosure of the experiment this subject reacted with the statement that he felt "exultant and relieved," adding, "I do not deny that at times I had the feeling: 'to heck with it, I'll go along with the rest.'"

Yielding. This subject went with the majority in 11 out of 12 trials. He appeared nervous and somewhat confused, but he did not attempt to evade discussion; on the contrary, he was helpful and tried to answer to the best of his ability. He opened the discussion with the statement: "If I'd been the first I probably would have responded differently"; this was his way of stating that he had adopted the majority estimates. The primary factor in his case was loss of confidence. He perceived the majority as a decided group, acting without hesitation: "If they had been doubtful I probably would have changed, but they answered with such confidence." Certain of his errors, he explained, were due to the doubtful nature of the comparisons; in such instances he went with the majority. When the object of the experiment was explained, the subject volunteered: "I suspected about the middle—but tried to push it out of my mind." It is of interest that his suspicion was not able to restore his confidence and diminish the power of the majority. Equally striking is his report that he assumed the experiment to involve an "illusion" to which the others, but not he, were subject. This assumption too did not help to free him; on the contrary, he acted as if his divergence from the majority was a sign of defect. The principal impression this subject produced was of one so caught up by immediate difficulties that he lost clear reasons for his actions, and could make no reasonable decisions.

A First Analysis of Individual Differences

On the basis of the interview data described earlier, we undertook to differentiate and describe the major forms of reaction to the experimental situation, which we shall now briefly summarize.

Among the *independent* subjects we distinguished the following main categories:

(1) Independence based on *confidence* in one's perception and experience. The most striking characteristic of these subjects is the vigor with which they withstand the group opposition. Though they are sensitive to the group, and experience the conflict, they show a resilience in coping with it, which is expressed in their continuing reliance on their perception and the effectiveness with which they shake off the oppressive group opposition.

(2) Quite different are those subjects who are independent and *withdrawn*. These do not react in a spontaneously emotional way, but rather on the basis of explicit principles concerning the necessity of being an individual.

(3) A third group of independent subjects manifest considerable tension and *doubt*, but adhere to their judgments on the basis of a felt necessity to deal adequately with the task.

The following were the main categories of reaction among the *yielding* subjects, or those who went with the majority during one-half or more of the trials.

(1) *Distortion of perception* under the stress of group pressure. In this category belong a very few subjects who yield completely, but are not aware that their estimates have been displaced or distorted by the

majority. These subjects report that they came to perceive the majority estimates as correct.

(2) *Distortion of judgment.* Most submitting subjects belong to this category. The factor of greatest importance in this group is a decision the subjects reach that their perceptions are inaccurate, and that those of the majority are correct. These subjects suffer from primary doubt and lack of confidence; on this basis they feel a strong tendency to join the majority.

(3) *Distortion of action.* The subjects in this group do not suffer a modification of perception nor do they conclude that they are wrong. They yield because of an overmastering need not to appear different from or inferior to others, because of an inability to tolerate the appearance of defectiveness in the eyes of the group. These subjects suppress their observations and voice the majority position with awareness of what they are doing.

The results are sufficient to establish that independence and yielding are not psychologically homogeneous, that submission to group pressure (and freedom from pressure) can be the result of different psychological conditions. It should also be noted that the categories described above, being based exclusively on the subjects' reactions to the experimental conditions, are descriptive, not presuming to explain why a given individual responded in one way rather than another. The further exploration of the basis for the individual differences is a separate task upon which we are now at work.

EXPERIMENTAL VARIATIONS

The results described are clearly a joint function of two broadly different sets of conditions. They are determined first by the specific external conditions, by the particular character of the relation between social evidence and one's own experience. Second, the presence of pronounced individual differences points to the important role of personal factors, of factors connected with the individual's character structure. We reasoned that there are group conditions which would produce independence in all subjects, and that there probably are group conditions which would induce intensified yielding in many, though not in all. Accordingly we followed the procedure of *experimental variation,* systematically altering the quality of social evidence by means of systematic variation of group conditions. Secondly, we deemed it reasonable to assume that behavior under the experimental social pressure is significantly related to certain basic, relatively permanent characteristics of the individual. The investigation has moved in both of these directions. Because the study of the character-qualities which may be functionally connected with independence and yielding is still in progress, we shall limit the present account to a sketch of the representative experimental variations.

THE EFFECT OF NONUNANIMOUS MAJORITIES

Evidence obtained from the basic experiment suggested that the condition of being exposed *alone* to the opposition of a "compact majority" may have played a decisive role in determining the course and strength of the effects observed. Accordingly we undertook to investigate in a series of successive variations the effects of *nonunanimous* majorities. The technical problem of altering the uniformity of a majority is, in terms of our procedure, relatively simple. In most instances we merely directed one or more members of the instructed group to deviate from the majority in prescribed ways. It is obvious that we cannot hope to compare the performance of the same individual in two situations on the assumption that they remain independent of one another. At best we can investigate the effect of an earlier upon a later experimental condition. The comparison of different experimental situations therefore requires the use of different but comparable groups of critical subjects. This is the procedure we have followed. In the variations to be described we have maintained the conditions of the basic experiment (*e.g.*, the sex of the subjects, the size of the majority, the content of the task, and so on) save for the specific factor that was varied. The following were some of the variations we studied:

1. *The presence of a "true partner."* (a) In the midst of the majority were *two* naive, critical subjects. The subjects were separated spatially, being seated in the fourth and eighth positions, respectively. Each therefore heard his judgment confirmed by one other person (provided the other person remained independent), one prior to, the other subsequently to announcing his own judgment. In addition, each experienced a break in the unanimity of the majority. There were six pairs of critical subjects. (b) In a further variation the "partner" to the critical subject was a member of the group who had been instructed to respond correctly throughout. This procedure permits the exact control of the partner's responses. The partner was always seated in the fourth position; he therefore announced his estimates in each case before the critical subject.

The results clearly demonstrate that a disturbance of the unanimity of the majority markedly increased the independence of the critical subjects. The frequency of pro-majority errors dropped to 10.4 per cent of the total number of estimates in variation (a), and to 5.5 per cent in variation (b). These results are to be compared with the frequency of yielding to the unanimous majorities in the basic experiment, which was 32 per cent of the total number of estimates. It is clear that the presence in the field of *one other* individual who responded correctly was sufficient to deplete the power of the majority, and in some cases to destroy it. This finding is all the more striking in the light of other variations which demonstrate the effect of even small minorities provided they are unanimous. Indeed, we have been able to show that a unanimous majority of three is, under the given conditions, far more effective than a majority of eight containing one dissenter. That critical subjects will under these conditions free themselves of a majority of seven and join forces with one other person in the minority is, we believe, a result significant for theory. It points to a fundamental psychological difference between the condition of being alone and having a minimum of human support. It further demonstrates that the effects obtained are not the result of a summation of influences proceeding from each member of the group; it is necessary to conceive the results as being relationally determined.

2. *Withdrawal of a "true partner."* What will be the effect of providing the critical subject with a partner who responds correctly and then withdrawing him? The critical subject started with a partner who responded correctly. The partner was a member of the majority who had been instructed to respond correctly and to "desert" to the majority in the middle of the experiment. This procedure permits the observation of the same subject in the course of transition from one condition to another. The withdrawal of the partner produced a powerful and unexpected result. We had assumed that the critical subject, having gone through the experience of opposing the majority with a minimum of support, would maintain his independence when alone. Contrary to this expectation, we found that the experience of having had and then lost a partner restored the majority effect to its full force, the proportion of errors rising to 28.5 per cent of all judgments, in contrast to the preceding level of 5.5 per cent. Further experimentation is needed to establish whether the critical subjects were responding to the sheer fact of being alone, or to the fact that the partner abandoned them.

3. *Late arrival of a "true partner."* The critical subject started as a minority of one in the midst of a unanimous majority. Toward the

conclusion of the experiment one member of the majority "broke" away and began announcing correct estimates. This procedure, which reverses the order of conditions of the preceding experiment, permits the observation of the transition from being alone to being a member of a pair against a majority. It is obvious that those critical subjects who were independent when alone would continue to be so when joined by another partner. The variation is therefore of significance primarily for those subjects who yielded during the first phase of the experiment. The appearance of the late partner exerts a freeing effect, reducing the level to 8.7 per cent. Those who had previously yielded also became markedly more independent, but not completely so, continuing to yield more than previously independent subjects. The reports of the subjects do not cast much light on the factors responsible for the result. It is our impression that having once committed himself to yielding, the individual finds it difficult and painful to change his direction. To do so is tantamount to a public admission that he has not acted rightly. He therefore follows the precarious course he has already chosen in order to maintain an outward semblance of consistency and conviction.

4. *The presence of a "compromise partner."* The majority was consistently extremist, always matching the standard with the most unequal line. One instructed subject (who, as in the other variations, preceded the critical subject) also responded incorrectly, but his estimates were always intermediate between the truth and the majority position. The critical subject therefore faced an extremist majority whose unanimity was broken by one more moderately erring person. Under these conditions the frequency of errors was reduced but not significantly. However, the lack of unanimity determined in a strikingly consistent way the *direction* of the errors. The preponderance of the errors, 75.7 per cent of the total, was moderate, whereas in a parallel experiment in which the majority was unanimously extremist (*i.e.,* with the "compromise" partner excluded), the incidence of moderate errors was reduced to 42 per cent of the total. As might be expected, in a unanimously moderate majority, the errors of the critical subjects were without exception moderate.

THE ROLE OF MAJORITY SIZE

To gain further understanding of the majority effect, we varied the size of the majority in several different variations. The majorities, which were in each case unanimous, consisted of 16, 8, 4, 3, and 2 persons, respectively. In addition, we studied the limiting case in which the critical subject was opposed by one instructed subject. Table III contains the means and the range of errors under each condition.

TABLE 3

Errors of Critical Subjects with Unanimous Majorities of Different Size

Size of majority	Control	1	2	3	4	8	16
N	37	10	15	10	10	50	12
Mean number of errors	0.08	0.33	1.53	4.0	4.20	3.84	3.75
Range of errors	0–2	0–1	0–5	1–12	0–11	0–11	0–10

With the opposition reduced to one, the majority effect all but disappeared. When the opposition proceeded from a group of two, it produced a measurable though small distortion, the errors being 12.8 per cent of the total number of estimates. The effect appeared in full force with a majority of three. Larger majorities of four, eight, and sixteen did not produce effects greater than a majority of three.

The effect of a majority is often silent, revealing little of its operation to the subject, and often hiding it from the experimenter. To examine the range of effects it is capable of inducing, decisive variations of conditions are necessary. An indication of one effect is furnished by the following variation in which the conditions of the basic experiment were simply reversed. Here the majority, consisting of a group of sixteen, was naive; in the midst of it we placed a single individual who responded wrongly according to instructions. Under these conditions the members of the naive majority reacted to the lone dissenter with amusement and disdain. Contagious laughter spread through the group at the droll minority of one. Of significance is the fact that the members lack awareness that they draw their strength from the majority, and that their reactions would change radically if they faced the dissenter individually. In fact, the attitude of derision in the majority turns to seriousness and increased respect as soon as the minority is increased to three. These observations demonstrate the role of social support as a source of power and stability, in contrast to the preceding investigations which stressed the effects of withdrawal of social support, or to be more exact, the effects of social opposition. Both aspects must be explicitly considered in a unified formulation of the effects of group conditions on the formation and change of judgments.

THE ROLE OF THE STIMULUS-SITUATION

It is obviously not possible to divorce the quality and course of the

group forces which act upon the individual from the specific stimulus-conditions. Of necessity the structure of the situation moulds the
group forces and determines their direction as well as their strength.
Indeed, this was the reason that we took pains in the investigations
described above to center the issue between the individual and the
group around an elementary and fundamental matter of fact. And
there can be no doubt that the resulting reactions were directly a
function of the contradiction between the objectively grasped relations and the majority position.

These general considerations are sufficient to establish the need of
varying the stimulus-conditions and of observing their effect on the
resulting group forces. We are at present conducting a series of investigations in which certain aspects of the stimulus-situation are systematically altered.

One of the dimensions we are examining is the magnitude of discrepancies above the threshold. Our technique permits an easy variation of this factor, since we can increase or decrease at will the deviation of the majority from the given objective conditions. Hitherto
we have studied the effect of a relatively moderate range of discrepancies. Within the limits of our procedure we find that different magni-
tudes of discrepancy produce approximately the same amount of
yielding. However, the quality of yielding alters: as the majority becomes more extreme, there occurs a significant increase in the frequency of "compromise" errors. Further experiments are planned in
which the discrepancies in question will be extremely large and small.

We have also varied systematically the structural clarity of the task,
including in separate variations judgments based on mental standards. In agreement with other investigators, we find that the majority effect grows stronger as the situation diminishes in clarity. Concur-
rently, however, the disturbance of the subjects and the conflict-qual-
ity of the situation decrease markedly. We consider it of significance
that the majority achieves its most pronounced effect when it acts
most painlessly.

SUMMARY

We have investigated the effects upon individuals of majority opinions when the latter were seen to be in a direction contrary to fact. By
means of a simple technique we produced a radical divergence between a majority and a minority, and observed the ways in which individuals coped with the resulting difficulty. Despite the stress of the
given conditions, a substantial proportion of individuals retained

their independence throughout. At the same time a substantial minority yielded, modifying their judgments in accordance with the majority. Independence and yielding are a joint function of the following major factors: (1)The character of the stimulus situation. Variations in structural clarity have a decisive effect: with diminishing clarity of the stimulus-conditions the majority effect increases. (2)The character of the group forces. Individuals are highly sensitive to the structural qualities of group opposition. In particular, we demonstrated the great importance of the factor of unanimity. Also, the majority effect is a function of the size of group opposition. (3)The character of the individual. There were wide, and indeed, striking differences among individuals within the same experimental situation. The hypothesis was proposed that these are functionally dependent on relatively enduring character differences, in particular those pertaining to the person's social relations.

BIBLIOGRAPHY

1. Asch, S. E. Studies in the principles of judgments and attitudes: II. Determination of judgments by group and by ego-standards. *J. soc. Psychol.*, 1940, *12*, 433–465.
2. ——. The doctrine of suggestion, prestige and imitation in social psychology. *Psychol. Rev.*, 1948, *55*, 250–276.
3. Asch., S. E., Block, H., and Hertzman, M. Studies in the principles of judgments and attitudes. I. Two basic principles of judgment. *J. Psychol.* 1938, *5*, 219–251.
4. Coffin, E. E. Some conditions of suggestion and suggestibility: A study of certain attitudinal and situational factors influencing the process of suggestion. *Psychol. Monogr.*, 1941, *53*, No. 4.
5. Lewis, H. B. Studies in the principles of judgments and attitudes: IV. The operation of prestige suggestion. *J. soc. Psychol.*, 1941, *14*, 229–256.
6. Lorge, I. Prestige, suggestion, and attitudes. *J. soc. Psychol.*, 1936, *7*, 386–402.
7. Miller, N. E. and Dollard, J. *Social Learning and Imitation.* New Haven: Yale University Press, 1941.
8. Moore, H. T. The comparative influence of majority and expert opinion. *Amer. J. Psychol.*, 1921, *32*, 16–20.
9. Sherif, M. A study of some social factors in perception. *Arch. Psychol.*, N.Y., 1935, No. 187.
10. Thorndike, E. L. *The Psychology of Wants, Interests, and Attitudes.* New York: D. Appleton-Century Company, Inc., 1935.

MEASURING MOTIVATION IN PHANTASY:
THE ACHIEVEMENT MOTIVE

DAVID C. McCLELLAND

Department of Psychology
Wesleyan University

CONTEMPORARY PSYCHOLOGICAL THEORY stresses the importance of motivation, but provides no satisfactory method for measuring it, at least at the human level. The present research was begun with the idea of remedying this defect. Psychology needs a measure of human motivation and we set out to find one. This report represents a brief description of some of the main findings obtained by our entire research group which has included the following people: David Angell, John W. Atkinson, Robert C. Birney, Russell A. Clark, Gerald A. Friedman, Jules Holzberg, Alvin M. Liberman, Edgar L. Lowell, John Perkins, Thornton B. Roby, Benjamin Simon, Joseph Veroff, and Josef Zatzkis.

In retrospect, at least, our search appears to have been guided by three hypotheses. First, the method of measurement for maximum theoretical usefulness should be at least partially independent of the methods of measurement used to define the other two main variables in contemporary psychological theory, namely, perception and learning. The field of sensation and perception received a great boost when the psychophysical methods were invented or systematized and put into wide use over a century ago. Theoretical development in this field continues to draw heavily for its vitality on the application of these methods. Similarly, learning theory received a great boost around the beginning of the twentieth century when methods for studying problem-solving behavior (*e.g.*, conditioning, serial rote learning, maze learning, and the like) were developed. It seemed logical that motivation in turn would get its greatest lift as a theoretical variable if some methods for measuring it could be developed that were not identical with those that were already in use to measure perception and learning.

The second hypothesis which guided our search was that motives might be best measured in phantasy. There were two bases for this assumption. In the first place, phantasy fulfills our first requirement: it differs quite radically from problem-solving behavior on the one hand and veridical perception on the other. In the second place, clinical psychologists from Freud to Murray have found phantasy of immense practical value in developing the dynamic or motivational theory of personality. In fact, one could argue that the whole psychoanalytic school of thinking is built, operationally speaking, on an analysis of imaginative behavior, whether it be the free association of adults on a psychoanalytic couch or the imaginative play of children.

Our third hypothesis was that motives could be experimentally aroused by manipulating external conditions. Here we were guided by the immensely successful assumption of animal psychologists that motives are states of the organism which can be aroused normally by deprivation. While we felt that the animal model has so far not proven particularly useful in its direct application to measuring motivation at the human level, nevertheless it has proven so theoretically fruitful in the construction of elementary behavior theory that it should not be wholly ignored.

Quite simply then, our problem became one of attempting to arouse human motives experimentally and to measure the effects on phantasy. As a preliminary check we decided to test one of our basic hypotheses, namely, that phantasy would be sensitive to changes in conditions which everyone would agree were motivating. So Atkinson and McClelland conducted and reported [2] an experiment in which they demonstrated that human subjects deprived of food for one, four, and sixteen hours wrote brief imaginative stories which changed in a number of important ways as hunger increased. From the shifts in the content of the stories they were able to develop a composite score which gave a rough idea of how long the subjects had been without food. This preliminary evidence together with earlier work done by Sanford [9] seemed to clear the track for work on what became the main objective of the study, namely, the measurement of the strength of the achievement motive in phantasy.

PROCEDURE

How could the achievement motive be experimentally aroused in human subjects? This was our first problem. Fortunately, there are several standard laboratory procedures for producing achievement orientation which are usually lumped together under the heading of "ego-involvement." They have in common the attempt to orient the subjects around success in some task which is or should be of great importance to them. In our case, we decided to define certain tasks as achievement-related for the subjects and to control their experiences of success or failure on these tasks. In this way we hoped to be able to control the intensity of the achievement motive aroused in various groups of subjects and to measure the effects of the different intensities on subsequent imaginative behavior. Specifically, we worked finally with six different "arousal conditions": (1) a *relaxed* condition in which the tasks the subjects performed were introduced casually as part of the blind exploration of some graduate students into a new problem, (2) a *neutral* condition in which the tasks were seriously introduced as ones on which the department of psychology wanted some norms, (3) an *ego-involved* condition in which the tasks were described as measures of intelligence and leadership capacity, (4) a *success* condition in which the subjects were allowed to succeed on the ego-involved tasks, (5) a *failure* condition in which the subjects were caused to fail on the ego-involved tasks, and (6) a *success-failure* condition in which the subjects first succeeded and then failed on the ego-involved tasks. In this way we attempted to explore the effect of the entire range of achievement-related experiences on imaginative behavior, although in the end our primary attention focused on the difference between the relaxed and ego-involved orientations rather than on the specific effects of success and failure.

How were we to measure the effects of these various arousal conditions on phantasy? Since our design calls for the scoring of a large number of records from sizable groups of subjects, we necessarily had to eliminate the type of elaborate phantasy production normally used by clinical psychologists. Instead we decided in favor of getting small, relatively standardized samples of imaginative behavior from each subject. In time our routine procedure involved asking a group of subjects to write brief five-minute stories in response to each of four pictures exposed for twenty seconds on a screen in front of the group. The stories were written around the following four questions spaced on an answer sheet:

What is happening?
What has led up to this situation?
What is being thought?
What will happen?

The instructions given were the standard ones for the Thematic Apperception Test. Their general tone is to urge the subject to be as creative as possible and not to think in terms of right and wrong answers. There were four slides in all, two of which came from the Murray Thematic Apperception Test and two of which were made up especially for this test. They suggested respectively a work situation (two men working at a machine), a study situation (a boy seated at a desk with a book in front of him), a father-son situation (TAT 7BM), and a young boy possibly dreaming of the future (TAT 8BM). Considerable work has been done by Atkinson [1] with slides suggestive of other situations, but most of the work reported is based on these four which represent an attempt to sample the range of achievement-related activities.

The stories obtained by this method average about ninety words in length. How are they to be scored? Again we had to eliminate complex scoring systems and in the end hit upon the scheme of analyzing the stories in terms of the action sequence suggested by the questions on the answer sheet. That is, a plot or story usually has a beginning (or instigation), a middle (containing instrumental acts and obstacles), and an end (containing goal responses). Thus the categories we finally chose to score were aspects of the instigation action or problem-solving sequence commonly used as a model in contemporary learning theory. They included the following (arranged in accordance with the time order in which they normally appear in a story): statements of need or wish, instrumental activities, blocks or obstacles either internal or external in nature, anticipations of the outcome, positive or negative affect accompanying success or failure in reaching a goal, and the like. Details about scoring definitions and other aspects of the procedure can be found either in the published preliminary report by McClelland, Clark, Roby, and Atkinson [6] or in the monograph now in preparation by McClelland, Atkinson, Clark, and Lowell [5]. This scoring system is general enough to fit an action sequence centered around any motive and was also used in scoring for hunger in the Atkinson and McClelland study [2] previously mentioned. The critical problem is that of finding a scoring definition for deciding whether statements are related to the motive in question—in the present instance, the achievement motive. What constitutes achievement imagery? This presented many serious and complicated problems but in the end we were able to formulate a definition which stated that any imagery (*e.g.*, statement in the story) which suggests *competition with a standard* is achievement related. In its simplest terms this means that someone in the story is *trying to do better* in relation to some achievement goal such as doing a better job or getting ahead in the world.

RESULTS

METHODOLOGICAL

Scoring the stories for various achievement-related categories as finally defined is highly reliable. After training, two judges working together agreed on 91 per cent of the categories on two successive scorings of the same records. The agreement on individual n Achievement (need for Achievement) scores derived from summation of these categories is even higher. The correlation is .95 between n Achievement scores obtained on two different occasions by two judges working together. One judge, after experience with the system for three days, has obtained a correlation of .92 between his scores and those obtained by another judge more experienced with the system. Furthermore, after practice the system can be applied rapidly; it takes from three to five minutes on the average to score the four stories obtained for a given individual.

Many significant differences in the scoring categories were produced by the various methods of arousing the achievement motive. In general, there were large and significant increases in the number of subjects and number of stories showing achievement-related imagery as the experiences the subjects had just had became more achievement-oriented. For the sake of simplicity, we will disregard specific differences in the effects of success and failure and turn our attention only to the derivation of an over-all index of the strength of an individual's achievement motive, an index which we refer to as his n Achievement score, following Murray's convention [8]. First, we noted all those characteristics such as stated need for achievement, anticipation of success and failure, *etc.*, which increased significantly from a lower to a higher state of achievement arousal; then we argued that the number of those characteristics in the stories written by a subject under normal or non-ego-involved conditions would indicate the normal strength of his concern for achievement. That is, we could look for the characteristics in a person's stories which we had found to be sensitive to experimental changes in achievement orientation, sum them up, and derive an over-all n Achievement score for that individual.

One of our first concerns was to see whether or not a measure derived in this way was applicable to groups of persons other than the male college students who had been the subjects in the various arousal conditions. To test the generality of the n Achievement measure, Veroff [10] compared the stories written by high school students, both boys and girls, after neutral and ego-involving experiences. He found that the high school boys, representing a much larger segment of the population than our college men, also showed a significant over-all increase in mean n Achievement score from the neutral to the ego-involving condition. This strongly suggests that the characteristics scored are not peculiar to the highly selected portion of the population represented in college. In the second place, Veroff found no significant change in n Achievement score for girls following ego-involvement. There are many interesting explanations for this finding, but the conclusion it leads to here is that the method cannot be applied to women without some additional assumptions. Finally, we went outside our culture altogether and compared the stories written by Navaho high-school-age males under neutral and ego-involving conditions, and found once again that even in this different culture, our scoring system was applicable and showed a significant increase in mean n Achievement score from a condition of low achievement arousal to one of higher achievement arousal.

Our next concern was with the reliability of a person's n Achievement score. In other words, what are the chances that he will get the same or a similar score on two different occasions? Our reliabilities are on the whole low. A test-retest correlation for two three-picture measures taken a week apart was only .22 (not significant with N = 40). However, the two measures agreed significantly (72.5 per cent) in placing subjects above or below the mean on the two occasions, and the split-half reliability for a six- or eight-picture test runs over .70 (corrected for halving the test). On the whole, in the present state of development, the n Achievement measure appears adequate for classifying individuals into high and low achievement groups, or at the most into high, middle, and low achievement groups, but not for finer discriminations or for individual testing purposes. It is always possible, of course, that with a projective instrument of this sort high test-retest reliabilities cannot be obtained because the subject is "spoiled" by having taken such a test once previously. This may mean that the measure is more valid in the sense of being related to other types of behavior than it is reliable in the sense of being related to itself as obtained on a second occasion.

RELATION OF N ACHIEVEMENT SCORE TO OTHER KINDS OF BEHAVIOR

While our method of deriving the n Achievement score from differences in achievement arousal conditions gives the measure a kind of validity, the skeptical observer would still want to know more. In particular, is our presumed measure of motive strength related to other kinds of behavior in ways that on a theoretical or common-sense basis we would expect motivation to be related? For this reason, much of our energy has gone into exploring the relation of the n Achievement score to other variables. Chief among these are performance and learning. On theoretical, experimental, and common-sense grounds one would expect that more highly motivated subjects would, at least under cerain circumstances, perform more quickly, and, under certain others, learn more efficiently than poorly motivated subjects. Thus, if our n Achievement score is an index of the strength of the achievement motive in individuals, we should be able to demonstrate that people with high n Achievement scores show evidence of better learning and performance. Of the several studies designed to test this hypothesis, the one by Lowell [4] is perhaps the most definitive. He first administered a three-picture form of the TAT n Achievement Test to a group of male college students and then asked them to work on a twenty-minute Scrambled Words test which required them to rearrange a nonsense series of letters (for example, WTSE) until they had constructed a meaningful word (e.g., WEST). The test was arranged in such a way that the subjects worked for two minutes on each of ten different pages of Scrambled Words, which were randomized from subject to subject to equate for difficulties. One week later Lowell administered to the same group of subjects another set of three TAT pictures and asked them to work on solving some simple addition problems for ten minutes. The n Achievement score for an individual was obtained in the usual manner by summing the significant characteristics in the stories obtained from all six pictures on the two different occasions. Figure 1 summarizes how groups of subjects with high and low n Achievement scores performed in different periods of the scrambled words task.

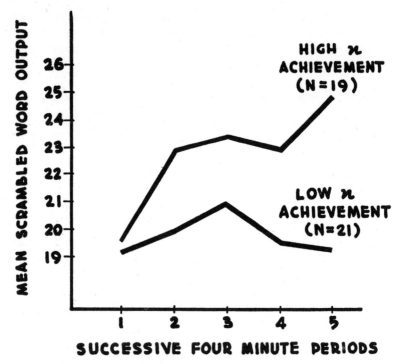

Figure 1. Mean output of scrambled words for subjects above and below the mean in n Achievement score in successive four-minute periods.

The rather regular increases in performance from the first to the fifth four-minute period for the high n Achievement subjects strongly suggest a learning curve, while variations in output for the low n Achievement subjects display no consistent trend. The high need group shows a mean gain in output from the first to the last period of 5.32 words, whereas the low need group shows a gain of only .43 words, a difference in gain of 4.89 words which is well beyond the 1 per cent level (t = 3.76). In short, our expectations are confirmed:

there is definite and statistically significant evidence for superior learning in the high as compared with the low n Achievement group.

Figure 2 shows the results for the addition task. Here it is clear that the high n Achievement subjects solved more problems at every point in the test so that their over-all output is significantly greater than for the low n Achievement subjects ($t = 2.40$, $P < .05$).

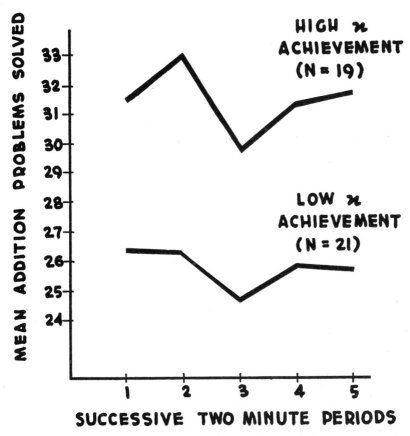

Figure 2. Mean output of addition problems solved by subjects above and below the mean n Achievement score in successive two-minute periods.

The difference in the findings reported in Figures 1 and 2 is important. Presumably the reason why the more highly motivated subjects showed learning in connection with the Scrambled Word task is because this task is sufficiently complex for the subjects to find new and better ways of performing at it as they practice it. The Additions task, on the other hand, is so simple that presumably subjects are about at their maximum level of efficiency when they begin; no new methods of adding are likely to be discovered in the course of a ten-minute task. Thus we can argue that where learning is possible in a complex task, the highly motivated subjects will show it; where it is not possible or at least not likely in a very simple task, high n Achievement produces faster performance but not learning. Both of these findings support the hypothesis that the n Achievement score is measuring motivational strength.

Another psychological variable to which n Achievement should be related is level of aspiration. Atkinson conducted a study [1] in which he obtained a four-picture measure of n Achievement on the day of a final examination in a course. He also asked the subjects to report the grade they *expected* to make on the examination on the back of the story form. The raw correlation between n Achievement score and *expected* examination grade was .24, which falls short of significance with a sample of thirty-eight subjects. Since asking the question in terms of expectancy calls for a reality estimate, he sought to eliminate some of the reality determinants of the level of aspiration by selecting from the thirty-eight subjects those twenty-three who, on the basis of past experience, might have been uncertain as to what to expect. The twenty-three consisted of those men who stood in one third of the distribution of general averages and a different third of the distribution of grades in this particular course. For these subjects the correlation between n Achievement score and level of aspiration was .45, which is significant at less than the .05 level. In other words, when the reality determinants of an aspiration judgment are ambiguous or in conflict, then motivation enters more largely into the determination of aspiration. This, too, confirms the hypothesis that the n Achievement score is a measure of motivational strength.

Motivation should also have some demonstrable connection with perception and memory. Out of several experiments done in this field, two are particularly striking and confirm each other. The first is the one reported by McClelland and Liberman [7] on the effect of n Achievement on the recognition of need-related words. Having previously obtained n Achievement scores on their subjects, they measured how quickly a subject could recognize achievement-related, security-related, and neutral words when they were exposed repeatedly at increasing illuminations for only .01 second. They found that subjects with high n Achievement scores were able to recognize positive achievement words like *success* and *strive* faster than subjects with low n Achievement scores. When they obtained a somewhat more stable measure of n Achievement by combining the score obtained from imagination with one based on a performance task to produce an over-all index of n Achievement rank, they were able to make a finer analysis of the data. That is, they found that subjects in the lowest third of the distribution of n Achievement ranks showed no particular trend with respect to recognizing either positive achievement words or negative achievement words like *unable* and *failure*. The subjects in the middle third of the distribution, however, showed a *slower* recognition time for the negative achievement words than did either the low or high thirds, and the high n Achievement third showed a much *faster* recognition of the positive achievement words than did either the middle or low thirds. In short, it looked as if, as n Achievement increased in intensity, it tended to orient subjects first around avoiding failure (decreased sensitivity to failure words) and then around attaining success (increased sensitivity to success words). Some further evidence that the middle n Achievement subjects were security-minded lay in the fact that they were also quicker at recognizing security-related words like *friend* or *comfort*. McClelland and Liberman concluded that "the group of subjects with moderate n Achievement are security-minded and chiefly concerned with avoiding failure, or with achieving a minimal level of aspiration, whereas the group of subjects with high n Achievement are concerned more directly with achieving success or attaining a maximum level of aspiration." [7, p. 251].

These findings were confirmed in a study reported by Atkinson [1] on the memory for completed and incompleted tasks. In addition to having subjects who could be classified low, moderate, or high with respect to n Achievement on the basis of their stories, he had three types of test situations: (a) a relaxed orientation in which the experimenter was introduced quite informally as a "graduate student who wants to try out some tasks"; (b) a task orientation in which the experimeter simply directed the students' attention to how the tasks were to be performed without any effort to create an experimental atmosphere; and (c) an ego orientation in which the experimenter described the tasks as being measures of intellectual ability, leadership, *etc.,* and urged the students to do their best. Atkinson found in line with work previously reported that the number of *completed* tasks recalled, irrespective of motivation, increased from relaxed to task to ego orientation. But when a breakdown was made according to n Achievement score, he found strikingly opposite trends for the subjects in the high and middle thirds of the n Achievement distribution with respect to the incompleted tasks. For the subjects with high n Achievement there was a regular *increase* in the number of incompleted tasks recalled, whereas for the subjects with moderate n Achievement there was a regular *decrease* in the number of incompleted tasks recalled. For the subjects with lowest n Achievement there was no trend in the number of incompleted tasks recalled. In short, the data look very much like those obtained with perception. The subjects with moderate n Achievement are defensive; they appear to regard their inability to complete a task as a failure as they become more ego-oriented, and consequently attempt to avoid remembering it. Subjects with high n Achievement, however, apparently tend to regard their incompleted tasks as *challenges* which they remember better as the situation becomes more ego-oriented, presumably in order to complete them. Both of these studies strongly suggest that there are at least two kinds of achievement motivation, one of which appears to be oriented around avoiding failure and the other around the more positive goal of attaining success. It cannot be stated, of course, which type of motivation is more efficient, since either an excessive concern with success or with avoiding failure may be maladaptive, depending on the requirements of the situation.

Having demonstrated the relation of our measure to important behavior variables, we come to the more traditional validity checks. Is the n Achievement score related in any significant way to how much achievement "drive" a person is judged to have either by himself or by a clinician after careful study? Apparently not. There is no significant relationship between imaginative n Achievement score and either a psychiatrist's judgment of n Achievement or a person's own judgment of his n Achievement intensity. This is not as disturbing as it might at first seem to be. If ratings of motivational strength were adequate measures of motivation (*e.g.*, were significantly related to performance, level of aspiration, *etc.*), there would be no need to develop any such elaborate system as this for measuring motivation. The fact of the matter is that such judgments must necessarily be complexly determined. When a psychiatrist, for example, attempts to estimate the strength of an individual's achievement motive he must take into account a great many factors—the person's actual performance, his goals in life at least as they are consciously realized, his relation to his father, *etc.* The final rating, whether it be the psychiatrist's' or the person's own, represents a synthesis or integration of these many factors and is not therefore, at least in the theoretical sense, "pure." That is, it does not represent any one aspect of personality but is a judgment involving many. It was just to avoid such complexly determined measures of motivation that the present research was undertaken.

The n Achievement score has been related to many other variables besides those so far reported, but the relationships obtained are either so complex or so tentative that they cannot be reported in any detail here. For example, we have obtained highly significant correlations between n Achievement scores and college grades on two occasions and an insignificant correlation on another occasion. The problem obviously needs further exploration. Similarly we have explored the relation of n Achievement score to other projective tests, namely, the Sentence Completion Test and the Rorschach, in both cases with some interesting but not completely comprehensible results. We have found that n Achievement score is significantly related to the kinds of linguistic categories that a person uses in attempting to express himself, at least in an achievement-related situation, and so forth. Rather than dwell on any of these findings, let us turn to our attempts to explore the origins of n Achievement, assuming for the moment that our measure of it is valid.

The first study in this area was a cross-cultural one performed by Friedman [3]. Quite surprisingly, he found that he could apply the n Achievement scoring system developed on male American college students to folk tales collected from eight different American Indian cultures. By selecting twelve such tales from each of the cultures and using the standard scoring system, he found he could obtain an over-all achievement index for each of the cultures which represented the amount of achievement-related imagery in the stories in his sample. He then correlated this index with ratings which had been made independently of data in the Yale cross-cultural files for a study by Whiting and Child on various child-rearing practices in the eight cultures. On theoretical grounds we predicted that n Achievement scores would be highly related to the amount of stress in the culture which was placed on independence training. Friedman found a relationship that was significant well beyond the 1 per cent level even with only eight cases, indicating that severity of independence training in childhood is highly correlated with the amount of achievement imagery in the folk tales current in a culture. This supports the hypothesis that achievement motivation develops out of parents' concern that children "stand on their own feet" rather early in life and learn to do things for themselves.

A more direct confirmation of this hypothesis was obtained by correlating n Achievement scores of male American college students with their own ratings of their parents' behavior toward them on several different dimensions, namely, Democratic-autocratic, Acceptance-rejection, Indulgence, and Casualness. The correlation for the Acceptance-rejection dimension was significant, being .49 for the father, .33 for the mother, and .48 for both parents combined. In other words, the higher the n Achievement score the more the student tended to rate both parents, but particularly the father, rejectant. Again this suggests that the son was either forced to stand on his own feet by his parents or *thought* he was forced to stand on his own feet (and therefore "rejected"). The sons were also asked to rate their parents on several different personality characteristics including the following: friendly, helpful, domineering, selfish, successful, clever, self-confident. Table 1 shows the results when the personality characteristics were grouped according to similarity.

TABLE 1

Correlations between n Achievement score and
personality traits attributed to parents (N = 30)

	Father	Mother	Combined
1. Friendly–Helpful	— .56	— .39	— .57
2. Domineering–Selfish	.10	.14	.14
3. Successful–Clever–Self-confident	— .37	— .41	— .44

Correlations of .36 and .46 are significant at the 5% and 1% levels respectively.

Apparently, again, the sons who rated their parents as unfriendly, unhelpful, and unsuccessful tended to have higher n Achievement scores. In reverse, the sons who found their parents (especially their fathers) to be helpful, nurturent, friendly, and successful tended to have low n Achievement scores. Again this makes theoretical sense. Apparently n Achievement develops out of an insistence on independence, or doing things for oneself which is interpreted by sons later on during college as rejection and unfriendliness. Contrariwise, boys who are greatly helped by clever fathers and mothers never get a chance to want to achieve by themselves. There are other bits of evidence in our data on this general point, but they all support the same conclusion: n Achievement score is significantly related to severity of independence training in childhood.

CONCLUSIONS

The general outcome of our research to date may be summarized briefly as follows:

(1) It has demonstrated the great potentiality of an n Achievement score based on phantasy as a measure of the achievement motivation of individuals irrespective of their cultural background.

(2) By providing an independent measure of motivation, it has opened up great new areas for further research, such as the relation between achievement motivation and school grades.

(3) It has demonstrated that the method of deriving a measure of motivational strength from experimentally produced changes in phantasy is a practical one which could theoretically be applied to the measurement of any motive.

(4) It has led us to question seriously prevailing theories of motivation and to attempt a revision of those theories, which is to be elaborated along with many more detailed research findings in a monograph now in preparation [5].

BIBLIOGRAPHY

1. Atkinson, J. W. The projective measurement of achievement motivation. Unpublished Ph.D. Thesis, Univ. Mich., 1950.
2. Atkinson, J. W. and McClelland, D. C. The projective expression of needs. II. The effect of different intensities of the hunger drive on thematic apperception. *J. exp. Psychol.*, 1948, *38*, 643–658.
3. Friedman, G. A. A cross-cultural study of the relationship between independence training and n Achievement as revealed by mythology. Unpublished A.B. Thesis, Harvard Univ., 1950.
4. Lowell, E. L. A methodological study of projectively measured achievement motivation. Unpublished M.A. Thesis, Wesleyan Univ., 1950.
5. McClelland, D. C., Atkinson, J. W., Clark, R. A. and Lowell, E. L. The achievement motive. Unpublished manuscript.
6. McClelland, D. C., Clark, R. A., Roby, T. B., and Atkinson, J. W. The projective expression of needs. IV. The effect of the need for achievement on thematic apperception. *J. exp. Psychol.*, 1949, *39*, 242–255.
7. McClelland, D. C. and Liberman, A. M. The effect of need for achievement on recognition of need-related words. *J. Personality*, 1949, *18*, 236–251.
8. Murray, H. A. *Explorations in Personality*. New York: Oxford Univ. Press, 1938.
9. Sanford, R. N. The effects of abstinence from food upon imaginal processes: a further experiment. *J. Psychol.*, 1937, *3*, 145–159.
10. Veroff, J. A projective measure of the achievement motivation of adolescent males and females. Unpublished. A.B. Thesis, Wesleyan Univ., 1950.

VERBAL BEHAVIOR IN RELATION TO
REASONING AND VALUES

CHARLES N. COFER

Department of Psychology
University of Maryland

IT HAS LONG BEEN HELD that the availability of symbolic processes in the human organism is a principal factor which accounts for some of the other differences between human and infra-human animals. Perhaps the most readily apparent relationship between symbolic factors and other behavioral functions is seen in the area of human reasoning, thinking and problem solving. D. M. Johnson [7] has recently pointed out that "The solution of complex problems, especially by human beings, often includes symbolic processes, such as the formation and use of verbal and numerical concepts, hypotheses, and plans of action. . . ." (p. 297). Other writers have been even more insistent on the essentiality of symbolic processes to such behavioral functions. Krout [9], for example, holds that "Language is the primordial stuff of mental behavior. Man can no more get away from language, once trained in its use, than he can dismiss his memories." Dewey and Bentley [2] seem to quote with approval the following statement by the philosopher, Charles Pierce: ". . . it is wrong to say that a good language is important to good thought, merely; for it is of the essence of it." Anthropological writers, like Lee [10], Thompson [14] and Whorf [15], likewise insist that the form and structure of a people's language determine in basic ways the nature of their concepts and their thinking.

Despite these and other assertions that symbolic processes, including language, may well be essential to human thinking, reasoning, and problem solving, there is relatively little experimentally obtained evidence to support them. Reviews of relevant literature, such as may be found in Woodworth [16], D. M. Johnson [7], Gibson and McGarvey [4] and the like seldom cite an investigation the design of which permits the isolation of language functions in reasoning activities. It has therefore seemed important to explore, in a series of studies, the importance of language processes in certain kinds of human reasoning situations and the way in which such processes function. A few studies of this type will be reported in this chapter. It may also be pointed out that, in addition to their concern with the language variable, these studies likewise may contribute to the more general problems of transfer of training and set, as they enter into the matter of human reasoning, problem solving, and thinking.

The general hypothesis that the content and structure of a language system (subject to variation among different individuals even within the same culture) may direct and limit the functions of problem solving, reasoning, and thinking bears some resemblance to a very general issue in individual psychology. This issue may be stated very briefly as follows. Human behavior shows a sufficient consistency and predictability under diverse situational circumstances and over long enough periods of time as to suggest that there are enduring properties of human organisms which mediate this consistency and make prediction possible. This is an obvious statement, but the identification and description of the properties (which, for the most part, must be constructs) in standard terms has not progressed very far, nor is there much agreement among theorists and investigators concerning such constructural properties as have been suggested. A number of terms in current use refer to constructs which have been assigned this function: habit, set, interest, value, attitude, belief, trait, drive, need, purpose, wish are some of the terms which have been so used.

The mechanisms by which such constructs as have been proposed perform their mediating functions have been little explored except in a few limited situations. It seems therefore that further work on this problem would be most desirable.

Now it is just possible that the mediating role of language processes suggested above for thinking and reasoning functions may be similar to the mediating role of other variables in this more general sense. Therefore, the study of language processes in reasoning may serve as a prototype of mediating processes in general. And, further, it is just possible that language processes may operate in a mediating role in behavioral functions other than reasoning. Some plausibility may attend this last statement, in view of the large number of other functions which are known to bear relationships of association to various language characteristics [see 13, 5, 8]. Hence, as a second general problem we may begin to explore the relationships between language functions and a personality construct (value) in an effort to determine the validity of this approach.

The foregoing paragraphs provide a general introduction to the specific research projects to be described in this chapter. The first group of studies is concerned with language factors and reasoning and the second group deals with value. Dr. A. J. Judson performed the first group of studies and Dr. M. D. Havron the second group.

INVESTIGATIONS OF REASONING

In the first study, the problem was to determine whether increasing the strength or the availability of relevant verbal responses would facilitate solution of a problem. Guetzkow's [6] group form of the Maier two-string problem was used as the problem task. The problem proposed is that two strings are suspended from the ceiling and the subject is to tie them together. The strings, however, are too short for the subject to grasp one, walk to the other one and tie the two together. There are several possible solutions to this problem, among which are the following: (1) to tie one string to an object nearly midway between the two, thus anchoring it while the other one is being obtained; (2) to hold one string in one hand while the subject "fishes" with an elongated object for the other; (3) to increase the length of one string; (4) to tie a heavy object to one string and then to set it in motion like a pendulum; the swinging string is caught while the subject holds the other one.

In this experiment it was decided to attempt to increase the proportion of pendulum solutions by means of pre-problem verbal experience. To provide this verbal experience three groups of subjects were asked during five successive class hours to learn eight five-word lists of meaningful words. One trial was given for each list on each day, and during the sixth class period the subjects were asked to solve the two-string problem. A fourth group (group D) received no verbal practice but did take the two-string test. The verbal experience provided the other three groups was identical except that in group A the words *rope, swing,* and *pendulum* occurred together in one list; in group B *rope* was associated with *hemp* and *twine,* but *swing* and *pendulum* did not occur in any list; and in group C *swing* was associated with *band* and *time, pendulum* with *clock,* and *rope* with *hemp* and *twine* in different lists. Theoretically, after this training, the subjects of group A on seeing the strings of the problem would have more available than would groups B and C the words *pendulum* and *swing* because of generalization [1] from *rope* to *string* and because of the specific associations to *rope* learned in the list. Therefore, group A should produce more pendulum solutions than the other groups.

The results support these expectations for male subjects. Sixty-eight per cent of the males of group A gave pendulum solutions as opposed to 58 per cent of group B, 47 per cent of group C, and 52 per cent of group D. The experiment was repeated with minor variations of method, and essentially the same results were obtained. This time 74 per cent of the males of group A, 56 per cent of group B, and 61 per cent of group C provided pendulum solutions. In each experiment, statistically significant differences were obtained between the results for group A and all other groups combined, and between group A and each other group with the exception of group B in the first experiment and of group C in the replication. There were no significant differences among these groups in the number of solutions other than the pendulum solution that appeared. Female subjects, however, provided relatively few pendulum solutions and the differences among the groups for females were not significant.

The study provides some confirmation for the hypothesis that strengthening verbal responses will affect problem solution. A second study was performed to determine whether verbal associations already in existence would similarly affect problem solution.

In this second study, twenty subjects were asked, individually, to give ten words in free association to each of ten stimulus words. Six weeks later each subject was recalled and went through the following procedure. First, he was given four words, presented individually on cards, and was asked to select the "correct" one. One of the four words was his first association given six weeks before to one of the stimulus words, and this one was the "correct" word. The other three words were new ones, *i.e.,* they had not appeared in the experiment before. After the subject made his selection, the experimenter said right or wrong as necessary, and this process was continued until the subject had made a correct choice in five consecutive trials. Following this, another set of four words was presented, consisting of three new words and another word from the associative chain. This time the subject was given only one trial, and after his choice another set of four words was presented. This was continued until all words of an association chain had been presented in combination with new words. This procedure will be clarified by an example. Suppose that, to the stimulus words *rose, sorrow* and *melody,* the subject has given the following associations:

Rose: flower, thorn, bush, stem, apple, tree, orange, lemon, grape-fruit, watermelon
Sorrow: tears, dry, weep, relax, sleep, snare, eyelid, eyebrow, ear, hear
Melody: tune, music, note, staff, sharp, flat, clef, range, gun, elevation

In the first test situation, *flower* is presented together with three new words. After the subject has learned that *flower* is the "correct" word, *thorn* is presented with three new words; then *bush,* and so on through *watermelon.* In none of these trials after he has learned that *flower* is correct is the subject told that his choice is right or wrong, and he is given but one trial on each set of words following the one including *flower.* Since these ten words were given in free association they presumably are interlinked associatively; the reinforcement of *flower* in the first test situation should therefore spread to the other words, and the associated words should be chosen more often as "correct" in the test trials than nonassociated words. As a control, each subject was also asked to learn that another word in a group of four (say, *tears*) was correct, and he was then given a number of test situations in each of which a word from a different associative chain (*e.g., music, note, staff,* etc.), was presented with three others. If the fact of associative linkage is important to performance in these problem situations, the associated words in this control situation should not be as frequently chosen as the words in the experimental situation.

The results obtained confirmed these expectations. Significantly more associated words were chosen in the tests when they were drawn from the same chain as was the word learned to be correct, than when they were not drawn from the chain to which the word learned to be correct was taken. This then suggests that extant verbal associative relationships may determine choice in simple verbal problems through transfer.

An important aspect of the process of reasoning, according to several writers, is set or direction. Studies were performed to determine whether, in the situations employed, the effects ordinarily attributed to these factors could be produced by language processes.

As a task for the study of this problem, a test was devised each item of which was capable of two correct answers. Consider the following item:

SKYSCRAPER TEMPLE CATHEDRAL PRAYER

The words in this item may be classified into two groups of three words each, one group being a "building" category and the other a "religion" category. If the subject is asked which one of the four words should be *excluded,* what factors in the situation will determine the set or the direction which will lead him to choose one as "not belonging?" We have postulated that the activation of a verbal response system will provide this "set" or "direction" and that the first unambiguous stimulus to occur will determine the course of problem solution through the activation of that verbal response system to which it is related.

To test this hypothesis, two forms of the same test were constructed. Each form consisted of forty-five items of the above type. Forms A and B were identical, save for twelve items distributed through the test. The word order in these twelve items was varied between Forms A and B. For example, if the order of the above example was used for Form A, the positions of the words PRAYER and SKYSCRAPER would be switched in Form B. As a control to obviate position preference development, the correct responses in the other thirty-three items were distributed through all four of the positions in the items.

Form A was administered to one group of sixty-five subjects and Form B to another group. The subjects were asked "to select the word that doesn't belong" in each item, to work rapidly and not to return to an item after it was finished. The results showed that for the thirty-three items which were unchanged between Forms A and B there were no significant differences in response distribution for any item in the two groups. For the twelve changed items, however, response distribution shifted significantly in nine instances. Thus, for example, in the above illustration, PRAYER would be chosen more frequently than SKYSCRAPER as the word which does not belong, but the reversal of the positions of these two words would lead to a greater frequency of choice of SKYSCRAPER than of PRAYER.

To explore this matter further, another study was performed in which a test consisting of forty-eight items was used. Twelve forms of this test were constructed, so that the effect of rotating the two unambiguous words through every possible position in the word groups could be studied. Six arrangements for the item given above, according to this scheme, would be:

SKYSCRAPER TEMPLE CATHEDRAL PRAYER
SKYSCRAPER TEMPLE PRAYER CATHEDRAL
SKYSCRAPER PRAYER TEMPLE CATHEDRAL
TEMPLE SKYSCRAPER PRAYER CATHEDRAL
TEMPLE CATHEDRAL SKYSCRAPER PRAYER
TEMPLE SKYSCRAPER CATHEDRAL PRAYER

The other six arrangements were identical with those above, except that PRAYER preceded SKYSCRAPER in each arrangement.

The twelve forms of this test were given to twelve groups of about twenty-five subjects each. Four statements summarize the statistically significant results: (1) As the first unambiguous word moved from the first to the third position in the series, it tended increasingly to be chosen as the word that did not belong, but it was chosen, even so, less frequently than was the second unambiguous word (2). As the second unambiguous word moved from the fourth position to the second position in the group, it tended to be chosen with decreasing frequency as the word that did not belong, but it was still chosen more frequently than the first unambiguous word (3). The foregoing two statements describe the results for each unambiguous word when it was either the first or second such word (4). When two ambiguous words stood between the two unambiguous words, the second unambiguous word was chosen as not belonging much more frequently than the first; this difference was less marked when one ambiguous word stood between the two and was still less marked but still present when the two were adjacent to each other.

These results seem clearly to indicate that, in simple verbal problems such as those used here, the determination of the direction of problem solution is a function of which unambiguous stimulus is first to be active. We further interpret these findings to mean that such a stimulus functions through its activation of a verbal response system to which it is related. As a further bit of evidence that, in this situation, verbal response systems may determine problem solution, we may cite results from another portion of the investigations just described.

The results obtained in word-recognition time studies by Postman, Bruner & McGinnies [12] and for association time by McGinnies [11] suggest that values, such as those measured by the Allport-Vernon Study of Values, are closely associated with verbal response systems. If this is so, it should be possible to counteract the stimulus activation of response systems by using subjects who have verbal response systems in a state of great strength, for example, those who have strong values. To test this possibility, twelve items were used, within the larger test of forty-eight items, which had a "religion" solution and a "non-religion" solution. The unambiguous words in these items were rotated through the word positions in the items in the manner described above. This test was given to subjects who were classed as "religious" and "nonreligious" by means of a measure to be described in the next section, and whose degree of religious observance was measured by means of a simple questionnaire. The religious subjects excluded the nonreligious word as not belonging in two of the religion items to a degree significantly greater than did the nonreligious subjects. On the thirty-six items not involving a religion solution, there were no significant differences in choice between the religious and nonreligious subjects. When degree of religious observance was studied in relation to performance, four of the religious items were significantly differently answered by religious subjects as compared to the less religious subjects, but there were no differences on the control items. These results tend to indicate that when a strong response system is present in the subject, it may counteract stimulus activation of response systems which would otherwise be dominant.

The foregoing studies are considered to be essentially exploratory, but they seem to indicate that there is some plausibility in the statement that verbal response systems or language factors may influence the course of human problem solving, reasoning, and thinking.

INVESTIGATIONS OF VALUE

In the latter part of the preceding section, it was mentioned that values, as measured by the Allport-Vernon Study of Values, seem to be closely associated with verbal response systems. Several studies were executed to explore this relationship further.

The first was an attempt to measure values by means of a simple word-association technique. If values are related to verbal response systems, it should be possible to measure them by associative means. A test was devised, consisting of items containing a stimulus word and two response words in the following form:

ethical

BE

aggressive

The final form of this test (the seventh form to be developed) contains sixty-four items. The subject is instructed to draw a line from the stimulus word to the response word which he thinks best "goes with" it. Forty of the items present an alternative choice between a word tapping a religious value (such as *ethical*) and a word tapping a political-economic or power oriented value (such as *aggressive*). The other twenty-four items are neutral or "buffer" items. Two test-retest checks of the reliability of scores on this test yielded reliability coefficients of .81 and .87. To test the validity of this word-association technique, two groups of college subjects were given the test and the Allport-Vernon Study of Values, scored for its political-economic and religious values. Correlations between the resulting sets of scores were .68 and .69. It therefore appears that the word-association test tends to have some degree of validity, in the sense of correlation with the Allport-Vernon. Other, more direct checks of this technique need to be done, however.

If values are associated with verbal response systems, one can hypothesize that a high value score should be associated with a highly available verbal response system. On the other hand, if a subject has two values in approximately equal strength, it can be surmised that the associated verbal response systems likewise would be of approximately equal strength. To test this hypothesis, time for completion of the word association form was recorded for (a) subjects with high value scores and (b) for subjects with intermediate scores. It is assumed that a strong, available verbal response system would lead to rapid response, whereas the existence of two verbal response systems of equal strength (postulated for those subjects with intermediate scores) would lead to delay of decision due to conflict. These records were made in two groups of subjects, and it was found in each case that the group with strong values completed the word-association test in significantly less time than did the subjects with intermediate values.

A study was conducted of the relationships of values to learning. Following the arguments of this section, it would be predicted that verbal materials consistent with a subject's value should be more readily learned than materials inconsistent with those values. Subjects whose measured values were high in either the religious or political-economic directions were asked individually to learn two lists of paired associates. In one list, all of the response members had a religion connotation and in the other a political-economic connotation. Four learning trials were given each subject for each list, and appropriate techniques were employed to rule out practice effects, *etc.* For the learning trials as a whole, a chi-square analysis showed significantly that learning was more readily performed when the response word was consistent with the subject's values than when it was inconsistent with his values. Differences were obtained for number of words correct, latency of response, and number of covaluant errors. A trial by trial analysis yielded differences which, in all cases, were consistent with expectations but which did not, in all instances, reach statistical significance. However, the consistency of the obtained differences, together with the results for the analysis of the learning task as a whole, tend to support the expectation that values may influence learning.

These studies seem to support the general hypothesis that there is a close relationship between values and verbal response systems. The exact nature of this relationship, however, will require further research for its explication.

DISCUSSION

The evidence summarized above, together with other evidence in the literature (which could not be reviewed here because of limitations of space), suggests two general conclusions: (1) that verbal processes may influence human reasoning, problem solving and thinking, at least insofar as the tasks studied are representative of such functions; (2) that there is a close relationship between values, as measured in terms of a standardized test, and verbal processes, again within the limits of such situations as have been investigated.

A basic question concerning these investigations arises with respect to the role of language in human behavior. It was suggested in the introductory paragraphs of this paper that a central problem of psychological inquiry concerns the nature and kind of variables which must be postulated for the mediation of behavior, and further concerns the processes by which such variables perform their mediating function. It is perhaps justifiable to suggest that in certain of the reasoning experiments reported here language variables may mediate, in part at least, human reasoning in some situations. Whether language processes can or do serve a mediating role in other behavioral functions must remain an open question, to be answered by future investigation.

In the broadest terms, the next steps in research of the kind reported here should be devoted to a further exploration of the possible mediating role of language processes, together with a comprehensive study of the ways in which language processes work and the laws under which they function. We should like to suggest, as a brief, introductory theoretical statement to such a research program, some hypotheses that seem fairly well to describe the results of the studies reported in this paper, in their general outlines at least.

We should postulate that in most human individuals there exists a large array of potential verbal responses and that these verbal response tendencies possess different potential or availability for evocation or emission, both within an individual and among different individuals. We further assume that for reaction (overt or covert) to take place an interaction between a stimulus and a response potential may occur, and the response will be made. Under conditions of minimal or ambiguous stimulation, however, we assume that the individual will tend to give that response or those responses whose potential for action at any given time is highest. Finally, it is recognized that individual verbal responses, isolated from other verbal responses, probably are rare, so that what happens to one verbal response will no doubt affect other verbal responses as well. One possible way in which verbal responses may be organized into verbal response systems has been suggested by Cofer and Foley [1] in terms of semantic generalization gradients.

Now if it should be that a stimulus activates a verbal response system, the resulting covert or overt verbal responses may well exercise a controlling or directing function with respect to imaginary, attitudinal [see Doob, 3], or other verbal kinds of behavior and also with respect to responses of other parts of the musculature to which they have been associated. A similar role would be assigned to verbal responses being "emitted" by the organism in the relative absence of external stimulation or in the presence of ambiguous stimulus conditions.

The foregoing formulation has been developed in connection with the studies reported here, but much further research is required in order to determine its validity, especially as to the directing or mediating function suggested for verbal responses.

BIBLIOGRAPHY

1. Cofer, C. N., & Foley, J. P., Jr. Mediated generalization and the interpretation of verbal behavior: I. Prolegomena. *Psychol. Rev.,* 1942, *49,* 513–540.
2. Dewey, J., & Bentley, A. F. *Knowing and the Known.* Boston: The Beacon Press, 1949.
3. Doob, L. W. The behavior of attitudes. *Psychol. Rev.,* 1947, *54,* 135–156.
4. Gibson, E. J., & McGarvey, H. R. Experimental studies of thought and reasoning. *Psychol. Bull.,* 1937, *34,* 327–350.
5. Goodenough, F. Semantic choice and personality structure. *Science,* 1946, *104,* 451–456.
6. Guetzkow, H. An analysis of the operation of set in problem solving behavior. Ph.D. dissertation, University of Michigan, 1947.
7. Johnson, D. M. Problem solving and symbolic processes. In Stone, C. P. (Ed.), *Annual Review of Psychology,* vol. 1, pp. 297–310. Stanford, California: Annual Reviews, Inc., 1950.
8. Johnson, W. *People in Quandaries.* New York: Harper, 1946.
9. Krout, M. H. *Introduction to Social Psychology.* New York: Harper: 1942.
10. Lee, D. Notes on the conception of the self among the Wintu Indians. *J. abnorm. soc. Psychol.,* 1950, *45,* 538–543.
11. McGinnies, E. Personal values as determinants of word association. *J. abnorm. soc. Psychol.,* 1950, *45,* 28–36.
12. Postman, L., Bruner, J. S. and McGinnies, E. Personal values as selective factors in perception. *J. abnorm. soc. Psychol.,* 1948, *43,* 142–154.
13. Sanford, F. H. Speech and personality. *Psychol. Bull.,* 1942, *39,* 811–845.
14. Thompson, L. Science and the study of mankind. *Science,* 1950, *111,* 559–563.
15. Whorf, B. L. Science and linguistics. *Tech. Rev.,* 1940, *44,* 229–231, 247, 248.
16. Woodworth, R. S. *Experimental Psychology.* New York: Holt, 1938.

PREDICTING WHO LEARNS FACTUAL
INFORMATION FROM THE MASS MEDIA

CHARLES E. SWANSON

School of Journalism
University of Minnesota

THIS PROJECT WAS DESIGNED IN ORDER TO learn more about the use of language and other symbols in the mass media and the responses of mass audiences. This is mass communications research, an area which advances through the cooperation of psychology, the social sciences, and journalism.

Such inter-disciplinary research with people in their every-day lives can be doubly rewarding: it can test theory developed in the laboratory and it can suggest principles for improving the effectiveness of those who try to communicate with invisible publics through newspaper, magazine, radio, film, television.

SUMMARY OF 1947–49 RESEARCH

A broad program of research in mass communications in a Division of Research was started in 1944 at the University of Minnesota's School of Journalism by its director, Dr. Ralph D. Casey. The Office of Naval Research project was directed from September, 1947 to September, 1949 by Dr. Ralph O. Nafziger, and since then by Dr. Charles E. Swanson. The latter is indebted to his research associates for their assistance in planning and executing the work: Dr. Robert L. Jones, Malcolm S. McLean, Jr., Warren C. Engstrom, and Harry Benenson.

Dr. Nafziger began in 1947 to study the problems raised by these questions [9]: "Who is the reader? What are his characteristics? What does the reader read in a newspaper? What relationship exists, if any, between the basic characteristics of the reader and what he reads? What type of newspaper content is made available to the reader? What is the relationship, if any, between the newspaper reader and other communication media?"

Dr. Nafziger [9, 10] used personal interviews, quota sampling surveys, and statistical techniques. He developed a system of categories, or classes, for analyzing newspaper content. He was able to classify newspaper content and measure differences in who reads what. A number of his findings were based upon this system of categories: adults who had attended four or more meetings in the four weeks prior to an interview had read more in most classes of news and had more information. Many other factors had some relationship to what people selected from newspaper or radio and what they knew about current events. These factors included occupational levels, sex, age, and education. No one factor was related to significant differences in what the samples read in all categories. No single population group failed to read some news and obtain some information.

To test the accuracy of individuals in reporting what they had read in a newspaper, Dr. Nafziger used information questions based on newspaper items. His staff re-interviewed a sample of newspaper readers. In every instance he found that persons who said they had read "all" of the items had higher information scores.

At Dr. Nafziger's suggestion, Carl V. Goossen [4] developed a hidden intelligence test for a doctoral dissertation under the direction of Dr. Walter W. Cook. This test was designed with two forms: one with five questions and another with five additional items, or a total of ten questions. The questions were administered in an opinion interview, so the respondents did not know their intelligence was being tested. Combined with the highest grade reached in school, the five-question test gave a multiple correlation coefficient of .88 with the criterion, scores of the respondents on the Pressey Classification Test, a standard intelligence test.

Development of Hypotheses, 1949–50

For the year 1949-50 a panel study had been planned. (In August, 1949, the present investigator became director of the Research Division and responsible for this project as successor to Dr. Nafziger, who became director of the University of Wisconsin School of Journalism.) The panel study proposed to use various tests to explore "what in the individual is related to his choice of media categories and what is the effect on him of exposure to various categories."

The present investigator sought, then, to design the 1949-50 project with these research aims in mind:

1. *External criteria.* Dr. Nafziger had found that the readership interview was subject to a varying amount of error. Besides reading behavior, a superior yardstick, or external criterion, was needed to assess the relative importance of variables.

2. *Predictive utility.* If the content categories, or classes, were to stand up under application by others, this project should include a test of their utility in predicting human behavior.

3. *Categories and dimensions.* What kinds of categories would have the greatest predictive utility? Should the categories be concerned only with the content of the message, *i.e.,* subject matter, style, source? Or should the categories cover such factors as photograph, illustration and other ways of transferring information through the media? Before the study could advance to the panel stage, it was necessary to compare the utility of the several kinds of categories.

4. *Measuring of interest.* Another major goal of the 1949–50 study was to test the extent to which an individual could be questioned directly about his interest in news or other items and how his verbal behavior could be used to predict what he would read or learn about similar items at some future time.

Two programs prepared the way for the field work. One involved the testing of several hypotheses and a system of categories on the results of interviews with three samples, each totaling two hundred adult readers of three Minneapolis newspapers (surveys done under a grant by the newspapers to the Research Division). The other program utilized the case study approach to predicting reading behavior.

As a result of statistical analysis of the differences in newspaper-reading behavior of the Minneapolis adults as related to the various categories, these reading patterns were established: the subject matter categories offered a more important area for research than two other catgeories—locale or vocabulary difficulty. Supposedly, people read more news about their home city, but somewhat smaller percentages of the Minneapolis adults—about 5 per cent—read the local news than read the national-foreign items. Also, such small correlations (about .20) were found between vocabulary difficulty, as measured by a readability formula, and amount of reading that further study did not seem merited at this time. (Swanson [11] previously had investigated with a controlled experiment the relationships of vocabulary difficulty to reading behavior.) Almost any item with factual information, *i.e.*, current issues, acts of government, scientific knowledge, had a much smaller audience than the entertainment categories: crime-adventure, sex-love, humor. On the average, photograph and illustration had larger audiences than prose.

In the testing of the case study approach to predicting reading behavior, ten newspaper readers were selected from the six hundred previously interviewed, and these were engaged in interviews three to six hours long during one to three sessions. In these lengthy interviews each individual was shown newspaper items from such broad categories as sports, comics, public affairs. As he read each item, the subject told what the item reminded him of and his responses were recorded. Next, he told what he had done the previous day and what he had selected from radio, newspaper, television, magazines, movies. He then took the Gates Reading Survey Test. The recorded associations were studied for hypotheses on improving the system of subject matter categories. Scores on reading speed, comprehension and vocabulary were used for predicting reading behavior. These results were compared with the utility of scores on interest in items in the broad categories.

As a result of this pre-testing, the Gates Reading Survey was not used in the panel because of the length of time (forty-five minutes) required to administer it. The system of subject matter categories also was found too long to use with an adult sample.

It was necessary to limit the panel study to careful analysis of two subject matter categories. Comics and news about government (international, national, state, and local) were selected as the two subject matter categories. It was expected that comics would offer an example of a category where items were much more alike, or a relatively homogeneous category. Items in the category "news about government" would often be dissimilar except for their likeness in subject matter. These two categories also are easily available in the average issue of an American daily newspaper.

Problem defined. Following the rationale of Horst [5], the basic problem was restated as follows: The problem is to identify factors in a category of news or other media content and personal elements in the individual which are associated with his success or failure in learning from an item or items in the category.

These content factors and personal characteristics then can be used to predict the degree of learning success of a given individual before he is exposed to items in a category.

It is intended to establish and to test a system of categories which can be used to predict who will read, listen to, or learn from classes of items in newspapers, magazines, radio and other media.

Two responses will be analyzed: (a) selection, *i.e.*, reading or listening to items in a category offered by newspapers or other media, and (b) learning, as measured by information tests.

In the panel study, then, two yardsticks, or external criteria, were used for testing the predictive utility of categories and audience variables. The external criteria were (a) reading behavior and (b) learning, or information, in a category.

The unique feature of a panel study is the repeated interviewing of the same individual over an extended period. As a result, other problems could be investigated in this study, including the following:

1. How consistent is an individual's reading behavior on two widely separated days? Does he consistently read the same comics, the same kinds of news and other information about government? Knowing what a man read on one day, how accurate will predictions be on what he reads at some future time?

2. Can social learning and perception theories be applied to analyzing content and predicting differences in learning, for example, factual information about government?

3. What factors are most important in predicting who learns factual information about government? Education? Occupation? Age? Sex?

4. If a man is shown items in two categories, *i.e.*, comics and news about government, will his verbal ratings of interest in these items have any utility in predicting what he reads or learns from like items at some future time?

Design of the Study

By December, 1949, the study design had been completed and the pre-testing and field work scheduled.

Subject matter categories. The two categories, comics and news about government, were defined. The extent to which naive subjects could agree on putting items in or out of the governmental news category was tested.

Information tests. Two information tests were devised as measures of success, or external criteria, on how adequately an individual could follow the news and learn about the acts of government. The tests were based upon a sampling of the news about government (international, national, state, and local) which appeared in the news in January, February, and March, 1950. One test required the individual to identify seventeen persons in foreign, national, state, and local governments. The other tested how much an individual knew about three major news events.

The sample. A probability sample of 448 dwelling units in Minneapolis was drawn. Sample design and technical details followed procedures outlined by Deming [1], Jessen [7] and others and applied by Watson [12]. The representativeness of this sample was checked by comparing sample data with various census benchmarks. Within each dwelling unit an adult was chosen by a random process, suggested by Goodman and Kish [3], which reduced interviewer bias in respondent selection to a minimum.

The interviews. Four waves of interviews were conducted in April and May, 1950. The first wave obtained demographic data on each respondent and data on what he had read in a metropolitan afternoon newspaper on April 19. On the second wave of interviews respondents were given the two information tests, the five-question disguised intelligence test, were asked a series of attitude questions, and told what they had selected from radio, television, film, magazines, books. The third wave interview consisted of a second readership test, this time on the May 1 issue of the metropolitan afternoon newspaper, and "forced reading" and interest ratings on selected items. In the fourth wave each respondent estimated "usual' reading and interest in selected governmental news and comics items; these items had been selected from previous audience studies as typical of the two categories and reprinted in a test booklet. An information test was given on the items which the respondents had read in the third wave "forced-reading" session. A total of 209 cases was interviewed on each of the four waves.

SUMMARY OF FINDINGS

At this time (September 19, 1950), some conclusions and hypotheses for future research can be reported but analysis of the data will continue for six to eight months. For example, the study of the differences in learning from material read voluntarily and similar items read under an interviewer's direction is not completed. Other results are available, however.

Category reliability. Twenty-two untrained subjects were given sixty minutes to read a three-page description of the category, news about government, and classify 185 newspaper items. They agreed with trained analysts in 70 per cent of their judgments on what items to include in the category, and in 90 per cent of their judgments on what items to class as "not governmental news."

Category validity. How useful was the category news about government in separating the "heavy" from the "light" readers? If this were a meaningful way of classifying news, more "heavy" readers should read every item of governmental news.

The April 19 and May 1 issues of the afternoon newspaper had been surveyed for readership by the panel. Each individual was given a score for reading a governmental news item. More "heavy" readers read every governmental news item. Every difference was significant at the 1 per cent level. This is positive evidence that even so simple a catgory can be used to predict who probably will read items in this class of content.

Difficulty of the tests. The Names Test used the names of seventeen persons in government. Every one of the seventeen items significantly discriminated high scorers from low scorers (the item analysis technique suggested by Kelley [8] was used). The median difficulty index was 38, indicating that the test was fairly difficult.

The Events Test was based upon three major events in governmental news during the first three months of 1950. At the international level the conflict of the West with Communism dominated the news. President Truman's budget message and debate over use of federal monies for national defense combined in a major national news event. In Minneapolis the most prominent news event was a conflict over a common learnings program in the public schools. A test of twelve multiple-choice items was built on these three events. Each item significantly discriminated high scorers from low scorers. The median difficulty index was 34.5, indicating the Events Test was slightly more difficult than the Names Test.

Reliability of the tests. Since the Names and Events Tests were to be used as criteria and since both were extremely short by most ability and achievement test standards, the question of their reliability was paramount. The perils of attempting to predict an unreliable criterion were clearly illustrated in the indifferent results obtained by Air Force psychologists during World War II in trying to predict bombardier success using circular error as a criterion.

No equivalent forms of the tests were built and the test-retest technique did not seem at all practicable in this kind of a study. Accordingly, analysis of variance approach to the calculation of a reliability coefficient as outlined by Hoyt [6] was utilized. The Names Test had a Hoyt reliability coefficient of .92 and the Events Test, only twelve items long and dealing with three events, had a Hoyt reliability of .65.

Homogeneity of the tests. One additional problem involved in the use of the Names and Events Tests as criteria concerned their homogeneity. Items at the international, national and state-local levels intentionally were included, both in the original item pool and in the final versions of the tests. It might be possible for a person to attain his particular total score on these tests by having knowledge of names and events at only the international or at the local level. Another person with the same total score might know the answers on national or state information items. A situation of this sort, if it occurred frequently, would raise serious doubts about the utility of such a category as news about government.

An index which shows how close a test comes to perfect homogeneity, 1.00, has been devised by Ferguson [2]. This simply involves plotting items vs. respondents. In 602 of 3,553 cells thus obtained on the Names Tests, items were answered in a way not in accord with perfect homogeneity, *i.e.*, easy items were missed by persons with a high total score or difficult items were answered correctly by persons with a low total score. This was the case in 17 per cent of the 3,553 cells. By subtracting .17 from the perfect homogeneity index of 1.00, an index of .83 was obtained for the Names Test.

As was true in the reliability measures, the Events Test did not measure up to the Names Test in homogeneity. The per cent departure from perfect homogeneity was 27 and the homogeneity index was .73.

Sex differences. Men and women differed sharply in their performance on these two tests. Men have more information about government when total score on the tests is taken as the criterion. To determine whether this same direction and extent of difference held true for all items in the two tests, another item analysis was undertaken. The proportion of men and women passing each item was determined and the significance of difference between these proportions was calculated.

Special attention was directed toward those items in the two tests which did not show significant differences in favor of men. As a result, three hypotheses were formulated for experimental study.

> Hypothesis I. Women will learn as much as or more than men from news with factual information about what women do or are expected to do.

This was suggested by the Events Test where the three questions dealing with the Minneapolis school dispute showed no sex differences. In two of the three items women tended to be slightly more informed. Almost as many women as men could identify the Superintendent of Schools.

Ability to identify the mayor of St. Paul showed no sex differences. In a 1950 campaign for re-election, he had been identified as a "family man' through photographs of his family and articles about his home life which appeared in the newspapers.

> Hypothesis II. Women will learn as much as men from news about persons or events which can be considered threats to basic security systems of the individual.

This was suggested by the lack of significant differences between men and women in identifying Mao Tse-tung, the Chinese Communist leader, and Klaus Fuchs, confessed atomic spy. Both had been labeled in the news as actual or potential threats to world peace during the weeks just before the interviews.

> Hypothesis III. Women will learn as much as men about a person or a concept which appears in varying contexts over a period of months or years.

Comparison of identification of Clement Attlee by Minneapolis adults in 1949 and 1950 resulted in this hypothesis. In 1949 Attlee was identified by 75 per cent of men and 57 per cent of women, a difference statistically significant at the 1 per cent level. In 1950, he was identified by 81 per cent of the men and 71 per cent of women, not a significant difference. A significant amount of learning from the news about Attlee had taken place, but the sex differences in favor of men had been obliterated, possibly because of the varying contexts in which Attlee's name had been mentioned.

Reducing the number of variables. One of the important findings of this study was the relative utility of a number of variables for predicting who would learn factual information from the news about government.

Data on more than thirty potential predictive variables were obtained. These included three areas of individual differences: intra-personal (intelligence and interests), behavioral (reading, listening, viewing of the media in the month prior to an interview), and demographic (age, sex, socio-economic status, *etc.*). A master intercorrelation matrix was prepared, using the Names and Events Tests as criteria.

One set of correlations utilized as predictors of the criterion variables was taken from individual difference areas (intra-personal and demographic). These variables were: (1) readership results on newspaper items categorized as news about government; (2) estimated intelligence obtained from the five-item disguised intelligence test; (3) self-estimate of usual amount of reading of news about government; (4) self-estimate of interest in this news category; (5) education; (6) occupational prestige level obtained from classifying the main wage earner's occupation [13].

With the Names Test as the criterion, variables 1 through 6 were combined in a multiple regression equation which yielded a coefficient of .54. Nonsignificant variables were dropped. Three significant variables survived: reading behavior, estimated intelligence and self-estimate of interest. This coefficient equalled .53.

The drop-out of education as a significant predictor of learning information about governmental news would appear incongruous, if it were not for the fact that the five-item disguised intelligence test makes use of years of schooling as one of its components. The test also measures other components of intellectual ability not provided by knowing how many years an individual went to school.

Item analysis results on the Names and Events Tests had shown large differences between men and women in knowledge about governmental news. It was decided to run sex as a seventh variable in combination with variables 1 through 6. This combination of seven variables yielded a multiple correlation of .65.

The two most important variables were intelligence, as estimated by the five-question disguised intelligence test, and sex. A two-variable multiple regression yielded a coefficient of .60. Similar analysis on the Events Test yielded a two-variable predictor, intelligence and sex, with a coefficient of .59. Both tests showed that the disguised intelligence test was the most useful predictor of information about government.

This suggests that intellectual ability is the most important trait for predicting who learns from this class of news, and that understanding the news about government imposes an intellectual task of significant dimensions upon the individual. Sex was the factor next most useful for predicting scores on these two tests. This is evidence that how the individual relates the news about government to the male or female social role has bearing on the amount of learning of factual information.

Several factors—intra-personal, behavioral and demographic—were "masked out" by the power of intelligence and sex as predictive variables.

Of the media behavior variables, magazine reading, book reading and general news reading were the most useful predictors. Type of magazines read—quality-news *vs.* pictorial-news *vs.* other types—gave an even higher correlation with the criteria. These data strongly suggest that quality-news and pictorial-news magazines are used by individuals seeking more news and information about government to supplement newspapers and radio newscasts.

Deviant cases. To find what other factors might have predictive utility, the three cases of extreme overestimates and the three cases of extreme underestimates of information were studied. The persons with more education were overestimated and those with less education were under estimated on information.

From the comments of these cases about news items, it appeared that methods of analyzing how information relates to various social roles or needs will increase the accuracy of predicting who learns from the news. Some individuals with apparently superior intellectual abilities or social prestige read and listened to the news but did not learn factual information. The model for this type was a "busy, busy" clubwoman (a college graduate and member of the League of Women Voters) who identified one out of seventeen persons in the Names Test.

Interest and prediction. Another purpose of this study was to test a method of asking an individual to look at sample comic strips and sample government news items, to say how frequently he had read similar items in the past seven days, and then to rate his intensity of interest in the sample items. These ratings were converted into scores for (a) self-estimate of frequency of reading, and (b) intensity of interest. The scores were used to test the utility of such direct questioning for predicting whether the individual would read the same items, such as comic strips, and like items in a category. If the correlations were high, this would be evidence that this direct approach and the category were useful for prediction of reading behavior. Low correlations would suggest either the need for more useful categories or re-finement of the questioning procedure.

Two samples of items were used. One sample was selected in October, 1949, printed in a booklet and submitted to the panel in May, 1950. The other sample of items was selected from a newspaper published the day of the third interview (May 1). This hypothesis was tested:

> Hypothesis IV. An individual's ratings of his interest and frequency of reading samples of items six months old and out of context are as useful for predicting his reading of like items as samples of items in the current newspaper, timely and in context.

Two samples of four comic strips were utilized. One set was six months old, the other appeared in the current newspaper. The scores for self-estimate of frequency of reading gave a correlation of .87.

Different news items were used in studying the governmental news category. Two samples formed the basis for this test. One sample included thirteen items which were printed in a booklet. The other sample was made up of fourteen items which appeared in the current newspaper. The scores for governmental news interest in the thirteen booklet items gave a correlation of .66 with the scores for interest in the fourteen different items in the newspaper. Scores on self-estimate of reading these two samples of items correlated .57.

These correlations indicate that similar items can be measured out of context, even after a considerable time period, and that the scores will be as useful as items measured in context for predicting what an individual probably will or will not read.

The predictive utility of the items was tested with this hypothesis:

> Hypothesis V. An individual's self-rating on frequency of reading and intensity of interest for samples of items can be used to predict what he will read of like items in the future.

Scores on estimated frequency of reading six comic strips in the booklet gave a correlation of .73 with the reading of twelve comic strips on April 19 and May 1. Interest scores gave a correlation of .54 with reading. On governmental news the scores on self-estimate of reading items like thirteen items in the booklet gave a correlation of .45 with the reading of twenty-eight items on April 19 and May 1. The interest scores gave a correlation of .35.

These results show that self-ratings on frequency of reading and interest can be used to predict whether an individual will read similar items. The correlations of these scores with comic reading were higher than those for governmental news. This means that the category "comics" has more utility for predicting behavior than the governmental news category.

SUMMARY

This study shows that intelligence and sex are two important variables in predicting who will learn how much factual information from the news about government. The following prediction statements are shown graphically in Figure I and are offered for further

Figure 1

PREDICTING WHO WILL BE INFORMED

MEN

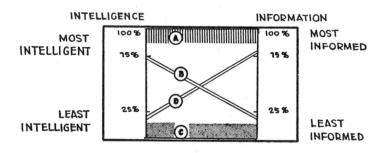

WOMEN

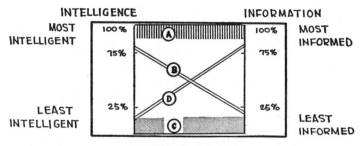

testing on this and other populations. They predict performance on information tests with reliability and homogeneity similar to the Names Test, and are accurate within two standard errors.

PREDICTION STATEMENTS

Of 100 men with intelligence estimates in the upper fourth, 58 (plus or minus 5) (see A) will have information scores in the upper fourth, and 8 (plus or minus 3) (see B) will have information scores in the lower fourth of the general population.

Of 100 men with intelligence estimates in the lower fourth, 4 (plus or minus 2) (see C) will have information scores in the upper fourth and 36 (plus or minus 5) (see D) will have information scores in the lower fourth of the general population.

Of 100 women with intelligence estimates in the upper fourth, 29 (plus or minus 5) (see A) will have information scores in the upper fourth, and 7 (plus or minus 3) (see B) will have information scores in the lower fourth of the general population.

Of 100 women with intelligence estimates in the lower fourth, 7 (plus or minus 3) (see C) will have information scores in the upper fourth, and 40 (plus or minus 5) (see D) will have information scores in the lower fourth of the general population.

The other major finding was that when an individual is shown items in two categories, *i.e.,* comics and news about government, his verbal ratings of self-interest and reading habits do have utility in predicting what he reads from like items at some future time. (Analysis is continuing to find the utility of such ratings for predicting learning, or information, in a category.)

OTHER HYPOTHESES AND FUTURE RESEARCH

These findings suggest hypotheses which can be investigated under experimental conditions. Among hypotheses which this and other research groups might find fruitful for study of communications problems are the following:

Hypothesis VI. Learning or nonlearning of an item or items in a given content category can be predicted within limits from analysis of how the content may relate or not relate to the social role or roles of individuals or groups.

Hypothesis VII. Certain words or combinations of words will cue association with a social role and, given such associations, a learning or nonlearning response can be predicted for individuals or groups.

Hypothesis VIII. A given concept, or factual information item, can be stated in different words, or different combinations of words, so the associations with different social roles will be made for contexts 1 . . . n, and the learning or nonlearning response can be predicted for individuals or groups.

Hypothesis IX. A given concept, or factual information item, can be stated in different words, or different combinations of words, so the comprehension difficulty, style factors and form factors can be measured, their relative importance tested and learning response predicted for individuals or groups.

Hypothesis X. A given concept, or factual information item, can be varied in still photographic form and word form so that factors relating to more or less successful communication can be measured, their relative importance tested and learning response predicted for individuals or groups.

These and other hypotheses from this project will be explored with a continuing study of the panel and with a series of experiments, similar in design to the one on vocabulary and reading behavior reported by Swanson [11].

APPLICATIONS

Research in mass communications may result in applications to theoretical analysis or to practice as in the following instances:

1. What is the utility of psychological and social theory about learning, perception, and language for predicting who will be informed?
2. How adequate is instruction in high schools and colleges as measured by information levels in the adult population?
3. How effective are teachers in increasing abilities to read and understand and increasing motivation to learn voluntarily about significant facts?
4. Which of the media—newspaper, magazine, radio, film, television—is most used by people as an informing medium?
5. How can complex, factual information be communicated to military personnel, low in ability and interest, so they will learn voluntarily the most in the least possible time?

To questions like these, research persons can turn for hypotheses with the knowledge that their findings will be important to basic social theory and to their society, provided that the findings will stand testing and will have utility in predicting what people in various cultures will do in their everyday lives.

BIBLIOGRAPHY

1. Deming, W. E. *Some Theory of Sampling.* New York: Wiley, 1950.
2. Ferguson, G. A. The factorial interpretation of test difficulty. *Psychometrika,* 1941, *6,* 323–329.
3. Goodman, R. and Kish, L. Controlled selection—a technique in probability sampling. *J. Amer. statist. Ass.,* 1950, *45,* 350–372.
4. Goossen, C. V. The construction and validation of a disguised intelligence test to be used in public opinion interviewing. Unpublished Ph.D. Thesis, University of Minnesota, 1949.
5. Horst, P., and others. *The Prediction of Personal Adjustment.* New York: Social Science Research Council, 1941.
6. Hoyt, C. Test reliability estimated by analysis of variance. *Psychometrika,* 1941, *6,* 153–160.
7. Jessen, R. J., and others. A population sample for Greece. *J. Amer. statist. Ass.,* 1947, *42,* 357–384.
8. Kelley, T. L. The selection of upper and lower groups for the validation of test items. *J. educ. Psychol.,* 1939, *30,* 17–24.
9. Nafziger, R. O. *Newspapers and Their Readers,* Volumes I and II. Minneapolis: University of Minnesota, 1948 and 1949 (Mimeographed).
10. ——. The reading audience. In W. Schramm (Ed.), *Communications in Modern Society.* Urbana: University of Illinois Press, 1948.
11. Swanson, C. E. Readability and readership: a controlled experiment. *Journalism Quarterly,* 1948, *25,* 339–343.
12. Watson, A. N. Respondent pre-selection. In D. M. Hobart (Ed.), *Marketing Research Practices.* New York: Ronald Press Co., 1950.
13. National Opinion Research Center. The quarter's polls. *Publ. Opin. Quart.,* Winter, 1947–48, *11,* 658–661.

SOCIAL AND PSYCHOLOGICAL FACTORS IN THE REHABILITATION OF THE TUBERCULOUS

DANIEL H. HARRIS

Saranac Lake Study and Craft Guild
Saranac Lake, New York

ORIENTATION AND STATEMENT OF PROBLEM

IT IS INCREASINGLY RECOGNIZED that rehabilitation constitutes a major problem in the treatment of illness, particularly chronic and recurring diseases and conditions resulting in disability.

It has been pointed out [1], that tuberculosis is of pivotal significance in this general problem, since it has so many aspects and effects which are common to other diseases and conditions of a chronic, recurrent and disabling nature. Tuberculosis is an *infectious* disease, necessitating isolation; it is a *chronic* disease, requiring prolonged and expensive treatment which few families can afford, with consequent social complications; it always produces a potential *handicap* in the form of the possibility of reactivation due to physical, hygienic, emotional or economic causes; it always produces an actual handicap —which may also be a vocational handicap—in the form of a limitation on physical activity, and frequently an additional physical handicap in the form of actual impairment of function; often associated with it are many *emotional and personality disturbances;* and generally it involves a social handicap arising out of the stigma attached to being an ex-tuberculous patient.

Tuberculosis thus affects people physically, psychologically and socially in such a variety of functions, with so many problems resulting which parallel situations arising from other conditions, that any findings concerning the rehabilitation of the tuberculous should be potentially applicable to the rehabilitation of a wide variety of other clinical entities.

We know that the tubercle bacillus is a *necessary but not sufficient* cause of tuberculosis. Its presence in an individual's tissues obviously does not, in itself, cause a tuberculous breakdown, since most people have been infected with it whereas only a small percentage ever develop a clinical case of tuberculosis. We know further that some objective factors—such as inadequate diet, poor working and living conditions, high population density, low economic status, and exposure to certain work hazards—have a demonstrable bearing; but they are clearly not the whole story, since the majority of people contending with a high concentration of such unfavorable factors still will not develop tuberculosis. It is pretty well agreed that it is strains and maladjustments in the personal, emotional and social lives of individuals, producing upsets in the bodily processes in the fairly well-established psychosomatic pattern, which usually undermine the individual's resistance to the point where, together with the presence of the tubercle bacillus, there exists the necessary *and sufficient* condition for a tuberculous breakdown [2, 9, 10].

In the treatment of tuberculosis, it is also taken as axiomatic that the "state of mind" of the patient has much to do with the success of the "cure." As a definite part of the treatment, the patient is supposed to relax and rest completely—mentally and emotionally as well as physically—so as to give his injured tissues a chance to heal. This is a prescription the self-administration of which is not too easy for many a patient, who (often suddenly) is facing a long siege by an easily fatal disease, added to whatever emotional stresses may have contributed to his breakdown—and all while flat on his back with plenty of time to brood. That many patients find it utterly impossible to follow the prescription is evidenced by the large percentage of tuberculous patients who terminate their treatment against medical advice, thus lessening considerably their chances for survival.

Even for patients who complete their treatment and are discharged with medical sanction, there is the possiblity of relapse. Relapse rates after initial discharge range from around 10 per cent or less to 80 and 90 per cent, depending on the kind of patient, the extent of the disease on admission, the duration and kind of treatment, the work-situation to which the patient returns, and other things about which we don't yet know too much in detail. There is good reason to believe that the same personal and social factors which played some part in bringing on the patient's first break—or other similar factors—will tend to bring on a second and third break if they are still present at discharge or should arise at a later time. In other words, psychological and social factors are no less important in the rehabilitation or relapse of tuberculous ex-patients than they are in the causation of the original breakdown and in the treatment of the disease.

While what has just been said is substantially agreed to be the case, in broad outline, the practical details of the picture remain to be filled in. The specific crucial question is something like this: *"What personal qualities and attitudes and emotional states, under what circumstances, and for how long continued, and combined with what pattern of age and sex and marital status and occupation and income and population density and so on, will reinforce the tubercle bacillus sufficiently to produce or reproduce a clinical tuberculous breakdown, in what percentage of cases?* And then, what can we do to alter those qualities, change those attitudes, ease those emotional states, and improve the circumstances, so that the tubercle bacillus will in the future get no aid or comfort whatever and will wither and become harmless in those people?

The answer to the second part of the question must of necessity wait on the answer to the first part. What are the social and psychological factors, in detail, in what combinations and under what circumstances, and with what kinds of people, which predispose individuals towards an initial breakdown or a later relapse, in how many cases in a hundred? That is what needs to be known, and that is what we are currently making a start towards finding out in the present project, under the joint auspices of the Office of Naval Research and the Saranac Lake Study and Craft Guild.

GENERAL PLAN OF RESEARCH

Since the factors tending toward an initial break cannot be too different from those tending toward a relapse following a cure, and since it would be impossible to study carefully everybody in the entire population and then wait to see who develops tuberculosis, we have adopted the procedure of studying carefully a fairly large number of people who are curing from a first break, and following them up. In outline, the plan is to:

>   1. study as thoroughly as possible the histories, characteristics, personalities, attitudes and circumstances of three hundred tuberculous patients who are homogeneous medically in

that they are all recovering from a first breakdown with tuberculosis and are all scheduled for discharge as arrested or apparently arrested within eight months (or less) from the time they become subjects; then—

2. follow them up carefully for seven years after discharge, (annually or oftener by mail, and in person three times during the seven years) gathering further data as suggested by current theories and actual developments; at the end of the seven years—

3. by comparing appropriate sub-groups of these patients who will have self-identified themselves—*i.e.*, by staying well and working, by relapsing one or more times, or by dying of tuberculosis during the follow-up period—to be in a position to—

4. demonstrate and quantify, both singly and in combination, the psychological and social factors affecting the rehabilitation or relapse of tuberculous ex-patients.

RATIONALE OF PROCEDURE

The material we are gathering consists of:

1. Data designed to test the validity of every relevant hunch, conclusion and opinion which the writer could find in the literature or glean from talking to numerous authorities in the field.

2. Information designed to give as complete and detailed a picture as possible of the individual subject's development, characteristics and circumstances. In selecting items to be included here, we have deliberately refrained from following any one school of psychological thought to the exclusion of others. Beyond the general assumptions that in the rehabilitation of the tuberculous there are psychosomatic aspects and that certain social and environmental factors are involved, we are not collecting data primarily designed to validate any theory of our own as to just what are the dynamics and factors operating. Some may regard this as a random and scientifically unsophisticated approach. To have started out with a specific theory, and collected primarily data designed to prove or disprove just that theory, would undoubtedly have made for a much neater research design and one involving a lot less work. It is the writer's conviction, however, that where a long-time longitudinal study is necessarily involved, and in the present state of our dependable knowledge concerning mind-body dynamics and personal-environmental interaction, the approach we are using is likely to yield much more in the way of usable results per unit of time and money invested.

PREVIOUS STUDIES

Previous studies of tuberculous patients have been mostly concerned with the medical course, treatment and outcome of the disease, and with relapse and mortality statistics. Actual studies of rehabilitation have been rather neglected. There have been many and diverse opinions expressed, based on uncontrolled clinical observation by tuberculosis specialists, which add up to the consensus that psychological and social factors are important in the rehabilitation of tuberculous ex-patients [2], but no experimental demonstration or quantification of any of these opinions has ever been made. There is evidence from the records of the Altro Workshops [3,5] that relapse rates and mortality rates are much less under favorable, supervised, part-time post-discharge employment conditions than are usually found in random discharges. There is supporting evidence for this from the Papworth Village Settlement in England [7]. The writer could find in the literature only one study which compared approximately matched groups (*i.e.,* on age, race, sex, marital status, and medical factors during original sanatorium stay and at discharge) of relapsed and nonrelapsed patients on social and psychological factors [4]. The study in question was based on data collected after the event of relapse for the experimental group, and at least a year following discharge for all subjects. The findings indicated higher intelligence, better social and emotional adjustment, slightly higher economic status, more education, and more extensive pre-tuberculosis work experience for the nonrelapsed group (N = 40 in each group). So far as is known to the present writer, no comprehensive controlled study of the factors affecting the rehabilitation *vs.* relapse of tuberculous patients has been previously initiated.

Milieu, Subjects, Method of Referral

The development of the Saranac Lake area as a center for the treatment of tuberculosis is an outgrowth of the establishment in 1884 by Dr. Edward Livingston Trudeau, just outside the village boundaries of Saranac Lake, of what is now known as Trudeau Sanatorium. At the present time there are within a twenty-mile radius of Saranac Lake six large and about forty small public and private tuberculosis sanatoria. In these, and in private homes and apartments in Saranac Lake under medical supervision, there can be found at any one time about fifteen hundred patients curing from tuberculosis. They represent almost every economic, vocational and educational grouping, are drawn from a wide geographical area, and comprise patients of both sexes, all ages, and all stages of the disease. Among the sanatoria and other places of treatment are found every type of treatment regimen, both medical and administrative.

The Saranac Lake Study and Craft Guild was organized in 1935 on a grant from the Carnegie Corporation by a group of ex-patients, physicians, and interested persons "to stimulate and promote inter ests of an educational and recreational character among confined and ambulant patients as aids to physical rehabilitation." In the intervening years the Guild's purposes and activities have developed and broadened, and it now carries on a rather unique program of education, demonstration, and research in the rehabilitation of tuberculous patients. Now incorporated into the public educational system of the state, the Guild's instructional services are available to all patients in the area. Not slighting educational and recreational activities, the Guild program now is oriented also towards the emotional, vocational, and broadly social aspects of rehabilitation. In addition to recreational activites and instruction—both bedside and in Guild classrooms—in a wide variety of academic, commercial, arts and crafts, and technical subjects, the Guild offers a general and vocational counseling service to all patients and ex-patients in the Saranac Lake area.

All of the subjects for this research are and will be patients referred by the tuberculosis specialists supervising their treatment. The medical directors of all the large sanatoria in the area and the private physicians caring for the patients in the small sanatoria, "cure cottages" and elsewhere in the village of Saranac Lake, are all members of the Guild Research Committee, and as such are taking an active interest in the progress of the research. They helped in the drawing up of the original outline of procedure for the project, are facilitating in every way the securing of the necessary subjects from among their patients, and are furnishing all desired information about those of their patients who become our subjects.

The referring physicians select subjects for the research in accordance with a set of criteria as follows:

1. Adult or re-infective type pulmonary tuberculosis.
2. An initial breakdown; no relapses.
3. Age at least eighteen on admission, and not over fifty-three at time of referral to research project.
4. Scheduled for probable discharge within eight months (or less) as arrested or apparently arrested.
5. Home residence in eastern half of United States and lower Canada.

Participation as subjects by the patients is of course voluntary, but cooperation so far has been excellent. Some advance publicity via the local newspaper and radio, together with the support of the referring physicians, brought about the initial participation of the first

few subjects, who apparently found the procedure sufficiently interesting to follow it through to completion and to recommend it to
others. We now anticipate the ready cooperation of all patients in the
area who meet our criteria for the selection of subjects.

DETAILS OF INITIAL PROCEDURE

Each subject is seen individually, twice a week, for about two hours
each session, until all our initial procedures and data have been
completed. This takes approximately a month. The project furnishes
transportation to and from our offices for all subjects who require it.
From January to June, 1950, the Principal Investigator on the project
working by himself completed the gathering of data on twenty-five
subjects. Since August, 1950, with additional staff of five Assistant
Investigators (Sidney Barasch, Lawrence D. Eskin, Melvin I. Fish-
man, Laura Musser-Floyd and Myra Rosen), we have been completing data on twenty-seven or twenty-eight cases a month, and should
complete initial data on our planned three hundred cases—possibly a
few more—before July 1951.

Interviews are held in individual offices, and each subject is seen
by the same Investigator throughout his whole series of visits. In addition to the usual office desk, table and chairs, each office has a very
comfortable upholstered armchair for the patient, a somewhat less
comfortable but matching upholstered chair for the interviewer, an
attractive drum-table on which cigarettes are available, and a couple
of ornamental as well as useful brass table-lamps; as well as other
items, varying with the interviewer (pictures, rugs, drapes, etc.),
which are also designed to give our interviewing rooms an informal
rather than office atmosphere.

The sixteen or eighteen hours spent with each subject are divided
more or less evenly between interviewing and testing. Mimeographed
outlines of topics and specific points to be covered in the interviews
are used, and a uniform battery of tests is administered for each subject; but there is no set order of procedure except for the priority
given to the establishment of good rapport during the first session.
The Thematic Apperception Test responses and certain parts of the
interview are recorded via Dictaphone thirty-minute memobelts.

The following standard instruments are being administered:

Wechsler-Bellevue Intelligence Scale, Form I
Rorschach Test
Minnesota Multiphasic Personality Inventory
Thematic Apperception Test (first 10 plates)

Cornell Index, Form N2
Vernon-Allport Study of Values
Kuder Preference Record

Additional (unstandardized) instruments being used include:

The Adjustment Index (from pp. 23–28 of: Wells, F. L. and
Ruesch, J., *Mental Examiners' Handbook*, Second Edition,
Psychological Corporation, 1945).

Questions on Imaginary Situations: a modified version of a sheet
devised some years ago by the Principal Investigator to investigate certain aspects of motivation, and concerning which he
presented a paper at the 1935 meeting of the Eastern Psychological Association, "Expressed Willingness to Take a
Chance."

A Sentence Completion blank, based on other blanks but with
changes, omissions, and additions to render it appropriate for
our subjects.

The interview procedure includes a set of fifteen Autobiographical
Topics, presented to the subject on 3 x 5 cards one at a time with the
request that he talk on each for five or ten minutes. Responses are recorded by Dictaphone. These topics cover some childhood memories,
a variety of emotional experiences, vocational history and attitudes,
pre-illness daily schedule, reaction to the diagnosis of tuberculosis,
and plans for the period following discharge.

Various rating scales and check-lists devised for use in this research
are filled out: by the subject himself on his attitudes towards various
aspects of his illness, by the interviewer on a wide variety of items,
and by the referring physician on the patient's adjustment during
treatment. The referring physician also furnishes detailed medical
information concerning each case at the time of discharge from treatment, on a form prepared for this purpose.

Planned Follow-up

The crucial data of the entire research will consist of comparisons
between those who achieve and maintain rehabilitation and those
who do not; therefore the follow-up procedure will merit careful
planning. As mentioned earlier, an annual mail follow-up and three
personal follow-ups with each subject are envisaged. Since the large
majority of relapses occur within the first two years after discharge
[6], it seems desirable to schedule the first personal follow-up visit
with each subject within the first eighteen months following discharge, so as to secure first-hand data at a critical time.

During the entire follow-up period it is planned to apply the best instruments for the measurement of the personal, vocational, and emotional adjustment of adults which will at that time be available. In preparing to assess rehabilitation, we propose to be guided by the definition adopted by the March 1946 Washington Conference on the rehabilitation of the tuberculous, which reads: "Rehabilitation in tuberculosis is the restoration of the tuberculous to the fullest physical, mental, social, vocational and economic usefulness of which they are capable." It may become necessary and desirable to construct our own scale for measuring the degree of rehabilitation attained by any individual at any given time-interval since discharge, basing it on a detailed item analysis of the definition quoted.

RESULTS TO DATE; OUTLOOK

As we are still in the initial-data-gathering stage, there are of course no substantial results to report at this time.

It may be of interest, however, to report the results of a preliminary study, designed to ascertain whether or not the records of a well-run sanatorium would be encouraging with respect to the main project, *i.e.*, whether analysis of such records would yield any items of a psychological and social nature which would differentiate between medically matched groups (at discharge) which differed sharply in the success of their post-discharge rehabilitation.

A group of twenty-three patients discharged between 1935 and 1942 from Trudeau Sanatorium who were alive and working in September 1948, with no recorded relapse since discharge, were matched for age, sex, marital status and occupation, and on all known ascertainable medical factors including family history of tuberculosis, extent of disease on admission, condition on discharge, surgery, complications, and medical prognosis at discharge, with another group of twenty-three patients discharged from Trudeau during the same period who had all relapsed and died of tuberculosis by September 1948. All records for the forty-six cases were then scrutinized for items possibly affecting or affected by psychological characteristics, family relationships and/or social experiences. In all, the two groups were compared on twenty-five such items.

The D (died) group, as against the R (rehabilitated) group, showed: more excessive drinkers and smokers; more pre-admission adjustment difficulties; more frequent dependence on relatives' contributions towards sanatorium expenses; more Catholics; fewer with admission history of nausea and vomiting, or of fainting; fewer who on discharge intended immediate return to employment. Table I shows the *t* ratios and confidence levels of these differences.

TABLE I

Differences Between D (Died) and
R (Rehabilitated) Groups of Trudeau Ex-Patients

Item	D N=23	R N=23	t ratio	confidence level
Fainting history	1	5	1.88	10 %
Intending immediate return to work	1	5	1.88	10 %
Excessive drinkers, smokers, etc.	9	3	2.07	5 %
Relatives Contributing	8	2	2.24	5 %
Catholics	12	4	2.85	1 %
Nausea-vomiting history	1	8	2.88	1 %
Pre-admission difficulties	18	7	3.73	0.1%

The second, third, fourth, and last of the differences listed in the table sound fairly logical, and consistent with what little we think we now know about rehabilitation and the problems confronting tuberculous ex-patients. The rationale of the first, fifth, and sixth items is not immediately clear, although a psychosomatically-based explanation has been suggested by a colleague for the differences in items one and six. It is the writer's guess that the difference in the fifth item may be an artifact due to a concomitant ethnic factor, rather than a difference due to religion. In any event, the results on this little preliminary study seem distinctly encouraging when one considers that the data we used were entirely ex-post-facto, and gathered in a nonpsychological setting for purposes rather unrelated to those of this research. They do demonstrate that a number of differences approaching reliability in social and psychological factors between groups of expired and rehabilitated ex-patients which were medically equivalent at discharge, can be found upon examining the records of a wellrun sanatorium. This certainly affords legitimate reason to expect that from our main study now going on, with plentiful data gathered at first hand for our purposes both during and following treatment, with a much larger number of cases and making use of psychological methods of inquiry, there should come clear-cut and definitive findings concerning the social and psychological factors affecting the rehabilitation and/or relapse of the tuberculous.

BIBLIOGRAPHY

1. Aitken, A. N. The institutional phase of rehabilitation. *J. Rehabilitation,* 1947, *13* (no. 6), 3–9.
2. Barker, R. G., Wright, B. A., and Gonick, M. R. *Adjustment to Physical Handicap and Illness.* New York: Social Science Research Council, 1946. Bull. No. 55, ch. 4.
3. Hochhauser, E. *Rehabilitation of the Tuberculous.* New York: National Council of Jewish Tuberculosis Institutions. Paper, 2nd annual meeting, Jan. 26, 1946.
4. Moore, M. G. A psychological study of 40 relapsed tuberculosis cases. Unpublished Master's Thesis, Western Reserve Univ., 1940.
5. Siltzbach, L. E. *Clinical Evaluation of the Rehabilitation of the Tuberculous.* New York: National Tuberculosis Assoication, 1944.
6. Trimble, H. G. Continuity of care. *Hospitals,* 1939, *13,* 46–48.
7. Varrier-Jones, P. C. The institutional treatment of tuberculosis. *J. state Med.* (Lond.), 1930, *38,* 268–277.
8. Wells, F. L. and Ruesch, J., *Mental Examiners' Handbook,* Second Edition, Psychological Corporation, 1945.
9. Wittkower, E. *A Psychiatrist Looks at Tuberculosis.* London: National Association for Prevention of Tuberculosis, 1949, 86–87.
10. *Irregular Discharge: the Problem of Hospitalization of the Tuberculous.* Wash., D.C.: Gov. Print. Off., 1948. Prepared by William B. Tollen for the Department of Medicine and Surgery, Veterans Administration. VA Pamphlet 10–47. Pp. 8–9.

AN INVESTIGATION OF NAVAL NEUROPSYCHIATRIC SCREENING PROCEDURES

WILLIAM A. HUNT

Department of Psychology
Northwestern University

THAT THE PRESENCE OF NEUROPSYCHIATRIC disorder renders the behavior of the individual less efficient and upsets the social organization in which he is existing may be considered a truism, since these two phenomena are generally accepted as basic in the very definitions of neuropsychiatric disorder itself. In general, society has accepted this opinion and has concluded that where an individual or group of individuals is set a task of achievement, their performance and chances of ultimate success in reaching their goal will be enhanced by the elimination or alleviation of any mental disorder among the individuals concerned. This is particularly true in a military organization engaged in military operations, for such operations demand peak individual efficiency in a highly intricate social organization, and at the same time are peculiarly conducive to the generation of those psychological pressures which precipitate or aggravate mental disorder.

Society has evolved many ways of handling the problem. The ideal solution would be the total abolition of mental disorder through a prophylactic program of biological eugenics and social reorganization directed toward the complete removal of all the causal agents concerned. While this goal has received, and should continue to receive, a large part of our efforts, we must realize realistically that at present we do not have the necessary basic knowledge for anything but a fragmentary prophylactic approach, and that even if we did have the scientific knowledge necessary for a complete and comprehensive attack upon the problem, there exists some doubt that we have either the economic resources necessary or the political wisdom to divert them to this use. It is, therefore, only reasonable to expect that for some time to come mental disorder will exist among our population and that our efforts must be directed not only to its prevention in the future, but to its treatment in the present.

The improvement of group efficiency through the elimination or alleviation of personality difficulty among its members has been approached from many angles, but I think the following three main trends can be recognized:

1. Identification of the maladjusted individual and his removal from the group. This is illustrated by the process of commitment to a state institution for custodial care.
2. Identification of the maladjusted individual and his selective placement in an environment where his maladjustment will not be incapacitating. This is seen in the common psychiatric use of environmental manipulation where vocational, marital, recreational, *etc.*, changes may be advocated for the patient.
3. Identification of the maladjusted individual and the use of therapy. As a case in point, we have the individual undergoing therapy while he is still occupying his former position in society.

These approaches are not mutually exclusive. Some therapy may be instituted in some custodial institutions; and selective placement most often issues from the therapeutic situation. The choice of any one or combination of these approaches is dictated by many complex social and practical considerations. Selective placement is seriously handicapped by the ignorance of the problem exhibited in many circles. Therapy is definitely limited at present by the shortage of professional personnel, and therapy in custodial institutions is still further limited by the economic restraints of inadequate budgets.

In World War II the military services concentrated largely upon the use of the first technique—detection of the maladjusted individual and his separation from the military services. This was accomplished by various diagnostic screening techniques designed to detect maladjustment, and by concomitant administrative procedures for the separation of the maladjusted individual from the service. At first these procedures were largely used on recruits at the preliminary training level, but as the war progressed the use of neuropsychiatric screening was extended, and re-screening at later points in the individual's period of service began to be adopted.

Since World War II the extensive educaton of the public in the principles of mental hygiene has resulted in greater public understanding of the neuropsychiatric problem. As a result, we can hope for a more enthusiastic reception for and use of selective placement in the future. Practical problems, however, still remain to limit its extensive use in any military emergency arising in the near future. Recent developments in therapeutic techniques also may make possible the more extensive use of psychotherapy in the future, but the professional manpower shortage in psychiatry and its ancillary disciplines shows few signs of abatement, and it appears inevitable that in any future military emergency the services will have to rely heavily upon neuropsychiatric screening as a major defense against neuropsychiatric problems.

The use of neuropsychiatric selection by the military services was instituted on a logical *a priori* basis. The apparent reasonableness of the procedure, its firm support by organized psychiatry and psychology, and the need for immediate action led to its adoption without previous experimental investigation; and once the nation was engrossed in its military effort, no facilities were available for its scientific validation. Such validation, however, ultimately had to be faced if we were to continue the use of neuropsychiatric selection procedures in the military services.

The present project has as its primary goal the over-all testing of the validity of neuropsychiatric selection in the Naval service. Did it accomplish what it set out to, the alleviation of psychiatric attrition in the Navy? As a secondary goal, we are investigating some of the specific screening procedures which played a part in the total selection process. Finally, it should be evident that the accumulation of masses of statistical data concerning neuropsychiatric selection will inevitably offer many insights into other general problems of mental hygiene. Thus the data gathered to date show differential effects of length of service on the incidence rate of the psychoneuroses as opposed to the psychoses, and apparent racial or cultural differences in incidence rates are appearing. These findings should lead to an increased understanding of the disorders involved.

Previous preliminary studies [1,2,8] had taught us some skepticism concerning the general reliability of neuropsychiatric statistics. It therefore seemed wise as a preparatory step to analyze the large amount of statistical material already collected and examine it in order to ascertain what common types of error existed and what safeguards against them might be taken. The results have been published in an article entitled "Some Sources of Error in ,the Neuro-

psychiatric Statistics of World War II" [3], which classifies and il-
lustrates the more common sources of error that we discovered. This
article is not only a compendium of errors which must be taken into
account by any investigator desiring to use military neuropsychiatric
statistics, but it offers many interesting, amusing, and sometimes de-
pressing sidelights on the contemporary practice of psychiatry. The
cumulative effect of this study of error is a grim one, but error which
can be recognized can be compensated for, and the situation is not
hopeless for the investigator willing to proceed with painstaking
caution.

As a result of these findings, we adopted a policy of concentrating
on material from sources known to us, where we are familiar with
the professional training and habits of the personnel involved, as well
as the particular situational demands and administrative framework
within which they functioned. Samplings of recruits handled in these
known situations are then obtained and direct access is had to the
medical and service records of the men involved. Any available internal or cross-checks are then utilized, and proper caution is used in
interpreting the results.

Our purpose was to answer the question: Was the neuropsychiatric
selection program instituted at all Naval Training Stations in 1941
[6] worthwhile? The specific form of the hypothesis in which this
question was cast and the experimental design selected for testing it
were dictated by the peculiar conditions under which we had to work.
It was not possible to set up controlled conditions in advance and
then follow the progress of a selected population under these conditions. The events in which we were interested had all transpired at
some previous time. We had to use what the sociologists have called
the "ex post facto" method, designed for use in historical situtations
where the conditions in question have all taken place previously. It
involves the setting up of an hypothesis and the devising of one or
more experimental designs suitable for testing the hypothesis. History is then examined carefully to discover, if possible, a time when
the events which occurred fitted the demands of the experimental
design. If a time can be found when the required series of events did
transpire, data is then collected as a check on the hypothesis. We
prefer the term "historico-experimental" to "ex post facto," since we
feel the former designation more precisely stresses the genuinely experimental nature of the method and the necessity of adequate historical knowledge if it is to be used.

The final hypothesis selected was a simple one—if neuropsychiatric selection was efficacious in reducing the number of psychiatric casualties during Naval service, an inverse ratio should exist between the number of military recruits screened out during preliminary training and the number of psychiatric casualties during subsequent military service.

The experimental design involves the selection of a series of comparable experimental groups with differing screening discharge rates during training. The subsequent history of these groups during military service should also reveal comparable differences in psychiatric attrition rate in inverse ratio to the differences in screening discharges. That is—the higher the original screening rate, the less subsequent neuropsychiatric disorder to be expected. As necessary controls, the experimental groups should be comparable in quality and should be screened by the same techniques used by personnel of equal ability. The difficulty lies in the fact that ordinarily when such controls are fulfilled, one expects to find equal screening rates, which would destroy our experimental design.

Fortunately, the peculiar conditions necessary for testing our hypothesis existed in the United States Navy during the first part of 1943. The training stations at Great Lakes, Newport and Sampson were operating under conditions where the quality of the recruit populations, the professional competence of the staffs engaged in neuropsychiatric screening, and the examination procedures in use were all roughly comparable. The actual screening discharge rates, however, varied widely owing to different attitudes of support on the part of the commanding officers at these stations. At Great Lakes, with the full cooperation of the Command, the psychiatric unit was allowed to discharge as many men as it saw fit. The discharge rate at Newport was held by the Command to approximately 4 per cent of all incoming recruits. At Sampson the Command was not sympathetic to neuropsychiatric screening and relatively few discharges were permitted.

Samples of approximately thirteen hundred men each were taken from each of these three training stations for the month of April, 1943. The same procedure was then repeated for the months of June and July. This provided three repetitions of the basic experiment under conditons known to fulfill the demands of our design. The recruit samples were selected at random from microfilm copies of the original muster lists of all new recruits arriving at the stations. We then obtained the health records of the recruits involved and determined directly from them both the psychiatric screening discharge rate during training and the neuropsychiatric attrition rate during two and one-half years of subsequent Naval service. If our hypothesis is correct, we should expect to find a subsequent attrition rate in inverse ratio to the original screening rate; that is, the more men screened out during training, the fewer subsequent discharges during service.

These experiments have been reported at greater length elsewhere [4,5], but the data can be summarized in Table I. Inspection of this

TABLE I

SCREENING RATE IN RELATION TO SUBSEQUENT
ATTRITION

	N	S%	A%	N	S%	A%
	April 1943			June 1943		
Great Lakes	1525	4.5	1.5	1347	5.9	3.2
Newport	1173	2.6	1.8	1294	4.2	3.0
Sampson	2823	0.7	3.0	1284	0.7	3.7
	July 1943			January 1943		
Great Lakes	1350	5.2	3.3	1310	4.4	2.6
Newport	1310	3.0	3.6	1255	5.0	3.7
Sampson	1354	1.3	5.0	1350	0.7	4.1

N = number in sample
S% = percent screened during training
A% = percent subsequent neuropsychiatric attrition

table shows that in general the expected inverse ratio between screening and attrition rates appears, thus for April, 1943 the screening rates were: Great Lakes, 4.5 per cent; Newport, 2.6 per cent; Sampson, 0.7 per cent, and the subsequent attrition rates were: Great Lakes, 1.5 per cent; Newport, 1.8 per cent; Sampson, 3 per cent. All the differences between stations in neuropsychiatric screening rate are statistically significant as are those in subsequent attrition between Great Lakes and Sampson, and Newport and Sampson. These differences are significant at the 2 per cent level or less (less than two chances out of a hundred that the differences are due to chance factors). The difference in subsequent attrition rate between Great Lakes and Newport, however, while in the expected direction, does not attain statistical significance. This is a phenomenon which we will notice recurring elsewhere in the table and which suggests that there is a curve of diminishing returns beyond which increasing the number of men discharged during training does not significantly reduce subsequent neuropsychiatric attrition. Stated colloquially, it seems possible to get too much of a good thing. The figures for June are not quite so clear. There is a small inversion in subsequent attrition between Great Lakes and Newport, and the differences between Great Lakes and Sampson, and Newport and Sampson, while in the expected direction, do not attain satisfactory statistical significance. The results for July, however, are completely as expected and all the differences are significant at less than the 1 per cent level except for the difference in subsequent attrition between Great Lakes and Newport. Again, while this is in the expected direction, it does not attain statistical significance indicating once more the appearance of a curve of diminishing returns. Apparently there is an optimal rate above which the efficiency of screening diminishes. This is confirmed by extensive studies that we have made of groups of recruits who were studied on the neuropsychiatric ward at the Newport NTS and subsequently sent to duty with some misgivings among the psychiatric staff. While the subsequent attrition rate is always greater for such groups than for "normal" recruits, it is sufficiently low to justify the manpower saving involved in sending the men to duty. Summarizing these data then, we can conclude, I think, that they bear out the serviceability of neuropsychiatric screening and confirm our hypothesis that discharge of men for neuropsychiatric reasons during training does result in a lessened incidence of psychoneurotic disturbance during their subsequent service.

A further check on our work was then attempted. The validity of the "historico-experimental" method rests in part on our ability to recognize historical periods suitable for experimental analysis. It seemed advisable to check our ability to select "favorable" conditions by attempting to pick a period at which time conditions were "unfavorable" and to see whether or not this judgment would be reflected in the results. We therefore selected a further sample from these three training stations during the month of January, 1943, when conditions at Great Lakes and Sampson seemed adequate for the research, but conditions at Newport did not. It would then be expected that the results from Newport under these circumstances would upset our previous findings. Inspection of Table I shows that this inference is confirmed. Although Newport, during this month, screened out more men than either of the other two training stations, its subsequent attrition rate was relatively high and not significantly different from that at Sampson which had a screening rate only one-seventh as great. It should be noted, however, that the expected relationship between screening and subsequent attrition is found for Great Lakes and Sampson where conditions were considered adequate. This difference is significant.

Our results justify neuropsychiatric selection as practiced in the United States Navy under the conditions represented in this experiment. They do not justify anything and everything that goes under the name of "screening." We feel that the screening in our study was representative and adequate since it was done by competent professional personnel using proven techniques under relatively favorable conditions. It is this "relatively" good screening that has been validated.

The word "relatively" is used deliberately, as Naval neuropsychiatric screening as it existed during World War II could never be called ideal. We seriously doubt whether such screening ever took place under completely favorable conditions. In practice it was continually handicapped by a shortage of personnel, inadequate space, unfavorable working conditions, and a lack of sympathetic understanding and cooperation that sometimes went as far as actual administrative sabotage [3]. Had all these difficulties not existed, the results reported above might have been more impressive.

Neuropsychiatric screening, however, should obviously not be undertaken too enthusiastically, as our curve of diminishing returns indicates. There would seem to be an optimal rate for screening discharges above which increased severity in screening does not yield comparable results in decreased subsequent attrition. We have discussed this point elsewhere as follows: "In general, severe disability is relatively easily detected and its unsuitability to most conditions of service can safely be predicted. Borderline disability is more difficult to detect and its unsuitability for service is more definitely a function of certain environmental conditions whose control and prediction are difficult for the examiner. As our selection problems become more subtle, our error rises. Somewhere along the line screening is no longer profitable" [5]. The specific point at which the curve of diminishing returns renders screening impractical is a difficult point to establish. It depends on many changing conditions, such as the relative shortage of manpower and the severity of the combat conditions to be undergone. Such a point will change with changing conditions and must always be established at the time, but we must be mindful of it in planning any selection program.

Moreover, we can agree that neuropsychiatric selection accomplished its purpose of diminishing psychiatric attrition during service, and still ask whether it was worth the cost. The actuarial complexities of this question are tremendous, and they are still further complicated by the humanitarian values involved. If we remember that every case of neuropsychiatric breakdown during service means a dangerous focus of inefficiency in an organization that depends upon efficient functioning for its very physical existence, and add to this the subsequent financial drain to the nation when such a patient becomes a pension case, the answer would seem indubitably to be "yes," even without considering the broader humanitarian values involved.

In the course of our work we have also investigated the relation of length of service to rate of neuropsychiatric attrition and find them clearly connected as would be expected. The longer the period of service of any group, the higher its neuropsychiatric attrition rate. Moreover, this is a gradually accelerating curve which seems to begin a sharp rise somewhere in the fourth or fifth year of service. If the general category of neuropsychiatric disorder, however, is split into those disorders classed as psychoneurotic (including disorders of personality) as opposed to the frank psychoses, we find that this increase in incidence seems to occur only for the psychoneuroses and not for the psychoses. Since the Naval psychotic rate is not high, however, the absolute number of psychotics included in our study is not great, and our findings may be a statistical artifact dependent upon inadequate sampling.

We have also investigated the relation between length of service and the rate of disciplinary discharge, lumping together under the category "disciplinary" all discharges labeled "bad conduct," "undesirable," or "dishonorable." Here the numbers involved are sufficiently large to make the findings reliable. We do not find the same increase in rate with length of service that exists among the neuropsychiatric disorders. Discharges for disciplinary reasons do not seem to rise as length of service increases.

Basic to the neuropsychiatric screening procedure is the psychiatric interview with its attendant psychiatric judgment of "suitability" or "unsuitability" for military service. The validity of such subjective judgments has often been questioned, particularly by the adherents of objective procedures such as group testing devices. Our validation of Naval neuropsychiatric screening would seem indirectly to validate the psychiatric interview as a selection device, since it played such an important part in the total neuropsychiatric selection process. In view of the importance of the question, however, we have been watching for opportunities for more direct validation.

Such a chance arose at a Naval receiving ship in 1944 [7]. A group of 944 seamen returning from overseas duty and being interviewe⌐

for reassignment by technicians in the Classification Department were referred to a psychiatrist for a psychiatric interview because of suspected neuropsychiatric difficulties. As a result of the psychiatric interview, the psychiatrist classified these men into three categories: symptomatology mild or absent, fit for general duty; symptomatology moderate, fit for limited duty ashore; symptomatology severe, hospitalization necessary. The health records for this group of 944 seamen were obtained and their subsequent medical histories were followed for the course of one year of service. The neuropsychiatric attrition rates for these three groups justify the psychiatrist's classification. Of those in the group with mild symptomatology, 6.5 per cent received neuropsychiatric discharges during the following year, while 20.2 per cent of the moderate group were thus discharged, and 89.7 per cent of the severe group required hospitalization. These differences are statistically reliable.

Since these seamen were all referred to the psychiatrist after a placement interview given by vocational specialists in the Classification Department, it is of interest to note that the attrition rate of the total group for the subsequent year was 15.6 per ccent which is roughly ten times the over-all Naval attrition rate of 1.6 per cent for that year. It would thus seem that such specialists are capable of operating as a rough preliminary psychiatric screen. Unfortunately no formal control group from among those seamen not referred to the psychiatrist is available.

We are also interested in the performance of certain groups within the Navy who were inducted as a result of special administrative decision. One of these is a group of illiterates. At the beginning of the war illiteracy was considered disqualifying for the Naval service, but as a manpower shortage gradually developed, selection standards were lowered and illiterates were acccepted for the Naval service. They were sorted out at the training stations and then sent to special literacy training programs, after which they proceeded to the fleet. We felt it would be of interest to know whether the subsequent service rendered by these illiterates justified their extra training. We selected a group of 940 illiterates chosen directly from the muster lists of illiterates arriving at one of the literacy training centers. Their medical histories through training and through one subsequent year of duty were followed. While we have no means of evaluating the quality of their routine service in the fleet, the psychiatric history of these illiterates was felt to be of interest because of the fact that illiteracy is symptomatic in some mental disorders such as mental deficiency and

psychopathic personality, and because its very existence in an individual must be considered a social handicap increasing his chances of
eventual maladjustment. While the group must be considered highly
selected because they were screened at the training station level before being sent to the special literacy program, about 10 per cent of
them were psychiatric casualties during their literacy training, and
the psychiatric attrition rate during a year of subsequent service was
double that of the Navy as a whole for that year. It would appear that
illiterates are not a particularly good neuropsychiatric risk in the
Naval service. A further investigation of their value to the service
would seem advisable. We are similarly studying several other groups.

The next step that we hope to take is an analysis of the screening
practices of a particular training station. To accomplish this we have
obtained access to the complete records for the war years of the Psychiatric Unit at the USNTS Newport, Rhode Island. We have available all the recorded material on every man studied by the unit. In the
case of men admitted to the observation ward for careful study, this
includes the psychiatrists' examination notes, results of any neuro-
logical or special medical examination given, psychological test results, the case history material obtained from outside sources, the final
staff decision and disposition. At present we are particularly interested in following the histories of those men examined in the ward
who showed some signs of pathology but who were not considered
ill enough to be discharged and consequently were sent to duty. We
wish to study the relative undesirability of the various types of disorder, the diagnostic importance of different symptoms, the possibility of establishing more exact selection criteria, and in particular,
through assessing the performance of individual personnel, to get
some idea of the validity, reliability, and range of professional performance in what could be considered a representative medical group
in action. This phase of the work, however, is only beginning. Its reporting must wait for the future.

At first glance these studies appear somewhat remote from the
other work reported in this volume, but further thought will reveal
that this is not so. Our statistics represent not merely *what patients
do*, but they also are a study of *what people do to patients*. We are
dealing here with the gross results in social practice of many of the
processes studied in the experimental laboratories of our colleagues. Cofer's studies of verbal behavior in reasoning have direct
bearing on the diagnostic behavior of the individual clinician. Asch's
results will help understand the group dynamics of the staff diag-

nosis. The whole problem of leadership is basic to morale and adjustment, and is reflected in any figures on neuropsychiatric attrition. Finally, I should like to turn all our material over to Margaret Mead and ask her, "What cultural characteristics are revealed in these practices?" It is only through such integration that we can gain understanding of the psychiatric problems of the military services and eventually hope to establish our clinical procedures upon a sound scientific basis.

BIBLIOGRAPHY

1. Hunt, William A. Negro-white differences in intelligence in World War II—a note of caution. *J. abnorm. soc. Psychol.*, 1947, *42*, 254–255.
2. Hunt, William A. The relative incidence of psychoneurosis among Negroes. *J. consult. Psychol.*, 1947, *11*, 133–136.
3. Hunt, William A., & Wittson, Cecil L. Some sources of error in the neuropsychiatric statistics of World War II. *J. clin. Psychol.*, 1949, *4*, 350–358.
4. Hunt, William A., Wittson, Cecil L. & Burton, Henrietta W. A validation study of naval neuropsychiatric screening. *J. consult. Psychol.*, 1950, *14*, 35–39.
5. Hunt, William A., Wittson, Cecil L. & Burton, Henrietta W. A further validation of naval neuropsychiatric screening. *J. consult. Psychol.*, in press.
6. Wittson, Cecil L. & Hunt, William A. Three years of naval selection. *War Med.*, 1945, *7*, 218–221.
7. Wittson, Cecil L. & Hunt, William A. The predictive value of the brief psychiatric interview. *Am. J. Psychiat.* (in press).
8. Wittson, Cecil L., Hunt, William A. & Stevenson, Iris. A follow-up study of neuropsychiatric screening. *J. abnorm, soc. Psychol.*, 1946, *41*, 79–82.

AN OVERVIEW OF THE CONFERENCE
AND ITS CONTROVERSIES

JOHN G. DARLEY

I DISCOVERED MANY WAYS of trying to summarize and interpret the wide range of research reports presented here this week. Happily, all ways appeared to be equally unsatisfactory, and consequently I was relieved of any problem of choice among the methods. During the course of our meetings, I made a series of notes, which have been regrouped for use here. In addition, I drew heavily on the three summaries of groups of papers prepared by Dr. Kelly, Dr. DeVinney, and Dr. Eberhart.

In a situation like this, you will recognize immediately that the reviewer and summarizer brings to his task all of his own values and biases. So far as possible, I have made these explicit; where this has not been done, I am sure you will call them to my attention.

To begin, I should like to make an oversimplified distinction based on the research reports presented during the first two days of our conference. I believe we could see in these reports the espousal of three points of view about making new knowledge or doing research. One is a peculiarly American form of pragmatism, which stresses external criteria, which accepts certain values, and which proceeds immediately to the task of prediction and control. The reports by Dr. Marquis and Dr. Katz tended to fit this category.

Another point of view was the clearly inductive approach set forth by Dr. Cattell, where the essential solution to the problem depends on an internal criterion and the operations of a closed system of factor analysis. In this rigorously inductive approach, the research worker searches for a large number of logically or behaviorally defined variables, to be later reduced in number by the operations of factor analysis. Consider what this approach involves: the selection of the largest possible number of variables; the assessment of these variables over the full range of human talent; the massive matrix resulting from the intercorrelations; the electronic calculator required to reduce this matrix. Even at this point, the process would not be ended; it would be necessary to create pure measures of the resultant factors, which in turn would have to be put to field test and validation. Evidence in the field of psychometric research does not indicate the clear predictive superiority of tests produced under factor analytic methods; the evidence also indicates that the factors caught at one moment of human development may not be the same as those that would be found at another time. Thus, while factor analysis may be a useful device in reducing and defining the variables within a given experimental situation, it may be questioned as the primary approach of greatest promise in the new areas of problems with which we deal here.

The third point of view regarding research is equally rigorous in the emphasis it places on the formulation of the concepts between which relationships will be sought. The approach was illustrated in the reports given by Dr. Festinger and Dr. French. These reports involved a high level of participation and discussion on the part of the audience. If I sensed the undercurrents of this discussion, it appeared to involve disagreements not so much with the necessity of conceptualizing the problem but with the behavior samples chosen to be coordinate with the concepts presented. I think we may have been trying to argue that the behavioral samples were not the correct psychological equivalents of the concepts.

In attempting to delineate these three distinct ways of approaching research, I do not imply invidious comparisons. I seek only to highlight the differences residing in the research reports—differences which reflect the past experiences and predilections of the research workers.

Several other issues emerged within the first few days of the conference. One of these may be described as research oriented around the tasks required of groups, with emphasis on external criteria of accomplishment, as contrasted with research oriented around the satisfactions of individual needs resulting from group participation.

We also touched lightly on arguments concerning the relative contributions to research of the various social sciences. By common consent the only way out of such arguments appeared to be the acceptance on our part of considerable responsibility for improving the training of research social scientists, regardless of the discipline in which they were originally trained.

In the summary presented by Dr. Kelly, a fundamental research problem was clearly presented. Do we deal with a universe of groups, from which our particular samples of groups are drawn, or do we deal with groups which for the moment must be considered as a given universe? This issue is directly related to the degree to which we may make generalizations from our findings regarding group behavior. Dr. Kelly's development of this point leads me to another consideration. Why have we not undertaken any systematic study of the birth, development, adolescence, maturity, tension-resolving behavior, aging, and death of groups? To reason by analogy, we have neither a good taxonomy nor physiology of groups upon which to build our experimental designs. So far as I have been able to determine, these data are not available in the field of sociology, nor have we given adequate consideration to the problem in psychology. It may well be that such data would resolve some of our arguments about whether we are sampling from a universe of groups in a particular study or whether the groups used must themselves be treated as the universe.

Another point of interest was apparent early in the week—this time a point of similarity in the studies reported. The groups used in the research studies were either created by the experimenters or were chosen from work groups. These groups are, in a sense, involuntary groups to the extent that their existence is dependent upon some outside force such as the ability of a company to pay for the work being done. The range of behavior of such groups is restricted; one large element in such groups is the motivation resulting from an existing conflict situation—labor-management conflict, for example. Dr. Kelly noted this situation in his summary also. There are many groups in our society based on voluntary participation—groups not held together by employment conditions. Such groups may present a different order of phenomena for study and may have a substantial influence on social change. Yet they do not attract our experimental interest, apparently. Nor have we turned our attention to groups of children, where developmental phenomena might be more clearly seen.

Frequently, in the reports and discussions of the early days of the conference, we found ourselves attempting to reason by analogy from the individual to the group. Thus some of the group phenomena presented were described or explained in terms of theories of individual personality dynamics or animal experimentation, as if the group were subject to the same laws as the individual. I believe we should quite consciously consider the extent to which such reasoning will inhibit or facilitate psychological studies of group behaivor.

In the summary presented by Dr. Kelly, he pointed out that each study with which he dealt had employed statistics as a technique of analysis. I was struck with what is possibly an obvious point: we have all accepted the desirability or the essentiality of the rigorous tests of theory and validity implicit in the use of statistics. In the development of a relatively new science of socio-psychological phenomena, it is heartening to see us carry over this tough-mindedness with respect to the nature of proof or verification.

It seemed to me that the reports given in the first two days of the program showed insufficient consideration of the role of abilities, aptitudes, or interests as determinants of the behavior of the group. Psychology has had the greatest amount of successful experience in the realm of psychometric theory, learning theory, psychophysiology, and personality theory. But in our research on group phenomena we appear to have neglected these areas, except as they were touched upon in the reports presented by Dr. Carter, Dr. Cattell, and Dr. Shartle.

Time did not permit us to go too deeply into technical matters such as the use of sociometric measures and the development of the questionnaires or check lists reported in the various studies. Even so, it appeared that sociometric data were accepted rather uncritically and that some of our questionnaire devices may not have met adequate standards of coverage or consistency or validity. You will recall that Dr. Cattell mentioned this point also in one of the discussions.

When we turned to the block of studies dealing with leadership behavior and phenomena, it quickly became obvious that the line between the studies of group behavior and the studies of leadership was extremely difficult to draw and maintain. Leadership, or leading behavior as the alternative suggested by Dr. Heyns, seems to be inextricably related to our theories of group functioning.

The problem of the criterion emerged again in the leadership studies. Dr. Carter, for example, described his plans to follow his cases into later military situations to establish a criterion against which his earlier measures could be validated, in the traditional sense of validation. Dr. DeVinney, who summarized the group of studies on leadership, pointed out that the research workers had tended to use as criteria, ratings, self-estimates, feelings of satisfaction with the group performance, and similar personalized referents. It occurred to me that we may be setting too high a level of aspiration for ourselves in our constant search for an external criterion. Possibly all we need or can get in our early studies of group behavior is a criterion that adequately subsumes the satisfactions of the individuals in the group. Certainly the search for satisfactory criteria in the area of psychometric research should give us pause in this new area. The predictive correlations to be obtained in almost any piece of selection research are so likely to conform to modal values already known to us that we no longer expect miracles to follow from concentrating our efforts on improved criteria. The predictive ceiling is fairly well known for the practical situations we face in selection research. If this may be assumed to hold for research on the prediction of group behavior, we may be well advised to lower our sights regarding the importance of the external criterion.

In the report by Dr. Carter, we discussed his concept of persons who serve as facilitators or depressors of group functioning. The burden of the discussion bore considerable resemblance to the sociologist's analysis of status and role relationships, under conditions of designated or appointed leadership. It would be my hope that these two sets of concepts, emerging in two closely related social sciences, could be studied jointly in a research project that would permit translations from one field to the other.

Several times during the meeting, Dr. Mead faced us with the importance of viewing our findings in the reference frame that is characteristic of the anthropologist—a viewpoint which we as psychologists admittedly understand insufficiently well. In the report given by Dr. Sanford, however, a technical issue emerged on which anthropologists and psychologists might establish a common research solution. You will recall that Dr. Mead questioned the advisability of using what she called a "German scale" for studies of samples from a non-German culture. The psychologist would naively ask why this should not be done—why he should not work on the assumption, which is experimentally testable, of communality or common elements in two or more modern cultures. Here may be a field of profitable joint study for psychology and anthropology—the determination of the common and the unique features in two or more modern cultures.

The report by Dr. Sanford, and to some degree the methodological points emphasized by Dr. Hunt in his later report, opened up another possibility for interdisciplinary cooperation which might be fruitful. This is in the area of historical research. Suppose we could adduce or deduce the needs of followers at a given moment in history, using documentary data of the type in which the historian is skilled. Predictions, testable against other documents, could then be made of the leader characteristics for the same period. As an illustration of the hypothesis involved, consider Laski's book entitled *The American Presidency*. He postulates a simple relationship which is important enough to warrant experimental test: in good times, the American president is weak; in bad times the American president is strong. It would seem to me that hypotheses of this order, frequently found in the documentary social sciences, are approximately testable by modification of some of the techniques Dr. Sanford and Dr. Hunt illustrated in their reports. Dr. Sanford, in describing the needs of his sample of followers, left unanswered the questions regarding the origin and nature of these needs. They appeared to be derived social needs, in line with certain theories of personality. Such derived needs can be changed, either by events or by direction from the leaders. Thus a study of long-range factors affecting group or societal needs may again be a way in which historians and other social scientists may profitably collaborate.

We were handicapped by time pressures in assimilating the series of studies reported from the Survey Research Center. Dr. Katz introduced the series; Dr. Kahn, Dr. Jacobson, and Dr. Morse then reported briefly; and Dr. Campbell gave an overview of the program at the end of their reports. In the summary by Dr. Campbell, two points stood out: the probability that the concentration of resources and skills represented in the organization would produce significant results; and the difficulties attendant upon meeting the sponsors' limits and needs in field research. Dr. Campbell went on to state that his group hopes to move in the direction of closer contact with top management and more intensive transmission of the results of research throughout organizational structures. He also mentioned that the research teams hoped to do more in terms of depth analysis of individuals and studies of organizational structures.

The answers we seek may lie in the consideration of an administrative problem: what is the most effective way in today's society to use our resources in the behavioral social science fields? You will remember ONR's presentation of the needs of the military establishment in translating social science knowledge to a social technology.

Our options may be one or a combination of the following alternatives:

1. the allocation of almost all the resources of the Advisory Panel to concentrated work on one problem area;
2. the creation of physical centralization, a super social science institute, for research in this area;
3. general centralized planning and fitting together of the available resources and investigator interests into a meaningful over-all pattern;
4. creation within the military program of some form of social science corps, at appropriate echelons of administration and command;
5. detailed centralized planning, with a consequent search for contractors willing to carry out specific assignments.

This problem of the "total push" in social science research today occurred many times during the course of our discussions. I mention it here because it grows natually from a consideration of the statements presented by Dr. Campbell.

At the conclusion of the group of studies dealing with leadership phenomena, Dr. DeVinney presented a summary of them. He made direct reference to Dr. Campbell's points of intensified contact with top management and intensified effort on the transmission of results of social science research. He asked us to face the possibility that it might be too early to embark on a program of social technology, in consideration of our limited available fundamental knowledge of the phenomena with which we are dealing.

In the discussion following Dr. DeVinney's summary, his cautionary statement evoked replies ranging across almost the entire spectrum of opinion about the role of the social scientist. I paraphrase the main points on this spectrum:

1. The recommendations for action or administrative change made by the social scientist would in all probability be no worse than the decisions presently made in power centers.
2. The decision to apply findings is essentially a tactical one in the larger strategy of maintaining continuing support of basic research in the behavioral social sciences; findings may be applied if by so doing we maximize the chances of support that can be plowed back into basic research.
3. The rush to apply interim or *ad hoc* findings involves us in the risk of piling up results without integrating them into a theoretical framework of maximal meaning and long-range validity.
4. The criteria that would be dominant under the pressure to apply results would be essentially the sponsors' criteria, and

since the sponsors tend to be in the managerial category of
society, we run the risk of alienating employees in our research. The criteria of satisfaction or of security may in the
long run be as crucial as the criteria of productivity.

5. The solution to this problem is itself a separate research
task; to analyze the value systems of those who will apply our
knowledge before we transmit it.

I should like to point out that this same general problem appeared
in the comments I made when our conference started. It is well to
consider our own social position in the relative security of meetings
such as this than to endanger our joint enterprise by lack of consideration of the broad social directions in which we are moving.

The last group of studies that I shall mention in this summary included those oriented primarily to an understanding of some of the
dynamics of individual behavior, alone or in group situations. Dr.
McClelland described a program of research aimed at the isolation
of "need achievement" as a special case of motivational theory. Dr.
Cofer reported a series of studies on factors associated with verbal
responses as evidences of set or tendency toward behavior. Dr. Asch
described a series of studies on the effect of group pressure on individual judgments, leading to case studies of the characteristics of
yielders and nonyielders to group pressures.

These studies were carried out by relatively small research teams
at relatively low cost. They had other common characteristics: identification and careful delimitation of the problem; clear-cut experimental designs; clear-cut results; rapid proliferation of implications
and new hypotheses under the conditions of group discussion following each presentation. With specific reference to the research reported by Dr. Asch, another facet of the tactical or moral problem of
the social scientist arose: Dr. Marquis pointed out that publication of
research results using the method of "multiple stooges" would tend
to destroy the effectiveness of the method itself. Other participants
raised the question of the sequelae of conscious lying and acting in
experiments, either as they might affect the experiments themselves
or the participants therein. It would seem that the social scientist
must face his own "Arrowsmith" dilemna, in the terms described by
Sinclair Lewis.

It seemed to me that our feelings about and reaction to these so-
called individual studies were much different than our reactions to
the group studies reported earlier in the week. I cannot prove that we
felt differently about them; I judge only from the group discussions
following the presentations. If I am correct in gauging our reaction,

it may be well to consider its possible meaning. Admittedly we are more habituated, as psychologists, to studies of this kind; we feel more at home with them. We may also feel that such studies produce more knowledge than our attempts to flail away at the complex variables present in group phenomena. We may feel that the more clearly we understand the individual, the more likely it will be that we can predict his behavior in the group. Dr. Hunt illustrated this point when he said that the series of individual studies permitted him to forecast what a small group might do to an individual in its midst.

Yet to offset such feelings, we must face the possibility that these individual studies are necessary but not sufficient to account for the behavior of groups. Research on group phenomena is inescapable. We may then demand that the studies of groups be as carefully formulated and explicitly done as the studies of individuals. This does not mean that we favor laboratory research over field research, or "pure" research versus applied research. We would demand only that any experiment be carefully done, without immediate concern for pressures to produce, to solve practical problems, to eventuate in social change.

To this point, I have tried to present a running summary, covering the chronology of the conference. Bear with me a moment longer while I try to list the major points that emerged by the end of the week:

1. We have faced moral and ethical and value issues frequently this week; they appear to be inescapable in the work we do.
2. We have seen the presentation of rather divergent ways of making knowledge or establishing a science of socio-psychological phenomena; for each investigator, the method of choice appears to be the result of his own training and philosophy, even though the experimenters come from a rather narrow range of backgrounds.
3. We have not yet done the job of establishing a taxonomy and physiology of groups, including a study of what the sociologist might call role and status variables. Possibly this does not need to be done, but I am not satisfied that the problem should be dismissed so casually.
4. We appear somewhat undecided about the degree to which theoretical systems from individual psychology may be directly translated to the psychology of groups.
5. We seem to have omitted the consideration of some variables about which we know a great deal in terms of individual behavior—variables such as ability, interest, learning rates.
6. We have grappled, rather frustratingly, with the problem of

criteria of group behavior, either as a dependent variable or as a part of the implicit value system with which we attack our problems.

7. We have discussed, somewhat inconclusively, the ways in which our social science resources, which are not limitless, can most effectively be used.

It is too early to evaluate our accomplishments of this week. Certainly the process of living together has produced changes in our views and exchanges of ideas. In the long run, I think the projects will be modified in appropriate ways by this interaction. The Panel, as you know, hopes to review new and renewal requests during the winter rather than the spring, in order to expedite the planning of the contractors. The meeting has given Panel members a much better picture than we have had before of the total program supported by the Office of Naval Research. I know I speak for the Panel when I say that we have been tremendously excited and impressed by the job all of you have done.

MAKING MILITARY APPLICATION OF
HUMAN RELATIONS RESEARCH

J. W. MACMILLAN AND H. E. PAGE

Office of Naval Research
Washington, D. C.

THE RESEARCH DESCRIBED IN THE preceding sections of this report was undertaken by the Office of Naval Research in response to requests by Naval officers who had learned something of social science research during the war years and immediately thereafter, and who believed that research in human relations could produce results which were both applicable to and necessary in over-all military operations. These officers knew that psychologists and other social scientists who had been associated with the Navy during the war had been able to solve certain types of problems in connection with selection, classification, training, *etc.*, and were vitally interested in the continuation of research in the broader area under discussion. Other officers had encountered human relations problems in their own commands, and had realized their importance. They also were wise enough to know that there were no readily available solutions. Some had read reports or books in the social science fields, were aware that research techniques in the field of human relations existed, and were willing to participate in the support of a research program.

In general, however, Naval officers, while well oriented to physical science and operational research, have had but limited contact with social science research. They are concerned with personnel problems such as the percentage of failures, wastage of time through AWOL's, deserters, men who will not fight, *etc.* They want to understand why these problems occur, whose fault it is that they do occur, and what can be done to improve conditions. They are also concerned about the failure of training activities to turn out men who can perform at a high degree of competence. They are concerned over the decreased quality of the personnel available for training and duty. In addition, they are disturbed by the officer program and the frequent lack of appreciation of the true worth of reserve personnel.

Though these problems are apparent, their clear definition and solution are not. Thus, if social scientists are to be of use to the military, there is need for a more definitive statement of problems and the construction of a framework around which a research program can be developed. Darley's opening paper mentioned in some detail how this can be done, so no description will be repeated here.

While some areas of psychological and social science research have obtained wide acceptance in the military services (*e.g.*, personnel selection and classification procedures) and permanent organizations established to conduct such activities, this is not true of the areas outlined by the original Advisory Panel. Nevertheless, that the potential value of research in these areas has been realized to some degree is shown by the following:

1. A course in leadership is being given at the Naval Academy. This resulted from a research project conducted by Drs. Jenkins and Sanford at the University of Maryland which showed that midshipmen who attended the course demonstrated acceptable leadership qualities to a higher degree than those who did not attend. However, this course consists merely of a series of lectures and the lasting effects are as yet unknown.

2. Another series of lectures was given two years ago to senior Naval officers, and again to a hundred officers from each of the three services, under contract with the American Psychological Association. This course consisted of fourteen lectures in the various social science fields. Here again the results are unknown, but there is evidence that a broader understanding of the potentialities of social science research was developed. A number of the officers in attendance have asked for further information and have come to members of the Human Resources Division or to other social scientists with inquiries about the application of research to their problems.

3. The Secretary of Defense last year established a Human Relations Working Group, under the general supervision of the Personnel Policy Board and the Human Resources Committee of the Research & Development Board, to analyze research findings in human resources and to make recommendations concerning the utilization of such results in administrative policy formation. This group is functioning under the chairmanship of Captain P. E. McDowell, USN, and though no

reports have yet been submitted, preliminary evidence indicates that the findings will be of considerable value in military operations.

4. A great deal of emphasis has been placed on research in human resources fields by the U.S. Air Force. A Human Resources Research Institute has been established at the Air University, Maxwell Field, Alabama, and a considerable sum of money has been made available for the support of human relations research.

5. The Army has undertaken a number of studies in the field of human relations by contract with Johns Hopkins University through the Office of Research Operations.

6. A number of requests for information have been received from naval activities and civilian agencies in the government, including the Civil Service Commission and the State Department. Research results have been made available wherever possible and there are indications that interest in the application of these results is increasing.

7. The Navy Department, in response to a request from the Navy Secretary of the Research & Development Board and the Chief of the Bureau of Naval Personnel, has established a human resources desk in the Office of the Chief of Naval Operations with one man responsible for the coordination of human resources research and development activities.

The above examples show that people in responsible positions are becoming more and more cognizant of the current and potential value of research of this type. Nevertheless, lack of familiarity with the subject matter of much of human relations research makes it difficult for them to grasp the applicability of such research to military problems. In the following paragraphs, an effort is made to focus on some of the military problems to which human relations research is applicable.

Career-wise, the problems of the military can be said to begin with manpower availability. Procurement, recruitment and induction problems follow, which in turn lead to all of the ramifications involved in the transfer of individuals from civilian to military life. Indoctrination, basic training and specialization, including classification and assignment, may be considered to follow in order. Assimilation into the larger military unit and the utilization of abilities and skills in noncombat and career planning each raise major problems for the military. The cycle may be considered as complete with problems raised by attrition of motivation, skills, capacities and personnel, and transitional problems resulting from the return to civilian from military life.

This, then, seems to provide a framework within which problems related to attitudes, motivations, communications and group organization and dynamics—problems in human relations—may be profitably discussed.

Attitudes toward the services are important in the consideration of manpower and human resources. Unification, the use of minority groups, and the willingness to support a large defense program are only a few items showing how national character and efforts to document that character are related to the military.

Problems of motivation are at once apparent in the use of inducements and incentives for mobilization, within both military and industrial establishments. Motivating a civilian population for an all-out war effort is certainly a subject for research with potentially great application. So also are the restriction of disaffected and disloyal personnel, and the creation of attitudes of acceptance for policy concerned with their control.

Reorganization of the civilian structure, both within industry and within the family as a result of mobilization, creates problems where research findings related to group organization and dynamics and the emergence of leadership are applicable. The need for organizing new civilian structures, *e.g.,* civil defense, offers opportunity to apply research findings in group dynamics and leadership. Problems of communication are likewise paramount as they relate to problems such as how to inform the public, and the spread and control of rumor. Directly related are problems of subversive propaganda and countermeasures.

If one turns from manpower resources to procurement, recruitment and induction, one encounters additional problems. The influence of group attitudes on individual attitudes toward the service, and the determination of and effective use of inducements for enlistment and re-enlistment are examples. Knowledge of group organization and structure has direct bearing on how best to integrate and utilize National Guard, Reserve, and Regulars in the national effort. Similar problems will likewise become apparent as international cooperation within the military becomes more commonplace.

If one ignores the transition from civilian to military life, one finds opportunities for application of research findings to indoctrination and basic training. Motivation and incentives for basic training are very pertinent to the military task. Much of our knowledge on reward and punishment is applicable to these problems. The use of indoctrination films for incentive purpose has been widespread, but little has been done to evaluate either the films or the effectiveness of the method for increasing the motivation and morale of troops. How to organize groups for instruction purposes, individual versus group instruction, formal versus informal instruction, and methods of communicating information to individuals and groups, are indicative of areas in need of further investigation.

In the areas of classification and assignment, preferences and interests in relation both to branch of service and to technical assignment are directly related to motivation and to military proficiency. Other examples are the use of special rewards for hazardous duty.

Additional problems are encountered in connection with crew formation, crew-served weapons, and the composition of particular military units. Here, knowledge of group organization, the emergence of leadership, and group versus individual goals should find ready application.

As individuals or groups become assimilated into larger organizations, problems related to traditions of units, identification with the group, pride in unit, discipline, group mores and ethics, are areas where research can lead to better solutions. How to communicate, both formally and informally, within a unit, is another aspect of group organization. In the utilization of the total abilities and skills of individuals and groups within the service, it is important to know about attitudes toward war, toward occupation duty, toward national and international policy, and toward our allies. How to organize joint and combined forces, how to prevent group disorganization and panic in one unit and to bring about such disorders in other units as well as in individuals, are indicative of areas where application of research in human relations is feasible.

Finally, one might mention the transition from military to civilian life as an area where research may find application. Changes in motivation resulting from establishing minimum service requirements for separation, types of discharges awarded and retirement privileges are important and subject to controlled investigation. Equally important are the assimilation into the civilian community and family reorganization.

An attempt has been made in the preceding pages to show the origin of the human relations program, the current status of the research, and some of the areas where additional research and its application would be profitable. Undoubtedly, many questions have arisen in the mind of the reader regarding the future of the program. For instance, can basic research be continued during an emergency period? What further moves should be made to implement the utilization of research results? What are the major obstacles to be overcome in such utilization? Some questions can be answered directly, others can be answered only tentatively due to the continually changing national and international situation.

The Office of Naval Research has long affirmed that basic research is essential to progress in science and that without it technological progress soon comes to a halt against the barriers of ignorance. Consequently, the Chief of Naval Research has recently issued the following statement in discussing the role of research and development under emergency and wartime conditions. "The Navy's present position and leadership in this field and careful analysis of the definite role which basic research plays in all development activities at all times leads to the conclusion that basic research must continue at a well considered high level." This policy has been stated because pressure has been exerted to reduce the basic research program in the interests of immediate application.

The application of research results to operating problems can be accelerated through their increased dissemination to military and civilian agencies. However, one of the major obstacles in a program of this kind is the lack of personnel competent to translate results into practice. There is an acute shortage of "social engineers," due in part to the tendency on the part of universities to train students to the "research level" with little time being spent on techniques of application. This is a problem for both universities and military departments.

An expanded educational program for military officers has been envisaged and one or two of the departments are now sending officers to universities for training in social science fields. It has further been suggested that a program be established whereby a number of officers could be sent to research projects in universities for periods of three to twelve months. This would train a number of individuals to understand the techniques employed and to develop a more open-minded attitude. It would probably not materially increase the degree to which such officers could apply research results, but would enable them to recognize more easily problems requiring human relations research techniques for their solution.

Other suggestions have included the preparation of suitable correspondence courses for service personnel, and indoctrination lectures by qualified social scientists. Here again the results would be useful, but would probably not be sufficient to insure maximum effectiveness of research utilization. Another suggestion is that social science facilities be established with considerable mobility. Such groups might move into military establishments for varying lengths of time to conduct research on service problems and to train personnel at the establishments in the utilization of social science techniques in their operations.

Even if a major effort is made during the next few years to train many more individuals at this level, there will still be a shortage of personnel. Consequently, a program of manpower conservation must be undertaken. The three services, civilian agencies, and business and industry are in keen competition for social scientists. This competition is currently increasing, and if the present limited emergency develops into an all-out effort, this shortage may have tragic results. It is necessary, therefore, to undertake some program of allocation of social scientists to prevent unnecessary duplication and to insure that each person is placed in a position of maximal effectiveness with his services available across the board in the Department of Defense and in other agencies. No plan as yet exists to effect this conservation. Professional societies, the National Security Resources Board, and other agencies responsible for scientific and technical manpower must be alerted to the urgent necessity for such a plan.

The problems of the application of human relations research are far from solved but several worthwhile approaches are under consideration. Action must be taken by both military organizations and social scientists because the uncertainties of the international situation and the increased demand for personnel trained in the social sciences create a dual responsibility.

APPENDIX

SUGGESTED GUIDE FOR THE PREPARATION OF RESEARCH PROPOSALS FOR THE OFFICE OF NAVAL RESEARCH

1. A brief statement of the experimental frame of reference from which the proposal developed, or from which the idea originated. This might be the past experimental program of the investigator, the work of others in the area, or possibly a seminar discussion.

2. A clear statement of the problem. What is the hypothesis that is being tested? What is the relationship of this problem to other knowledge in the field? What is the expected contribution to scientific knowledge or theory? If an applied problem, what is the expected end-product, or expected modification in procedures now being used?

3. A reasonably clear and complete statement of the methodology. What is the experimental design and the technique(s) for data analysis?

4. List all equipment required. This includes equipment already available, as well as equipment that must be acquired by the institution or supplied under the terms of the contract either as government furnished equipment or purchase.

5. Estimated duration and cost. Cost includes equipment, expendable material, direct labor, number of persons employed and percentage of them on projects, estimated overhead, *etc.* (It should be understood, of course, that the overhead is to be negotiated by Contracts Division, ONR, Washington, so that a mere statement of the proposed overhead is sufficient in proposals.)

6. A description of the available facilities for performing the contemplated work. Buildings and modifications thereof are not generally authorized, it being expected that institutions will pay these costs.

7. Each proposal should indicate something of the scientific training and background of the principal investigator and *must* carry his signature. Also, the proposal *must* show by signature of the business

representative or other comparable official of the institution, that the proposal has the approval of the institution.

8. The original and three copies of proposals should be submitted to the Chief of Naval Research through the area Branch Office of ONR. In addition to the above, fifteen copies should be forwarded direct to the Branch Head. These copies are for distribution to the Advisory Panels of the cognizant Branch, and will expedite the decision on the proposal.

AN EXPLANATION OF SOME TERMS
FOR THE GENERAL READER

According to a pre-test made on the readibility of the papers presented in this volume, the general reader will have little difficulty in grasping the essential generalizations presented by the authors. Some may be more insistent, however, and want further understanding of some terms and analysis techniques which are used in a number of the papers in this volume. This short essay attempts to present their meaning in a non-technical way.

VARIABLE

The social scientist often uses the term *variable* to designate the factors or elements in the situation he is describing. Thus in McClelland's paper each of the measures to which the estimate of achievement need was related—level of aspiration, memory for completed and incompleted tasks, performance on the scrambled words test, *etc.*—is considered a *variable,* a factor which may vary in its amount or strength.

Sometimes a variable is described as being *independent* or *dependent.* This means merely that the factor is being considered by the author or experimenter as having a special relationship to other variables in the situation. *Independent* variables are those elements taken as givens, factors which vary in ways that are looked upon as causing changes in the *dependent* variables. In his discussion of morale variables, Katz at first attempts to isolate the independent variables, such as size of work groups, and demonstrate their relation to the dependent variable, morale. Then later, he regards the morale factors as independent and uses them to predict worker productivity, which then is taken as the dependent variable. Because of the ever pervasive tendency of variables in the social sciences to be linked through circular causal chains, the distinction between independence and dependence is arbitrary. For instance, in the Katz example, one can postulate that morale affects productivity which in turn affects morale, and so forth round the chain. In an experimental situation, what has been the independent variable might later be used as the dependent variable.

STATISTICAL TESTS OF SIGNIFICANCE

As soon as the social scientist attempts to make estimates of the extent to which a variable exists in a given situation, he is confronted with measurement problems. Because his techniques are relatively crude, he must in some way recognize the error in his measurement. In addition, the researcher wants to make generalizations which he and others know are repeatable and are not the result of chance. In statistics, he finds a tool which enables him to estimate the frequency with which the results he obtains might have occurred by chance. There are a number of devices used to obtain these estimates, the commonest being the so-called *Chi-Square* and *t-tests* or *t-ratios*. These devices yield an estimate of the number of times out of 100 the results might have been obtained by chance. In Harris' paper, his first table lists the t-ratios and then tells what percentage of times, had his comparison of the two groups of ex-patients been repeated, he might have expected to have obtained these results by chance. Most researchers do not place much confidence in their results, unless the estimates for obtaining them by chance are 5 out of 100, or less. It is customary to report the *test of significance* by merely citing the finding and then saying, "These results are significant at the such-and-such level of confidence." This means that application of an appropriate statistical device has revealed the likelihood of obtaining these results by chance are only so many out of 100. A quite complicated elaboration of these tests of significance, called *analysis of variance,* enables the experimenter at times to separate his error variations from variations due to other more determinable causes.

CORRELATION COEFFICIENT

It is often useful when comparing two measurements on the same person or group to be able to indicate by a single number or index the extent to which the two different aspects are associated with each other. Statistical devices used for this purpose are called correlation coefficients and are often symbolized by an r. There are many kinds that are used depending upon the particular situation. The ones used in this volume range from -1.00 through zero to $+1.00$. When the coefficient is relatively high, in the .60's, .70's, or .80's, concomitance in the two measures is considerable. When the correlation is low, in the .10's, .20's, or .30's, there is little consistent relationship between the measures. When the r is prefixed with a negative sign, as in $-.75$, the relationship between the two measures is "negative" or inverted, that is, high values of the one variable tend to correspond to low values on the other. When the coefficient stands alone or is prefixed by a plus sign, as .75 or +.75, the correlation is positive or direct, that is, high values on the one measure tend to correspond to high values on the other. For instance, in Marquis' paper on conferences, the satisfaction of the group was correlated positively with its cohesiveness but negatively with its members' self-oriented needs. That is, groups high in satisfaction consistently tended to be high in cohesiveness but low in the extent to which their members exhibited self-oriented needs. r's hovering around zero indicate there is practically no correspondence between the measures.

FACTOR ANALYSIS

One of the problems plaguing the social scientist is the extent to which his variables overlap each other and are contaminated by irrelevant elements. The technique of *factor analysis* has been developed within the last quarter-century to ferret out the underlying factors or dimensions which might be useful in describing the original variables in simpler and more parsimonious terms. A factor analysis is a rather complicated procedure, begun by getting the correlations of each of the variables with all the others. Then by means of statistical devices, a smaller set of factors are extracted in terms of which the original variables may be described. Sometimes these new factors are called *dimensions*, the original variable then being said to be *loaded* to such-and-such a degree on these dimensions. This means that the original measure then is thought of as containing so much of the first factor, so much of the second, *etc.* Some variables are relatively pure, having a large loading on only one dimension; other variables are mixtures, having small loadings on all factors. Thus, in the factor analysis reported by Carter in his second table, he was able to find two factors underlying the six different group tasks. He found some of the tasks largely "intellectual" as Reasoning; others largely "doing things with one's hands" as Mechanical Assembly; and still others a mixture of the two components, as Clerical.

To understand the results presented in this volume, it is not necessary for the reader to know the technical processes by which the investigator achieves his findings. However, in many instances the methodology is so intimately connected with the conclusions that it is difficult, if not impossible, to report the one without the other. This note has attempted to supply background which may help the general reader grasp the results more easily when they are so intermingled with methodological considerations.

OFFICE OF NAVAL RESEARCH

INDEX

(Note: Page numbers in italics refer to bibliographical items.)